D1220682

VISIONS
Language ✦ Literature ✦ Content

Mary Lou McCloskey

Lydia Stack

THOMSON

HEINLE

Australia ✦ Canada ✦ Mexico ✦ Singapore ✦ United Kingdom ✦ United States

THOMSON

™

HEINLE

VISIONS STUDENT BOOK A
Mary Lou McCloskey and Lydia Stack

Publisher: *Phyllis Dobbins*
Director of Development: *Anita Raducanu*
Director, ELL Training and Development: *Evelyn Nelson*
Developmental Editor: *Tania Maundrell-Brown*
Associate Developmental Editor: *Yeny Kim*
Associate Developmental Editor: *Kasia Zagorski*
Editorial Assistant: *Audra Longert*
Production Supervisor: *Mike Burggren*
Marketing Manager: *Jim McDonough*
Manufacturing Manager: *Marcia Locke*
Photography Manager: *Sheri Blaney*
Development: *Proof Positive/Farrowlyne Associates, Inc.; Quest Language Systems*
Design and Production: *Proof Positive/Farrowlyne Associates, Inc.*
Cover Designer: *Studio Montage*
Printer: *R.R. Donnelley and Sons Company, Willard*

Cover Image: *© Danny Lehman/CORBIS*

Printed in the United States of America.
6 7 8 9 10   08   07   06   05   04

For more information, contact Heinle, 25 Thomson Place, Boston, Massachusetts 02210 USA, or you can visit our Internet site at http://www.heinle.com

For permission to use material from this text or product contact us:
Tel   1-800-730-2214
Fax   1-800-730-2215
Web   www.thomsonrights.com

ISBN: 0-8384-5247-7

Reviewers and Consultants

We gratefully acknowledge the contribution of the following educators, consultants, and librarians who reviewed materials at various stages of development. Their input and insight provided us with valuable perspective and ensured the integrity of the entire program.

Program Advisor

Evelyn Nelson

Consultants

Deborah Barker
Nimitz High School
Houston, Texas

Sharon Bippus
Labay Middle School
Houston, Texas

Sheralee Connors
Portland, Oregon

Kathleen Fischer
Norwalk LaMirada Unified
    School District
Norwalk, California

Willa Jean Harner
Tiffin-Seneca Public Library
Tiffin, Ohio

Nancy King
Bleyl Middle School
Houston, Texas

Dell Perry
Woodland Middle School
East Point, Georgia

Julie Rines
The Thomas Crane Library
Quincy, Massachusetts

Lynn Silbernagel
The Catlin Gabel School
Portland, Oregon

Cherylyn Smith
Fresno Unified School District
Fresno, California

Jennifer Trujillo
Fort Lewis College
Teacher Education Department
Durango, Colorado

Teresa Walter
Chollas Elementary School
San Diego, California

Reviewers

Jennifer Alexander
Houston Independent School District
Houston, Texas

Susan Alexandre
Trimble Technical High School
Fort Worth, Texas

Deborah Almonte
Franklin Middle School
Tampa, Florida

Donna Altes
Silverado Middle School
Napa, California

Ruben Alvarado
Webb Middle School
Austin, Texas

Sheila Alvarez
Robinson Middle School
Plano, Texas

Cally Androtis-Williams
Newcomers High School
Long Island City, New York

Minerva Anzaldua
Martin Middle School
Corpus Christi, Texas

Alicia Arroyos
Eastwood Middle School
El Paso, Texas

Douglas Black
Montwood High School
El Paso, Texas

Jessica Briggeman
International Newcomer Academy
Fort Worth, Texas

Diane Buffett
East Side High School
Newark, New Jersey

Eva Chapman
San Jose Unified School
    District Office
San Jose, California

Elia Corona
Memorial Middle School
Pharr, Texas

Alicia Cron
Alamo Middle School
Alamo, Texas

Florence Decker
El Paso Independent School District
    (retired)
El Paso, Texas

Janeece Docal
Bell Multicultural Senior High School
Washington, DC

Addea Dontino
Miami-Dade County School District
Miami, Florida

Kathy Dwyer
Tomlin Middle School
Plant City, Florida

Olga Figol
Barringer High School
Newark, New Jersey

Claire Forrester
Molina High School
Dallas, Texas

Connie Guerra
Regional Service Center 1
Edinburg, Texas

James Harris
DeLeon Middle School
McAllen, Texas

Audrey Heining-Boynton
University of North Carolina-
    Chapel Hill
School of Education
Chapel Hill, North Carolina

Carolyn Ho
North Harris Community College
Houston, Texas

Donald Hoyt
Cooper Middle School
Fresno, California

Nancy A. Humbach
Miami University
Department of Teacher Education
Oxford, Ohio

Marie Irwin
University of Texas at Arlington Libraries
Arlington, Texas

Mark Irwin
Cary Middle School
Dallas, Texas

Erik Johansen
Oxnard High School
Oxnard, California

Marguerite Joralemon
East Side High School
Newark, New Jersey

Karen Poling Kapeluck
Lacey Instructional Center
Annandale, Virginia

Lorraine Kleinschuster
Intermediate School 10 Q
Long Island City, New York

Fran Lacas
NYC Board of Education (retired)
New York, New York

Robert Lamont
Newcomer Center
Arlington, Texas

Mao-ju Catherine Lee
Alief Middle School
Houston, Texas

Leonila Luera
Pharr-San Juan-Alamo ISD
Pharr/San Juan, Texas

Gail Lulek
Safety Harbor Middle School
Safety Harbor, Florida

Natalie Mangini
Serrano International School
Lake Forest, California

Linda Martínez
Dallas Independent School District
Dallas, Texas

Berta Medrano
Pharr-San Juan-Alamo ISD
Pharr/San Juan, Texas

Graciela Morales
Austin Independent School District
Austin, Texas

Karen Morante
School District of Philadelphia
Philadelphia, Pennsylvania

Jacee Morgan
Houston ISD
Houston, Texas

Lorraine Morgan
Hanshaw Middle School
Modesto, California

Dianne Mortensen
Pershing Intermediate School 220
Brooklyn, New York

Denis O'Leary
Rio del Valle Junior High School
Oxnard, California

Jeanette Page
School District of Philadelphia (retired)
Philadelphia, Pennsylvania

Claudia Peréz
Hosler Middle School
Lynwood, California

Yvonne Perez
Alief Middle School
Houston, Texas

Penny Phariss
Plano Independent School District
Plano, Texas

Bari Ramírez
L.V. Stockard Middle School
Dallas, Texas

Jacqueline Ray
Samuel High School
Dallas, Texas

Howard Riddles
Oak Grove Middle School
Clearwater, Florida

R.C. Rodriguez
Northside Independent School District
San Antonio, Texas

Randy Soderman
Community School District Six
New York, New York

Rita LaNell Stahl
Sinagua High School
Flagstaff, Arizona

Dean Stecker
School District of Palm Beach County
West Palm Beach, Florida

Mary Sterling-Cruz
Jackson Middle School
Friendswood, Texas

Rosemary Tejada
Carlsbad High School
Carlsbad, California

Camille Sloan Telthorster
Bleye Middle School
Houston, Texas

Vickie Thomas
Robinson Middle School
Plano, Texas

Claudio Toledo
Lynwood Middle School
Lynwood, California

Christopher Tracy
Garnet-Patterson Middle School
Washington, DC

Lydia Villescas
Pharr-San Juan-Alamo ISD
Pharr/San Juan, Texas

Stephanie Vreeland
T.A. Howard Middle School
Arlington, Texas

Jennifer Zelenitz
Long Island City High School
Long Island City, New York

We wish to thank the students at the following schools who helped us select high-interest readings at an appropriate language level. Their feedback was invaluable.

Student reviewers

Cooper Middle School
Fresno, California

De Leon Middle School
McAllen, Texas

Garnet-Patterson Middle School
Washington, D.C.

Hanshaw Middle School
Modesto, California

Intermediate School 10 Q
Long Island City, New York

Jackson Middle School
Friendswood, Texas

L.V. Stockard Middle School
Dallas, Texas

Liberty Middle School
Pharr, Texas

Martin Middle School
Corpus Christi, Texas

Memorial Middle School
Pharr, Texas

Newcomer Center
Arlington, Texas

Nimitz High School
Houston, Texas

Oak Grove Middle School
Clearwater, Florida

Oxnard High School
Oxnard, California

Pershing Intermediate School 220
Brooklyn, New York

Samuel High School
Dallas, Texas

Serrano International School
Lake Forest, California

Silverado Middle School
Napa, California

T.A. Howard Middle School
Arlington, Texas

Trimble Technical High School
Fort Worth, Texas

Contents

UNIT 6 Connections   350

To the Student

We hope you like *Visions*
We wrote it for you
To learn speaking, reading, writing,
And listening, too.

You'll read all kinds of things —
Stories, poems, and plays,
And texts that will help you understand
What your content teacher says.

Mary Lou McCloskey

Use this book to "grow" your English,
To talk about what you write and read.
Use it to learn lots of new words
And new reading strategies you'll need.

Good authors, good activities,
And especially your good teachers,
Can also help you learn grammar and writing,
And lots of other language features.

Lydia Stack

So please open this book
And learn everything you can.
Then write and show us how far you've come
Since you first began.

M.L.M. and L.S.

http://visions.heinle.com

UNIT 1

Traditions and Cultures

Children Asking for "Posada" (La Procesión), Diego Rivera, oil painting. 1953.

View the Picture

1. What are the people in this picture doing?
2. Do you know about this tradition?
3. What other traditions do you know about?

In this unit, you will read poems, personal narratives, a folktale, and historical fiction about different traditions and cultures. You will learn about the features of poems, narratives, and fiction. You will also practice writing these forms.

1

Into the Reading

Family Photo

a poem by Ralph Fletcher

Birthday Barbecue

a personal narrative and a painting by Carmen Lomas Garza

Objectives

Reading Compare and contrast a poem and a personal narrative.

Listening and Speaking Tell about and act out a party activity.

Grammar Use present continuous tense verbs.

Writing Write a personal narrative.

Content Math: Analyze a bar graph.

Use Prior Knowledge

Discuss Family Celebrations

Prior knowledge is something that you already know. Use your prior knowledge to help you understand new information.

Families often come together to celebrate a holiday or an important event.

1. With a partner, list events that families celebrate in different regions and cultures.
2. Talk about a family celebration that your culture has.
   a. What event do you celebrate?
   b. How do you celebrate?
3. Use a storyboard to show pictures of a family celebration. Label each picture.
4. With your classmates, compare and contrast your storyboards.

Family Celebration

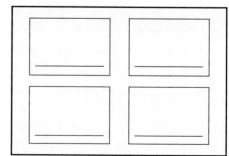

Build Background

Piñatas

Background is information that can help you understand what you hear, see, or read.

A *piñata* is a clay or paper container that people fill with candy or gifts. It is often shaped like an animal or a star. At birthday parties in Mexico and some other countries, people hang a piñata from the ceiling or a tree. Children try to break open the piñata by hitting it with a stick while their eyes are covered.

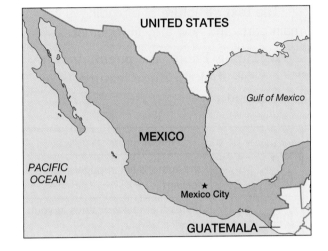

 **Content Connection**

Mexico is a country to the south of the United States.

Build Vocabulary

Learn Words for Family Members

When you learn new words, you **build your vocabulary.**

1. In your Personal Dictionary, draw the web shown.
2. With a partner, fill in words for family members.
3. If you don't know a word, ask other students or your teacher for help.
4. For help with pronunciation, ask your teacher or a classmate for help.

Text Structure

Poem and Personal Narrative

The **text structure** of a reading is its main parts and how they fit together.

1. "Family Photo" is a **poem.** As you read, look for these features of a poem:

Poem	
Experiences	the author's life, thoughts, and feelings
Images	words that make pictures in your mind
Structure	sections called "stanzas"; stanzas are not always complete sentences

2. "Birthday Barbecue" is a **personal narrative.** A narrative tells about things that happen. As you read, look for these features of a personal narrative:

Personal Narrative	
Experiences	the author's life, thoughts, and feelings
Details	words that describe true information, things, and actions
Pronouns	use of *I, we, us,* or *me*
Structure	paragraphs

Student
CD-ROM

Reading Strategy

Compare and Contrast

A **reading strategy** is a way to understand what you read. You can become a better reader if you learn good reading strategies.

When you **compare** two or more things, you see how they are similar. When you **contrast,** you see how they are different.

1. As you read or listen to the audio recording of "Family Photo" and "Birthday Barbecue," compare and contrast the characters (the people) and the events (the things that happen) in the two stories.

2. Copy the Venn Diagram on a piece of paper. Use it to compare and contrast as you read.

Family Photo **Birthday Barbecue**

poem — both describe a family event — personal narrative

Student
CD-ROM

Family Photo

a poem by Ralph Fletcher

Birthday Barbecue

a personal narrative and painting
by Carmen Lomas Garza

Audio
CD 1, Tr. 1

Family Photo
a poem by Ralph Fletcher

1. One last picture
before we head off
in different directions.

2. One last group shot of
all of us, **smirking,**
with **rabbit ears.**

3. Three **generations,**
kids on shoulders,
a baby cousin on my lap.

4. And in the middle
Grandma and Grandpa
who started all this.

5. We're all **ripples** in a pond
spreading out
from a stone they threw.

Compare and Contrast

Who are the characters in this poem? After you read "Birthday Barbecue" on page 8, compare and contrast the characters.

---

smirking   smiling in a way that shows you feel smarter or better than someone else

rabbit ears   when people hold their fingers in the shape of a "V" behind someone's head, like the ears of a rabbit

generations   any of the different age levels in a family, such as grandparents, parents, and grandchildren

ripples   little waves

About the Author

Ralph Fletcher (born 1953)

Ralph Fletcher grew up in a big family. His family members told many stories. Fletcher started writing in junior high school. After college, he traveled around the world. Then he went back to school and studied writing. Now Fletcher writes poems, novels, and nonfiction. He says, "I love to write. I love getting up every morning and . . . playing with stories, trying to build my city of words."

➤Based on "Family Photo," how do you think Ralph Fletcher feels about his family?

Audio
CD 1, Tr. 2

Compare and Contrast

Compare and contrast what happened in "Birthday Barbecue" with what happened in "Family Photo."

Birthday Barbecue

a personal narrative by Carmen Lomas Garza

1   This is my sister Mary Jane's birthday party. She's hitting a piñata that my mother made. My mother also baked and decorated the cake. There she is, bringing the meat that's ready to cook. My father is cooking at the **barbecue,** which he designed and built himself. My grandfather is **shoveling** in the coals of **mesquite wood.**

---

barbecue   a place for cooking food outdoors
shoveling   using a shovel to move or pick up something

mesquite wood   a type of wood used in cooking food outdoors

2   Underneath the tree are some young **teenagers,** very much in love. My great uncle is **comforting** my young cousin, who was crying, and **encouraging** him to hit the piñata. My grandmother is holding a baby. She was always holding the babies, and feeding them, and putting them to sleep.

---

teenagers people between the ages of 13 and 19

comforting making someone feel better

encouraging giving strength or hope to, urging

About the Author
Carmen Lomas Garza (born 1948)

Carmen Lomas Garza was born and grew up in Texas. She is a painter. She has also written books with her stories and her paintings. Garza first discovered art from her mother, who was a painter. She says, "My mother Maria was the first artist I saw paint. I thought she was making magic." Garza's artwork and stories help her celebrate her Mexican-American culture.

➤ Why do you think Carmen Lomas Garza wrote about and painted a picture of her sister's birthday party? Describe the colors, shapes, and lines in the painting. How do they influence Garza's message?

Beyond the Reading

Reading Comprehension

Question-Answer Relationships (QAR)

You can understand readings better if you answer different kinds of questions about them.

"Right There" Questions

1. **Recall Facts** In "Family Photo," who is in the family photo?
2. **Recall Facts** In "Family Photo," where are Grandma and Grandpa sitting?
3. **Recall Facts** In "Birthday Barbecue," who is Mary Jane? What is she celebrating?

"Think and Search" Questions

4. **Identify** In "Birthday Barbecue," name three things that the mother did.
5. **Draw Conclusions** In "Birthday Barbecue," where do you think the mother is bringing the meat?

"Author and You" Questions

6. **Interpret** Look at stanza 5 of "Family Photo." What do you think the author means?
7. **Compare and Contrast** How are the painting and the text in "Birthday Barbecue" similar and different?
8. **Draw Conclusions** In "Birthday Barbecue," how do you think the grandmother feels about babies? Explain.

"On Your Own" Question

9. **Identify Mood** Do you think "Family Photo" and "Birthday Barbecue" are happy readings? Why or why not?

Activity Book
p. 2

Student
CD-ROM

Build Reading Fluency

Rapid Word Recognition

Rapidly recognizing words helps increase your reading rate. It is an important characteristic of effective readers.

1. With a partner, review the words in the box.
2. Read the words aloud for one minute. Your teacher will time you.
3. Count how many words you read in one minute.

one	built	threw	who	threw	one
cousin	who	built	threw	who	threw
who	made	cousin	one	made	cousin
threw	threw	who	cousin	one	made
made	cousin	one	made	built	who

Listen, Speak, Interact

Tell About and Act Out a Party Activity

When people listen and talk to each other, they **interact.**

In "Birthday Barbecue," the author describes what people are doing at a birthday party.

1. Work with a partner. Choose a birthday party activity.
2. What happens during the activity? Write or draw the details in order.
3. Practice telling and acting out the activity with your partner.
4. Tell the class about your activity. Then act it out if possible.

5. What birthday activities did you learn about? How are they similar to and different from the activities in the selection?

> *Break a Piñata*
> 1. *Hang a piñata.*
> 2. *Cover someone's eyes.*
> 3.
> 4.

Elements of Literature

Recognize First-Person Point of View

Literature is something that an author writes for someone to read. Authors use many different ways to express themselves. These ways are the **elements of literature.**

A kind of literature is a **genre.** Poems and personal narratives are examples of genres.

In the narrative genre, the **narrator** tells the story. Sometimes the narrator is a person in the story.

> I hang a piñata. I cover my sister's eyes. My sister tries to hit the piñata. The piñata breaks. We pick up the candy.

A story written like this has **first-person point of view.** Look at the underlined words in the example. When the narrator uses words like *I, my,* and *we,* the story is in **first-person point of view.**

In your Reading Log, write one sentence from "Birthday Barbecue" that shows first-person point of view.

First-Person Point of View	
Who	**Pronouns that Are Used**
The narrator describes events.	I, me, my, we, us, our

Reading Log   Activity Book
p. 3

Student
CD-ROM

Word Study

Identify Compound Words

Words can have several parts. In this section, you will learn what the different parts mean.

A **compound word** is a word made of two words. Look at the chart.

1. Copy the chart in your Personal Dictionary.
2. Find compound words in "Birthday Barbecue" that fit the meanings.
3. Write the separate words and the compound words in the chart.

First Word	Second Word	Compound Word	Meaning
birth +	day ⇒	birthday	the day of your birth
+	⇒		the mother of one of your parents
+	⇒		the father of one of your parents

Personal Dictionary

Activity Book
p. 4

Student
CD-ROM

Grammar Focus

Use Present Continuous Tense Verbs

Grammar is the way that a language is put together.

A **present continuous tense verb** tells about an action that is happening now. It uses the verbs *am, is,* or *are* plus a verb ending in *-ing*. For example:

My father is cooking.

Present Continuous Tense		
I	**am**	cook**ing.**
He/She/It	**is**	cook**ing.**
We/You/They	**are**	cook**ing.**

1. Find two more sentences in paragraphs 1 and 2 of "Birthday Barbecue" that use present continuous tense verbs. Write them on a piece of paper. Circle the present continuous verbs.
2. Write your own sentence about something happening in the classroom right now. Use a present continuous tense verb. Circle it.

Activity Book
pp. 5–6

Student
Handbook

Student
CD-ROM

From Reading to Writing

Write a Personal Narrative

After you read literature in school, you often write about it. This section shows you how to do this.

Draw a picture of a family celebration or a party. Put yourself in the picture, too. Write a personal narrative about the picture.

1. Write in the first-person point of view. Use *I, me, my, we, us,* or *our* to show that you are the narrator.
2. Use present continuous tense verbs.
3. Write one paragraph.

Activity Book
p. 7

Student
Handbook

Across Content Areas

Analyze a Bar Graph

Content areas are the subjects you study in school. Math, science, social studies, language arts, and other arts such as music and drawing are content areas.

A **bar graph** is a graph that shows amounts. This bar graph shows the number of different family members in Pablo Garcia's family. To read the bar graph, look at a family member at the bottom of a bar. Then find the number that corresponds to the top of the bar.

1. How many aunts does Pablo have?
2. How many sisters does he have?
3. Which bar has the most members?
4. Which bar has the fewest members?
5. Make a bar graph like this to show your own family members.

Activity Book
p. 8

Student
CD-ROM

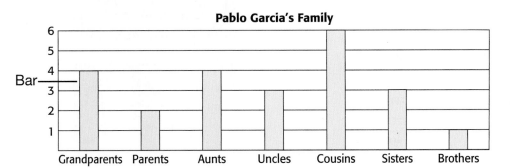

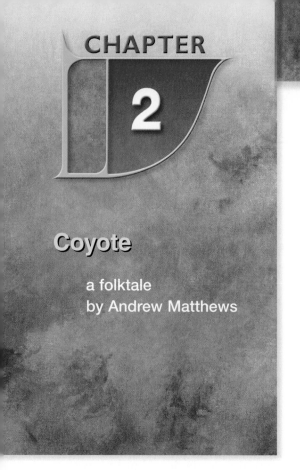

Coyote

a folktale
by Andrew Matthews

Objectives

Reading Read aloud to show understanding as you read a folktale.

Listening and Speaking Present a dramatic reading.

Grammar Identify subjects and verbs in sentences.

Writing Write a narrative.

Content Science: Learn about food chains.

Use Prior Knowledge

Share Knowledge About Coyotes

What do you know about coyotes?

1. Copy each statement below on a piece of paper.
   a. Coyotes live in many parts of the United States.
   b. Coyotes have no fur.
   c. Coyotes hunt for food during the night.
   d. Coyotes can live in very cold places.
2. Decide if each statement is true or false. Write *T* if you think a statement is true. Write *F* if you think a statement is false.

3. Share your answers with a partner. Do your answers match? Ask your teacher if you need help.

Coyote

Build Background

Stories with Animals

People of all cultures tell stories. Some of these stories have animals in them. Sometimes the animals talk and do other things that animals cannot do.

Some stories tell about nature. For example, they might tell about the beginning of the ocean or Earth. Most people do not believe that these stories are true.

In the story you are going to read and listen to, the first coyote creates Earth. After you read or listen to "Coyote," talk about stories you have heard from different regions of the United States and other cultures. How are they similar or different?

SOCIAL STUDIES
Content Connection

Culture includes the ideas, activities (such as art, foods, clothing), and ways of behaving that are special to a country, people, or region.

Build Vocabulary

Learn Words for Animal Sounds

Animals make sounds, and languages have words for those sounds. Here are some words for sounds that dogs, coyotes, and wolves make.

1. Listen as your teacher says the words.
   a. howl
   b. growl
   c. yelp
   d. bark
2. Now listen as your teacher makes the animal sounds. Can you match the words above with the sounds?
3. Work with a partner. Make one of the animal sounds and have your partner say the word for it.
4. Write the words in your Personal Dictionary.
5. Do you know the word for *bark* in another language? What is it?

Personal Dictionary

Activity Book
p. 9

Student CD-ROM

Text Structure

Folktale

"Coyote" is a **folktale.** A folktale is a **narrative** (a story) that people tell to their children and grandchildren.

Look at the chart. It shows some distinguishing features of a narrative.

Look for and analyze these features as you read or listen to "Coyote."

Narrative

Beginning
Who is in the story? These are the **characters.**
Where and *when* does the story take place? This is the **setting.**

↓

Middle
What happens? This is the **plot.**

↓

End
How does the story end? Are the characters happy? Sad?

Student
CD-ROM

Reading Strategy

Read Aloud to Show Understanding

When you do not understand something you read, try reading it aloud to yourself. Follow these tips:

1. Reread the part of the selection aloud.
2. Ask yourself these questions:
   a. What happened in this part of the reading?
   b. What will happen next?

3. Go on to the next part of the reading.
4. Use this strategy as you read "Coyote."

Student
CD-ROM

Coyote

a folktale by Andrew Matthews

Prologue

This story is from the folktales of the American Indians of the western and southwestern United States.

1   At the start of things, it was dark. Dark lay on dark and all was black and **still.** Then, into the stillness came a small sound, a quiet sound. It got bigger, louder, and stronger until it filled the darkness. The sound was Coyote's howl.

2   Coyote grew around the howl. First came his mouth with its sharp, white teeth, then his head with its bright eyes, then his body, bones, and fur. Last of all came a tail. Coyote blinked his eyes at the darkness.

3   "My legs want to run, but I can't run through the dark!" he said.

4   He breathed a wind in the shape of a shell. He turned the shell upside down and with a shake of his head he **flung** it into the air and made the sky.

Read Aloud to Understand

Read paragraphs 3 and 4 aloud. What does Coyote want to do? What did he make?

---

still   not moving

flung   threw with force, threw hard

5   Coyote took colors to the five corners of the Earth and then he waited. The colors grew into the sky and bent together in the first **rainbow.** The rainbow **divided** the day from the night.

6   Coyote howled a **disk** of burning gold and put it into the sky to be the Sun. He howled a disk of **gleaming** silver and put it into the sky to be the Moon.

7   "My legs want to run, but there's nothing to run on!" he said.

8   Coyote **bared** his teeth and growled. The hard sound of the growl turned into rocks and hills and mountains. Coyote growled more softly. His growl made forests and grassy **prairies.**

**Read Aloud
to Understand**

Read paragraphs 7 and 8 aloud. Coyote can't run. Why? What does Coyote make?

---

rainbow   a curve of bright colors that sometimes forms in the sky after a rainstorm

divided   separated, split

disk   a thin, flat circle

gleaming   shining brightly

bared   showed

prairies   large areas of flat or slightly hilly grassland with tall grasses and few trees

Beyond the Reading

Reading Comprehension

Question-Answer Relationships (QAR)

"Right There" Questions

1. **Recall Facts** What is the world like at the beginning of "Coyote"?
2. **Recall Facts** Who makes the world in "Coyote"?

"Think and Search" Questions

3. **Determine Sequence of Events** What is the first thing that Coyote creates?
4. **Identify** How many times does Coyote make things?
5. **Determine Causes and Effects** What happens after Coyote yelps?

"Author and You" Questions

6. **Identify** Name some things that Coyote does *not* create in this story.
7. **Analyze** How does the author organize and present his ideas?

"On Your Own" Questions

8. **Make Inferences** Do you think coyotes were important to American Indians of the southwestern United States? Explain.
9. **Compare Oral Traditions** Many folktales are told out loud. What stories have you heard that tell about something in nature? What culture or region is the story from? How is it similar to "Coyote"?
10. **Paraphrase Text** How would you tell someone what "Coyote" is about in your own words?

Activity Book
p. 10

Student
CD-ROM

Build Reading Fluency

Reading Key Phrases

Reading key phrases will help you learn to read faster. Fluent readers group or phrase words as they read.

1. Read these phrases aloud.
2. Raise your hand each time you read the phrase "Coyote howled."

Coyote howled	Coyote blinked	Coyote barked
Coyote yelped	Coyote barked	Coyote howled
Coyote barked	Coyote howled	Coyote growled
Coyote growled	Coyote yelped	Coyote yelped

Listen, Speak, Interact

Present a Dramatic Reading

Long ago, people told folktales like "Coyote" to each other. They probably used their voices and bodies to show meaning and make the story exciting for listeners.

1. The class will form four groups. Each group will present a reading of one page of "Coyote."
2. In your group, decide which part each person will read.
3. Practice your reading with your group. Use your voice and body to show meaning and make the presentation enjoyable.
4. Group members may act out certain events while you read.
5. Present your reading for the rest of the class. If possible, videotape your performance. Be sure to listen as the other groups present.
6. How did the readings affect you as you listened? What parts of the readings caused this effect? Did you interpret meaning from voices and body movements?

Elements of Literature

Understand Author's Purpose

An **author** is a person who writes something. When you write, you are an author. When authors write something, they have a **purpose.** The purpose tells *why* they wrote it.

Here are some purposes for writing.

a. *To entertain.* For example, the author has a funny or an unusual story to tell.
b. *To inform.* For example, the author tells us about how coyotes live.
c. *To express an opinion.* For example, the author tells us why he or she thinks coyotes are beautiful animals.
d. *To persuade.* The author writes because he or she wants us to do something. For example, the author wants us to give money to protect coyotes.

1. Work with a partner. What is the author's purpose in writing "Coyote"? Sometimes there is more than one purpose.
2. Think about "Birthday Barbecue" in Chapter 1. What is the author's purpose in writing it?

Activity Book
p. 11

Student
CD-ROM

Word Study

Use a Thesaurus or Synonym Finder to Find Synonyms

Synonyms are words with similar meanings. You can use synonyms to make your writing more interesting. Look at these synonyms from the selection:

Hares darted across the prairies.

Mice scuttled across the forest floor.

Both of these underlined words refer to a way of moving quickly.

You can find synonyms for words in a **thesaurus** or **synonym finder.** Both of these reference sources list words in alphabetical order, beginning with *A* and ending with *Z*. A list of synonyms is given next to each word.

You can find on-line versions of these references on the Internet.

1. Read the sentences and the list of words below.
   a. He flung the shell into the sky.
   b. Then a small sound filled the stillness.
   c. Coyote made heaps of clay.

ate	threw	smelled	quiet	car
	story	birds	stones	piles

2. Choose the word that is the synonym of each underlined word.
3. Use a thesaurus to check your answers. (For *flung,* look up *fling.*)

Activity Book
p. 12

Student
CD-ROM

Grammar Focus

Identify Subjects and Verbs in Sentences

A complete **sentence** has a subject and a verb. The **subject** of a sentence is who or what the sentence is about. The **verb** describes the action, or what happens in the sentence. Look at this example:

Coyote blinked his eyes.

Coyote is the subject. The sentence is about Coyote. *Blinked* is the verb. It tells what Coyote did.

Find the subject and verb in each sentence.

1. Coyote howled a disk of gold.
2. He found a river with a high bank.
3. The mice scuttled quickly.

Activity Book
pp. 13–14

Student
Handbook

Student
CD-ROM

From Reading to Writing

Write a Narrative

Use your imagination to write a narrative about an animal that creates something in nature. Your animal can talk and have other special abilities.

Tell your story in one or two paragraphs. Give it a title (a name).

1. Make sure your story has a beginning, a middle, and an end.

2. Choose your words carefully to be sure that your story makes sense.

3. Be sure to capitalize and punctuate your story correctly to strengthen its meaning.

Activity Book
p. 15

Student
Handbook

Across Content Areas

Learn About Food Chains

Some animals eat other animals. Coyotes, for example, hunt (chase and kill) and eat other animals such as hares. Animals that hunt are called **predators.**

What do hares eat? They eat plants. Plants, hares, and coyotes make up a **food chain.** A predator like a coyote is often at the top of a food chain. Coyotes eat hares. Hares eat plants.

Make another food chain with these three words:

Fish   People   Insects

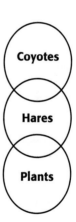

Activity Book
p. 16

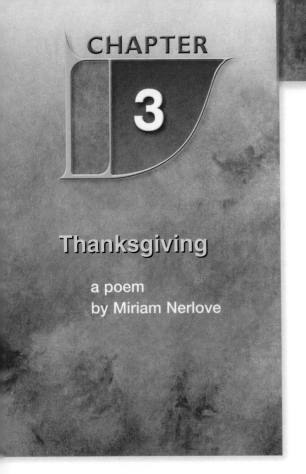

CHAPTER 3

Thanksgiving

a poem
by Miriam Nerlove

Use Prior Knowledge

Talk About Holidays

A holiday is a special day. It is a day to celebrate events or important people. For example, New Year's Day is a holiday in many cultures. People celebrate the beginning of the new year on New Year's Day.

In the United States, people say "Happy New Year" on that day. What do you say in your region or culture?

1. Copy the chart on a piece of paper.
2. Think about holidays that your family or friends celebrate. List two holidays.
3. Write what people celebrate on each holiday.
4. Share your chart with a partner.

Holiday	What People Celebrate
New Year's Day	the new year

Build Background

Thanksgiving

Thanksgiving is an important holiday in the United States. On Thanksgiving, people give thanks for the good things in their lives. Many people eat a big meal with family members and friends.

Content Connection

In the United States, people celebrate Thanksgiving on the fourth Thursday of November.

On Thanksgiving, people remember the story of the Pilgrims. The Pilgrims came from England to live in the Americas in the 1600s. At first, the Pilgrims did not have enough food. The Native Americans showed the Pilgrims how to grow and find food. Later, they shared a feast (a very big meal) together. The Pilgrims gave thanks for the food and their new home.

Build Vocabulary

Learn Words for Foods

On Thanksgiving, people eat many different foods.

Look at the food words and the pictures. Match each word with its definition. Use a dictionary to check your work.

| 1. pumpkin | 2. cornbread | 3. turkey |
| 4. cranberries | 5. nuts | 6. pie |

Definitions

a. bread made from corn

b. a type of meat from a bird

c. a dessert with a crust and a sweet filling

d. a big, orange fruit

e. seeds with a hard shell around them

f. small red fruit

The Heinle Newbury House Dictionary

Activity Book
p. 17

Student CD-ROM

Text Structure

Poem

"Thanksgiving" is a **poem.** A **poet** is a person who writes a poem. Look at some features a poem can have.

Poem	
Rhyme	words with the same ending sound; for example: The winter was **cold** and the house was **old.**
Rhythm	a beat, like a drum sound in music
Stanzas	groups of lines
Vivid Language	words that help you see, hear, smell, touch, and taste what the poet is describing

Look for these features as you read the selection. Think about how the vivid language helps you to make pictures in your mind and understand the poem. Also notice how the words rhyme and have rhythm.

Student
CD-ROM

Reading Strategy

Describe Mental Images

"Thanksgiving" has many words that help you form **mental images.** Mental images are pictures that you form in your mind. Read these lines from the poem:

so they held a great feast with plenty to eat.

There was <u>cornbread</u> and <u>nuts</u>, <u>berries</u> and <u>meat</u>.

The underlined words help you picture the feast in your mind. They tell you what foods were at the feast. Draw a picture of your mental image of this stanza.

Describing mental images can help you understand and enjoy a poem better. Follow these tips to describe mental images:

1. Stop after you read each stanza. Think about mental images that you formed.
2. Describe your mental images or present a dramatic interpretation of your images to the class.

Student
CD-ROM

Thanksgiving

a poem
by Miriam Nerlove

Audio
CD 1, Tr. 4

Describe Mental Images

What mental images do you form when you hear the word *Thanksgiving*?

1   Thanksgiving! It's time for Thanksgiving!

2   Each year in November we like to remember . . .

3   the Pilgrims, who came such a long time ago,
    to build and to live here, to work and to grow.

Describe Mental Images

What mental images do you form after reading stanza 4? What words help you form these mental images?

4 They hadn't much food and the winter was cold.
   The Pilgrims got sick—both the young and the old.

5 But Native Americans knew what to do.
   The Pilgrims were taught many things that were new.

6 They grew corn and pumpkins to last the whole year.
   They also caught fish, **hunted** turkey and **deer.**

---

hunted killed for food   **deer** an animal with hooves that lives in forests

7 The people were thankful for food they had grown . . .

8 so they held a great feast with **plenty** to eat.
There was cornbread and nuts, berries and meat.

9 Then **neighbors** and Pilgrims **gathered** to share the Thanksgiving meal they all had **prepared.**

---

plenty   more than enough
neighbors   people who live close to one another

gathered   came together
prepared   made

10　Now we remember that **feast** our own way,
　　with the special big dinner we're having today.

11　We work in the kitchen, Mother and I,
　　and **bake** not just one, but *two* pumpkin pies!

12　We're off to Grandma's. "Mother, let's go!
　　Please hurry up—we're going too slow."

Describe Mental Images

How do you think Mother and the boy get to Grandma's? Do they drive? Walk? What image do you form in your mind?

---

feast　a large meal

bake　cook in an oven

Describe Mental Images

How do you think the pumpkin pie tastes? Smells? Looks? What words help you form these mental images?

13   The warm pumpkin pies smell so good and so sweet,
I **sneak** a small piece of the **piecrust** to eat.

14   We finally arrive at a little past four—
the whole family's waving at Grandma's front door.

15   There's Grandma and Minnie, her little gray cat,
Uncle Bob, Aunt Marie, cousins Laura and Matt.

---

sneak do something so that other people cannot see you

piecrust the outside pastry that holds the filling of a pie

16   We sit down to eat in a **wonderful mood.**
We say that we're thankful for **plenty** of food.

17   Uncle Bob **carves** the turkey and uses a knife
that is one of the biggest I've seen in my life!

18   We **gobble** the food down, we eat till we're **stuffed.**
When Grandma says, "More?" we tell her, "Enough!"

Describe Mental Images

What do you think the table looks like after the family finishes eating? Which words help you form this mental image?

wonderful very good; very pleasing	**carves** cuts into pieces or slices
mood how someone feels	**gobble** eat in a quick and hungry way
plenty a lot of	**stuffed** a feeling of being very full from eating

19 But now comes the pie—and I know that it's good.
I waited to eat it as long as I could.

Describe Mental Images

What mental image do you form after you read this stanza? Are the people worried that Baby Laura will drop the cup?

20 When we're finished with dinner, it's time to clean up—
Watch out! Baby Laura has Uncle Bob's cup!

21 I pick up the **wishbone** that's dried on a dish.
Matt and I pull—will Matt get the wish?

---

watch out be careful

wishbone a bone in some birds that is shaped like a Y; people play a game with a wishbone: the person who breaks off the largest piece of the wishbone gets to make a wish

I win!
I make my own wish and I know what to say:
May next year's Thanksgiving be just like today!

Describe Mental Images

What mental image do you form when you read the words "I win!"? Is the boy smiling? Jumping up and down? Doing something else?

About the Author

Miriam Nerlove (born 1959)

Miriam Nerlove was born in Minneapolis, Minnesota. She started her career as an illustrator (a person who draws pictures to go with text). She now writes poetry for young people. Many of Nerlove's poems are about holidays. She also writes about history.

➤ Why do you think Miriam Nerlove wrote a poem about Thanksgiving? To entertain? To describe? To teach? What questions would you want to ask Nerlove?

Beyond the Reading

Reading Comprehension

Question-Answer Relationships (QAR)

"Right There" Questions

1. **Explain** Why did the Pilgrims get sick?
2. **Recall Facts** Who taught the Pilgrims how to grow food?
3. **Recall Facts** Where do the boy and his mother celebrate Thanksgiving?
4. **Recall Facts** What do they take to the dinner?
5. **Recall Facts** Who else is at the dinner?

"Think and Search" Questions

6. **Make Inferences** Who was living in America when the Pilgrims arrived?
7. **Compare** How is the family's Thanksgiving similar to the Pilgrims' Thanksgiving?

"Author and You" Questions

8. **Make Inferences** Do you think the main character likes Thanksgiving? Explain.
9. **Understand Author's Perspective** Do you think the author likes Thanksgiving? Explain.

"On Your Own" Questions

10. **Connect Your Experiences** Do you know of a celebration like Thanksgiving in another culture? How are they the same? How are they different?
11. **Form Questions** What information would you like to find out (research) about the Pilgrims?

Activity Book
p. 18

Student
CD-ROM

Build Reading Fluency

Echo Read Aloud

Effective readers learn to read with feeling. Echo reading helps you read with feeling and expression. Your teacher reads a line. Then the class reads (echoes) the same line aloud. Turn to page 30.

1. Listen to your teacher read.
2. Read the same line aloud with expression.
3. Continue listening and reading.

Listen, Speak, Interact

Tell What You Are Thankful For

When you are thankful, you are happy about the good things in your life.

1. List three things that you are thankful for on a piece of paper.
2. Choose one thing on your list. Tell the class why you are thankful for it. Give evidence and examples to support your ideas and to make them clear.

What I Am Thankful For
1. *my home*
2. *my big sister*
3. *my healthy family*

3. Take notes as you listen to your classmates. Write down their main ideas (the most important things that they say) and their supporting evidence (information that shows that the main ideas are correct).

Elements of Literature

Identify Rhyme

Poems often have words that **rhyme.** Words that rhyme have the same ending sounds. The words *bad* and *mad* rhyme.

1. With a partner, choose a page of the selection that you like.
2. Find the rhyming words on your page. Be sure you know how to pronounce them. Ask your teacher if you are not sure.
3. With a partner, practice reading these stanzas aloud. Ask your partner to tell you if you pronounce the rhyming words correctly or not.

4. As you read, show meaning with your voice and gestures.
5. Read your stanzas to the class.
   a. Read loudly enough for everyone to hear.
   b. Read slowly enough for everyone to understand.
   c. Use a medium pitch—your voice should not be too high or too low.
   d. Use a tone of voice that expresses your feeling about the poem.

Activity Book
p. 19

Student
CD-ROM

Word Study

Analyze the Suffix -ful

A **suffix** is a group of letters added to the end of a word. A suffix changes the meaning of the word. The suffix -ful means "full of."

thank**ful** means "full of thanks"

1. Copy the chart in your Personal Dictionary.
2. Match each word in the chart with the correct definition below. Write the definitions in the chart.
   a. full of wonder
   b. full of care
   c. full of joy
3. With a partner, write a sentence for each word.

4. Use resources, such as a dictionary, or ask your teacher to help you correctly spell other words that have the suffix -ful.

First Word	Suffix	New Word	Definition
thank +	-ful ⇒	thankful	full of thanks
care +	-ful ⇒	careful	
wonder +	-ful ⇒	wonderful	
joy +	-ful ⇒	joyful	

Personal Dictionary

The Heinle Newbury House Dictionary

Activity Book p. 20

Student CD-ROM

Grammar Focus

Use Subject Pronouns

A **noun** is a part of speech that stands for a person, a place, or a thing. *Girl, school,* and *backpack* are nouns.

A **pronoun** is a part of speech that takes the place of nouns. In Chapter 2, you learned about the subjects of sentences. **Subject pronouns** can be used in place of nouns that are subjects. The subject pronouns are *I, you, he, she, it, we,* and *they.*

Native Americans knew what to do.
They knew what to do.

They takes the place of Native Americans.

1. Rewrite these sentences so that they have a subject pronoun.
   a. The turkey was very big.
   b. The pies were delicious.
   c. My brother and I like turkey.

2. Write three sentences using subject pronouns.

Activity Book pp. 21–22

Student Handbook

Student CD-ROM

From Reading to Writing

Write a Narrative About a Holiday

Choose a holiday that your family celebrates. Write one paragraph about the holiday.

1. Ask yourself these questions:
   a. What is the important holiday? When do we celebrate it? Why do we celebrate it?
   b. How do we prepare for the holiday?
   c. How do we celebrate the holiday?
2. Write your narrative. Use the model to help you.
3. Write a title for your narrative.
4. Use singular and plural nouns and pronouns correctly to show people, places, or things.

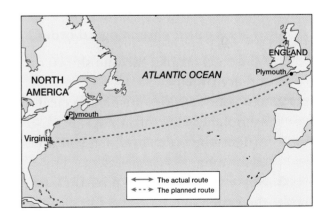

Title _____

_____ is an important holiday. My family celebrates it on _____. We celebrate it because _____. To prepare, we _____ _____. On the holiday, we celebrate by _____

5. Use a resource, such as a dictionary, to help you correctly spell words in your paragraph.

The Heinle Newbury House Dictionary

Activity Book
p. 23

Student Handbook

Across Content Areas

Read a Map

The Pilgrims came to the New World by ship. Because of bad storms, the Pilgrims did not land where they wanted to go. Look at the map and answer the questions.

1. Where did the Pilgrims want to go?
2. Where did they land?
3. Look in an **atlas** (a book of maps) or on the Internet to find out how far it is from Plymouth Colony to Virginia. Take notes.

Activity Book
p. 24

CHAPTER 4

Turkish Delight

a personal narrative
and recipe
by Hamdiye Çelik

Objectives

Reading Compare text events with your own experiences as you read a personal narrative.

Listening and Speaking Distinguish fact from opinion.

Grammar Use the verb *to be* with complements.

Writing Write a personal narrative.

Content The Arts: Design a Turkish rug.

Use Prior Knowledge

Discuss Everyday Activities

In "Turkish Delight," the narrator describes everyday activities. They are presented in the order in which they occur. This is called **chronological order.**

1. Make a chart like the one shown on a piece of paper.
2. List your activities during a typical school day. Use chronological order—the order in which you do each thing.
3. Share your chart with a partner. Is the order you do things the same or different from your partner?

Time	Activities
6:00 A.M.	
10:00 A.M.	
12:00 P.M.	
3:00 P.M.	
6:00 P.M.	
8:00 P.M.	
10:00 P.M.	

Build Background

Turkey

Turkey is a country that is partly in Europe and partly in Asia. Turkey has big cities and small towns. It also has rich farmland. Turkey is famous for its colorful ceramic dishes and tiles. Turkish handmade rugs are known around the world.

Content Connection

Turkish Delight is a sweet, chewy dessert made of nuts, fruit, and sugar. In Turkey, it is called *lokum*.

Build Vocabulary

Identify Words That Show Time

Sometimes an author organizes the story in chronological order. In "Turkish Delight," the author uses transition words that show this time order. Knowing the meanings of these words will help you analyze when events (things that happen) take place.

1. In your Personal Dictionary, write the following sentences.
   a. <u>After</u> school, I come home.
   b. <u>During</u> the week, I go to school in the mornings.
   c. <u>Then</u> I help my family with the housework.
   d. <u>After</u> the housework is finished, I do my homework.
2. Use clues in the sentences to rewrite the sentences into chronological order.

Personal Dictionary

Activity Book p. 25

Student CD-ROM

Text Structure

Personal Narrative

"Turkish Delight" is a **personal narrative.** The chart shows the distinguishing features of a personal narrative.

Look for these features as you read "Turkish Delight."

Personal Narrative	
First-Person Point of View	pronouns *I, me, we, us*
Personal Details	true information about the author

Student CD-ROM

Reading Strategy

Compare Text Events with Your Own Experiences

You can understand text events better when you compare them with your own experiences.

1. Read or listen to the audio recording of paragraph 1 of "Turkish Delight." How are you similar to Hamdiye? How are you different from Hamdiye?
2. As you read or listen to each paragraph in the selection, compare your experiences with Hamdiye's. Organize your answers in a Venn Diagram.

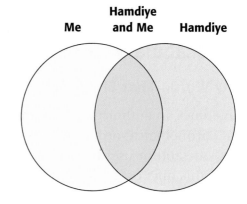

Student CD-ROM

Turkish Delight

a personal narrative and recipe
by Hamdiye Çelik

Audio
CD 1, Tr. 5

Compare Text Events with Your Own Experiences

How is your school day similar to or different from Hamdiye's?

1 My name is Hamdiye Çelik. I am 13 years old. I live in the town of Dargeçit in the southeastern part of Turkey. I have black hair and dark skin. I am a rather **reflective** and **clever** person. I respect my **elders** and love **youngsters.** I like reading poetry and playing volleyball.

2 During the week, I go to school in the mornings. When I return home at noon, I help my family with housework first and then eat lunch. I live with my four sisters and my mother. We all help each other. After the housework is finished, I do my homework, read, and play. Since my father died years ago, we live on a very **limited budget** and barely survive. But I have no **complaints.**

3 My mother is a hardworking, honest woman, who helps everyone, and for this reason, she is my **role model.** I am very happy to have such a family.

---

reflective very thoughtful
clever intelligent
elders people older than you
youngsters boys and girls older than babies and younger than teenagers

limited restricted, a small amount
budget money set aside for a purpose
complaints expressions of unhappiness about something
role model a person who is an example of success for young people

Compare Text Events with Your Own Experiences

Reread paragraphs 4 and 5. What do farmers grow where you live?

4   When spring comes, we go to fields in other **regions** to plow or collect cotton or **hazelnuts.** When winter approaches, we return to our town, and for the rest of the year, we live on the money we saved.

5   Our handmade Turkish kilims and carpets are famous worldwide. In **rural** villages, there are community centers especially for helping girls and women learn how to earn money. Two of my sisters took kilim and carpet weaving classes at one center. This is how they **contribute** to our family **income.**

What's a *kilim?* A kilim is a hand-woven rug that is exactly the same on the front as on the back. **Doubly** useful!

regions areas of a country	**contribute** give to
hazelnuts nuts from a hazel tree that you can eat	**income** money earned from working
rural related to the countryside, not the city	**doubly** twice the amount of

Compare Text Events with Your Own Experiences

Compare Turkish traditions with the traditions of your community.

6   In Turkey, our traditions and **rituals** have an important place in our lives. Some of our traditions are wedding celebrations for young couples, visiting sick people, and **funeral services.** They are signs of help and **solidarity** in our society. During religious holidays, people who are angry with each other forget and forgive old **misunderstandings** and, instead, live in **tolerance** and love.

Sweet Golden Treats

7   Turkey grows lots of **apricots.** People pick the apricots, then lay them out to dry—everywhere you look there's a beautiful orange glow! Here's a **yummy** way to eat Turkish apricots. Remember to ask an adult for help in the kitchen.

---

rituals   ceremonies to mark a serious or special event or day

funeral services   ceremonies for remembering people who have just died

solidarity   a feeling of togetherness or having the same opinions as others in a group

misunderstandings   disagreements, arguments

tolerance   acceptance, especially of beliefs and behavior that is different

apricots   small, peachlike fruits

yummy   good tasting

Kaymakli Kayisi (Cream-filled Apricots)

8 dried apricots
½ cup (1¼ **dl**) water
1 cup (2½ dl) sugar
2 **T** lemon juice
1 cup (2½ dl) whipped cream
1 T chopped **almonds**

Compare Text Events with Your Own Experiences

Have you ever made or eaten a recipe like this one? Explain.

8   Soak apricot halves in water for two hours to soften them. Mix water, sugar, and lemon juice in a pan and **bring to a fast boil** over medium heat. Carefully add the apricots using a spoon and cook for 5 minutes. Turn off heat. Scoop the apricots from the pan and arrange on a plate. Let cool. **Dab** some whipped cream on each apricot. Sprinkle with chopped almonds. **Dig in!**

dl deciliter, a unit of measurement in the metric system	**bring to a fast boil** heat the liquid until it bubbles a lot
T tablespoon, a large spoon used to measure recipe ingredients	**dab** put a small amount
almonds nuts often used in dessert recipes	**dig in** eat and enjoy

Beyond the Reading

Reading Comprehension

Question-Answer Relationships (QAR)

"Right There" Questions

1. **Recall Facts** Who tells this narrative?
2. **Recall Facts** In which city does Hamdiye live?
3. **Recall Facts** How do Hamdiye's sisters earn money?

"Think and Search" Questions

4. **Describe the Sequence of Events** What does Hamdiye do after she finishes the housework?
5. **Describe** Describe Hamdiye. What does she look like? What does she like?
6. **Determine Characteristics of Culture** What did you learn about Hamdiye's culture?

"Author and You" Questions

7. **Identify Themes** What are some important traditions in Hamdiye's community?
8. **Draw Conclusions** How do you think Hamdiye feels about the traditions she describes?

"On Your Own" Questions

9. **Connect** What do you think are the best parts of Hamdiye's life? What do you think are the hardest parts?
10. **Compare and Contrast** In what ways is your culture similar to Hamdiye's? In what ways is it different?

Activity Book
p. 26

Student
CD-ROM

Build Reading Fluency

Reading Chunks of Words

Reading chunks or phrases of words is an important characteristic of fluent readers. It helps you stop reading word by word.

1. With a partner, take turns reading aloud the underlined chunks of words.
2. Read aloud two times each.

> During the week, I go to school
> in the mornings. When I return home
> at noon, I help my family
> with housework first and then eat lunch.
> I live with my four sisters and my mother.
> We all help each other.

Listen, Speak, Interact

Distinguish Fact from Opinion

A **fact** is true information. An **opinion** is what someone thinks or believes. In "Turkish Delight," Hamdiye gives facts and opinions. Can you tell the difference? Here is an example:

Fact: I am 13 years old.
Opinion: I am a clever person.

1. With a partner, reread or listen to the audio recording of paragraphs 1, 2, and 3 of the selection.

Facts	Opinions

2. List facts and opinions in a chart like the one here.

3. Compare your list with another set of partners.

4. Share your list with the class.

Elements of Literature

Instructions

Authors use **instructions** to list the steps in doing something. The recipe in "Turkish Delight" gives instructions. It explains the steps needed to make an apricot dessert.

Recipes include a list of ingredients, or food items needed to make a recipe. Then the recipe explains what to do with the ingredients. People often write these instructions in a numbered list.

1. Reread the recipe for Cream-filled Apricots.

2. Rewrite the instructions in paragraph 8. Give each step a number starting with 1.

3. Use the list shown to help you organize the steps.

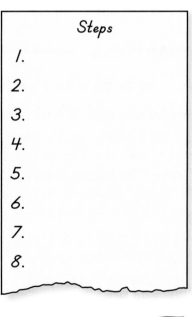

Steps

1.
2.
3.
4.
5.
6.
7.
8.

Activity Book
p. 27

Student
CD-ROM

Word Study

Recognize Root Words and the Suffix *-ish*

Many English words are made by combining a **root word** and a **suffix**. A *root word* is a word or part of a word that can be used to make other words. A *suffix* is an ending. The suffix *-ish* means "like" or "having to do with." The word *Turkish* means "having to do with Turkey."

Words	Definitions
childish	having to do with England
English	like the color red
foolish	like a child
reddish	like a fool

1. Work with a partner. On a piece of paper, match each word with its correct definition.
2. Check your answers with another pair of students.
3. Write sentences using three of the words.

4. Write the words and their definitions in your Personal Dictionary.

Personal Dictionary   Activity Book p. 28   Student CD-ROM

Grammar Focus

Use the Verb *To Be* with Complements

A **complement** describes or renames the subject of a sentence. A complement can be a noun, a pronoun, or an adjective. Complements can follow a form of the verb *to be*. Forms of *to be* include *am, is,* and *are*.

Look at these sentences. The underlined words are complements.

The dogs **are** <u>big and brown</u>.

She **is** <u>my sister</u>.

I **am** <u>older</u>.

1. Read paragraphs 1, 2, and 3 of "Turkish Delight." On a piece of paper, write two sentences that include a form of *to be* and a complement.
2. Circle the *to be* forms and underline the complements.
3. Write two sentences of your own using a form of *to be* and a complement. Be sure to use the correct forms of *to be* and to spell these forms correctly.

Activity Book pp. 29–30   Student Handbook   Student CD-ROM

From Reading to Writing

Write a Personal Narrative

Write a letter to a new pen pal. Your letter will be a personal narrative that tells about you. Write one paragraph.

1. Describe yourself and your family. Include details about how old you are, what you look like, your daily activities, where you live, and what you like to do.
2. Use the first-person pronouns *I, me, we,* and *us.*
3. Use time words to show order.

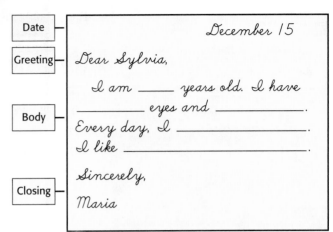

Date	December 15
Greeting	Dear Sylvia,
Body	I am _____ years old. I have _____ eyes and _____. Every day, I _____. I like _____.
Closing	Sincerely, Maria

Activity Book
p. 31

Student Handbook

Across Content Areas
THE ARTS

Design a Turkish Rug

People who make rugs are **weavers.** Weavers make **designs** in the cloth. A design can be a shape or a picture.

Sometimes weavers use **symbols** as their designs. A symbol is something that stands for something else. For example, a flying bird might be a symbol of freedom.

In "Turkish Delight," Hamdiye describes a kind of Turkish rug called a *kilim.* Turkish weavers make colorful designs in the rugs. These designs are often symbols.

The picture shows two common symbols found on Turkish rugs.

1. On a piece of paper, design a "Turkish rug." Draw symbols that you would weave on a Turkish rug.

2. Share your design with a small group. Explain what each symbol means and why you chose it.

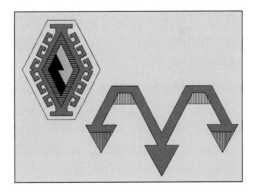

Activity Book
p. 32

CHAPTER 5

Sadako and the Thousand Paper Cranes

an excerpt from a novel based on a true story by Eleanor Coerr

Objectives

Reading Identify cause and effect as you read historical fiction.

Listening and Speaking Perform a dialogue.

Grammar Recognize possessive nouns.

Writing Write a fictional narrative.

Content Math: Learn geometric shapes and vocabulary.

Use Prior Knowledge

Describe a Sickness

In "Sadako and the Thousand Paper Cranes," the main character is named Sadako. She is in the hospital because she is very sick. She feels sad and lonely. Her family and friends come to visit her, and they cheer her up.

1. Think about a time when you or someone you know was very sick.
2. With a partner, write words that describe being sick. Use a web like the one shown. How does a sick person's body feel? What emotions and thoughts does a sick person have?

3. Draw pictures to go with your web of words. Show how a person looks when he or she feels sick, sad, or lonely.

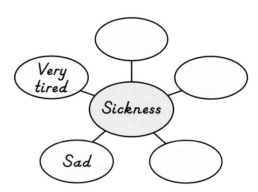

Build Background

Radiation Sickness

In 1945, during World War II, the United States dropped two atom bombs on the Japanese cities of Hiroshima and Nagasaki. The bombs spread radiation— harmful energy waves that come from atom bombs. Radiation made people very sick. They felt very weak and had trouble fighting germs. This reading tells a story about Sadako Sasaki. She was a Japanese girl who had radiation sickness.

SOCIAL STUDIES

Content Connection

Japan is a nation of islands. It is in the Pacific Ocean near the east coast of China.

Build Vocabulary

Identify Words About Setting

The **setting** of a story is its time and place. One way to learn new words is to relate them to a setting where they are used. The setting for "Sadako and the Thousand Paper Cranes" is a hospital. Work with a small group to learn words that relate to the setting of hospitals.

1. Read the words in the box.

nurse	shot	sick
hospital	visiting	hours

2. Work with your group to figure out what each word means. Use a dictionary if necessary. Write the meanings in your Personal Dictionary.

3. Write a sentence for each word.

Personal Dictionary

The Heinle Newbury House Dictionary

Activity Book *p. 33*

Student CD-ROM

Text Structure

Novel Based on a True Story

The reading selection is taken from a book called *Sadako and the Thousand Paper Cranes*. A story that fills a book is a **novel.** This is a special kind of novel. It is a novel based on a true story. The author did not make up the whole story. The story really happened, but it did not happen exactly the way the author wrote it.

We can also say that this story is **historical fiction.** In historical fiction, the author makes up some or all of the story. Look at the distinguishing features of this genre.

Historical Fiction	
Setting	the time and place of a story; some are made up
Characters	the people; some are made up
Plot	what happens in the story Beginning ↓ Middle ↓ End

Pay attention to and analyze the setting, the characters, and the plot as you read.

Student
CD-ROM

Reading Strategy

Identify Cause and Effect

The reason something happens is its **cause.** The event that happens is an **effect.** As you read the selection, think about why the events in the story happen.

1. One way to find a cause and an effect is to ask a question and then answer it. Use the word *because* in your answer to connect the cause and the effect.

2. Read these sentences:

   She got sick.
   She was in Hiroshima when the bomb fell.

   Why did she get sick?
   She got sick *because* she was in Hiroshima when the bomb fell.
   the cause = being in Hiroshima
   the effect = getting sick

3. Make a chart like this. As you read the selection, write causes and effects.

Causes	Effects
She was in the hospital.	She didn't hear her mother making breakfast.

Student
CD-ROM

SADAKO AND THE THOUSAND PAPER CRANES

an excerpt from a novel based on a true story

by Eleanor Coerr

Audio
CD 1, Tr. 6

Prologue

This excerpt is set in a hospital room in Hiroshima, Japan. It is around 1955—ten years after the atom bomb was dropped on the city. The main character is a 12-year-old girl named Sadako Sasaki. She becomes sick and is taken to the hospital. There Sadako learns that she has leukemia, which is a sickness of the blood. Her sickness is caused by being around the radiation that the bomb left behind.

The Golden Crane

Identify Cause and Effect

What causes Sadako to hope that yesterday was a bad dream?

1   The next morning Sadako woke up slowly. She listened for the familiar sounds of her mother making breakfast, but there were only the new and different sounds of a hospital. Sadako sighed. She had hoped that yesterday was just a bad dream. It was even more real when Nurse Yasunaga came in to give her a **shot.**

2   "Getting shots is part of being in the hospital," the **plump** nurse said briskly. "You'll get used to it."

---

shot   the use of a needle to put medicine into a vein   **plump**   full and round in shape

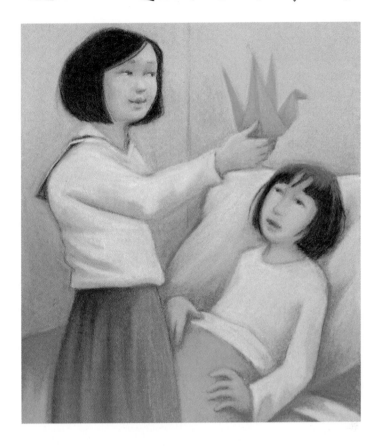

Identify Cause and Effect

Why does Sadako want the sickness to be over?

3 "I just want the sickness to be over with," Sadako said unhappily, "so I can go home."

4 That afternoon Chizuko was Sadako's first visitor. She smiled **mysteriously** as she held something behind her back. "Shut your eyes," she said. While Sadako squinted her eyes tightly shut, Chizuko put some pieces of paper and scissors on the bed. "Now you can look," she said.

5 "What is it?" Sadako asked, staring at the paper.

6 Chizuko was pleased with herself. "I've figured out a way for you to get well," she said proudly. "Watch!" She cut a piece of gold paper into a large square. In a short time she had folded it over and over into a beautiful crane.

7 Sadako was **puzzled.** "But how can that paper bird make me well?"

---

mysteriously in a secret way   **puzzled** confused, not understanding

Identify Cause and Effect

What does the old story say will happen if someone folds one thousand cranes?

8   "Don't you remember that old story about the crane?" Chizuko asked. "It's supposed to live for a thousand years. If a sick person folds one thousand paper cranes, the gods will **grant** her wish and make her healthy again." She handed the crane to Sadako. "Here's your first one."

9   Sadako's eyes filled with tears. How kind of Chizuko to bring a good luck charm! Especially when her friend didn't really believe in such things. Sadako took the golden crane and made a wish. The funniest little feeling came over her when she touched the bird. It must be a good **omen.**

10 "Thank you, Chizuko **chan,**" she whispered. "I'll never never part with it."

11 When she began to work with the paper, Sadako discovered that folding a crane wasn't as easy as it looked. With Chizuko's help she learned how to do the difficult parts. After making ten birds, Sadako lined them up on the table beside the golden crane. Some were a bit **lopsided,** but it was a beginning.

grant   give or allow what is asked for
omen   a sign of something that is going to happen in the future

chan   a Japanese suffix added to the end of a name to show affection
lopsided   with one side much larger or heavier than the other

Identify Cause and Effect

How does the golden crane make Sadako feel?

12   "Now I have only nine hundred and ninety to make," Sadako said. With the golden crane nearby she felt safe and lucky. Why, in a few weeks she would be able to finish the thousand. Then she would be strong enough to go home.

13   That evening Masahiro brought Sadako's homework from school. When he saw the cranes, he said, "There isn't enough room on that small table to show off your birds. "I'll hang them from the ceiling for you."

14   Sadako was smiling all over. "Do you promise to hang every crane I make?" she asked.

15   Masahiro promised.

16   "That's fine!" Sadako said, her eyes **twinkling** with **mischief.** "Then you'll hang the whole thousand?"

17   "A thousand!" Her brother groaned. "You're joking!"

18   Sadako told him the story of the cranes.

---

twinkling   shining

mischief   small, irritating acts or behavior, usually by children

19   Masahiro ran a hand through his straight black hair.
"You tricked me!" he said with a **grin.** "But I'll do it
anyhow." He borrowed some **thread** and **tacks** from Nurse
Yasunaga and hung the first ten cranes. The golden crane
stayed in its place of honor on the table.

20   After supper Mrs. Sasaki brought Mitsue and Eiji to the
hospital. Everyone was surprised to see the birds. They
reminded Mrs. Sasaki of a famous old poem:

> Out of colored paper, cranes
> come flying into
> our house.

**Identify Cause
and Effect**

Why did Mrs.
Sasaki choose the
tiniest crane?

21   Mitsue and Eiji liked the golden crane best. But Mrs.
Sasaki chose the tiniest one made of fancy green paper
with pink **parasols** on it. "This is my choice," she said,
"because small ones are the most difficult to make."

---

grin   a big smile
thread   a twisted fiber, such as cotton, wool, and so on

tacks   small sharp nails
parasols   light umbrellas used as protection from the sun

22 After visiting hours it was lonely in the hospital room. So lonely that Sadako folded more cranes to keep up her **courage.**

23 Eleven . . . I wish I'd get better. Twelve . . . I wish I'd get better . . .

Epilogue

Sadako continues to make cranes even though her sickness causes her to feel weak. After she makes 644 cranes, Sadako dies. People all over Japan learn about Sadako Sasaki's experience. As a result, a statue of her is built in the Peace Park of Hiroshima. People from all over the world visit the statue. They leave paper cranes to remember Sadako and to promote peace.

courage   the ability and strength to face difficulties

About the Author   Eleanor Coerr (born 1922)

Eleanor Coerr was born and grew up in Canada. She loved to write as a young girl. Coerr eventually became a reporter. She traveled a lot. She visited the Peace Park in Hiroshima. She decided to write a book about Sadako. Eleanor Coerr wrote, "Sometimes one book can change an author's life. *Sadako and the Thousand Paper Cranes . . .* has been that book for me . . . It has moved thousands of children around the world to fold cranes as wishes for peace."

➤ How do you think Eleanor Coerr felt about Sadako and her life? What makes you think that?

Beyond the Reading

Reading Comprehension

Question-Answer Relationships (QAR)

"Right There" Questions

1. **Recall Facts** Where is Sadako?
2. **Recall Facts** What does Chizuko bring to Sadako?

"Think and Search" Questions

3. **Compare and Contrast** How are Sadako's cranes different from the golden crane that Chizuko makes?
4. **Analyze Character Relationships** How do you think Sadako's visitors feel about her? How do you think Sadako feels about her visitors?
5. **Summarize Text** How would you summarize the important ideas in the selection?

"Author and You" Questions

6. **Understand Tone** How do you think the author feels about Sadako? How does this affect how you feel about her?

7. **Analyze Text Types** Why do you think the author chose to base the story on a true event?
8. **Analyze Text Types** What events in the story do you think are historically correct? What events do you think are fiction? Explain.

"On Your Own" Questions

9. **Form Questions** What questions would you research about the background of the story?
10. **Evaluate** How does the illustrator's choice of style, elements of art, and method of drawing help you to understand and gather more meaning from the text?

Activity Book
p. 34

Student
CD-ROM

Build Reading Fluency

Adjust Your Reading Rate for Quotations

Reading quotations (what characters say) helps you learn to adjust your reading rate. You must pause and read with expression. Learning to read with expression makes others want to listen.

Reread the conversation between Sadako and Chizuko. Look for the quotation marks (" . . . ").

1. With a partner, take turns rereading aloud paragraphs 4–7 on page 59.
2. Read the quotations with expression.
3. Pause after each quotation.
4. Choose the quotation you like best.
5. Read aloud with expression to the class.

Listen, Speak, Interact

Perform a Dialogue

In fiction, characters often say things to each other. This is called **dialogue.** You can find dialogue on the page because it has **quotation marks** (" . . . ") around the words the characters say.

> "Getting shots is part of being in the hospital," the plump nurse said briskly.

1. With a partner, find some dialogue in the story that you like. Copy several lines.
2. Be sure to put quotation marks around what the characters say.
3. Listen to the audio recording of the selection to help you distinguish and produce the intonation (changing voice level) of the words you use.
4. Practice saying the dialogue to each other. Speak clearly and slowly.
5. Say only the words in quotation marks. Don't read things like "he said" and "she said."
6. Present your dialogue to the class. Be sure to use effective rate, volume, pitch, and tone.

Elements of Literature

Understand Characterization

Characterization is the way an author creates a character. Eleanor Coerr describes what Sadako says, does, and feels to tell you what the main character is like. Read this sentence from the selection:

> Sadako was puzzled.

The sentence tells you how Sadako feels.

> Sadako's eyes filled with tears.

This sentence shows what Sadako does. (She cries.) The word *tears* also provides clues about how Sadako feels. The author also tells you how other characters in the story act toward Sadako.

This gives you more information about the main character. For example, Chizuko makes Sadako a crane to cheer her up. This tells you that the main character is loved and cared for by others.

1. Find a description in the story that provides information about Sadako.
2. Then find a description about another character that also helps you learn about the main character.
3. Write these descriptions in your Reading Log. Explain what they tell you about Sadako.

Reading Log

Activity Book
p. 35

Student
CD-ROM

Word Study

Recognize Adjectives Ending in *-ed*

Adjectives are words that describe a person, a place, or a thing. Some adjectives can be made from verbs by adding *-ed* to the simple form of the verb. A simple form of a verb is the verb without any endings.

Chizuko was pleas**ed** with herself.

Simple Form of Verb	+ed	Adjective
pleas~~e~~	+ ed	pleased

Notice that if the simple form of a verb ends in an *e*, you drop the *e* before you add *-ed*.

Find two more examples of adjectives ending in *-ed* in the reading. Write them in your Personal Dictionary. Look in paragraphs 7 and 20.

Personal Dictionary   Activity Book p. 36   Student CD-ROM

Grammar Focus

Recognize Possessive Nouns

A **possessive noun** is a noun that shows who has or possesses something. The author uses possessive nouns to show things that Sadako has.

That afternoon Chizuko was Sadako<u>'s</u> first visitor.

The word *Sadako* is a singular noun. A **singular noun** is a noun that stands for only one person or thing. To make a singular noun possessive, add *'s*.

1. Find two more examples of singular possessive nouns in the selection. Look in paragraphs 9, 11, and 13.

2. Explain what the character has in each example.

3. Look around the classroom. Identify three things that three different people have. On a piece of paper, write possessive nouns to describe what each person has. For example:

My teacher's desk is brown.

David's backpack is very large.

Activity Book pp. 37–38   Student Handbook   Student CD-ROM

From Reading to Writing

Write a Fictional Narrative

Write a three-paragraph fictional narrative set in a special time in history. You can choose a story that you have read about, or you can make it up.

1. Describe the setting—the time and place of your story.
2. Use characterization to tell readers about your characters.
3. Put your events in chronological order. Clearly connect the events by using words to show what happens next, such as *soon, next,* and *finally.*
4. Include dialogue with quotation marks.

Title	
1	*Setting:* time and place *Characters:* the people in the story *Problem:* what the people have to do
2	*Plot:* what happens
3	*Conclusion:* how the problem is resolved; how the characters change

Activity Book
p. 39

Student Handbook

Across Content Areas

Learn Geometric Shapes and Vocabulary

The art of making different figures from paper is called **origami.** If you unfold one of these figures, you will see that the folds make many different **geometric** shapes. Geometry is a type of math in which you study shapes, lines, and angles.

The following sentences show how geometry relates to origami. Complete each sentence with one of these words.

> **triangle** △
> **square** □
> **diagonal**—a line connecting opposite corners of a square or a rectangle
> **symmetrical**—the same on both sides

1. A _____ piece of paper is six inches long and six inches wide.
2. Connect the two opposite corners of the square and press to fold the paper. A _____ with three sides is formed.
3. Unfold the paper. The shapes on both sides of the fold are the same size and shape. They are _____ .
4. The line connecting one corner to the opposite corner is a _____ .

Activity Book
p. 40

Listening and Speaking Workshop

Present a Narrative About Your Favorite Holiday

Topic

Tell a story about the most fun you have had on a holiday. Describe the setting (the time and place), the characters (the people), and the events in the order in which they happened.

Step 1: Use a chart to get organized.

Make notes or draw pictures as you plan your story.

Holiday: _____	Notes and Pictures
Setting Place Time of day and year	
Characters	
Events What happened? Was there a problem? What was the solution?	
Ending How did you feel? Why was it a good time?	

Step 2: Answer questions.

1. Where did the holiday take place?
2. Who was with you?
3. What happened to make it fun? Describe the specific events in order. What feelings did you have?

Step 3: Think of an opening that will get the audience's attention.

1. Ask a question.
2. Say something funny.
3. Make an interesting statement.

Step 4: Use visuals.

Make some visuals to make your presentation more interesting. You can use a poster, some pictures, or a computer presentation.

Step 5: Practice telling your story to a partner.

1. Use your chart to help you.
2. Use your visuals.
3. Use the information from the checklists to revise your presentation.

Step 6: Present.

1. Speak loudly enough for everyone to hear. Speak slowly.
2. Use gestures (movements of your body).
3. Be expressive. For example, use your voice to show excitement.

Student
Handbook

Viewing Workshop

View and Think

Compare and Contrast Cultures

In this unit you read about people who were part of different cultures. A **culture** is a group of people who share something in common. For example, people who live in the same area and have the same traditions are part of the same culture.

1. Go to a library and borrow a video about a culture that is different from yours.

2. Before you view the video, prepare some questions. For example:
   a. What is the land like where the people live?
   b. What kind of work do many of the people do?
   c. What traditions do the people practice?
   d. What is the food like?

3. View the video and find out if your questions were answered. What other things did you learn from the video?

4. Think about your culture. Compare and contrast your culture with the culture on the video.

Further Viewing

Watch the *Visions* CNN Video for Unit 1. Do the Video Worksheet.

CNN Video

Writer's Workshop

Write a Personal Narrative About a Trip

Prompt

A personal narrative tells a story about something you did. Tell about a trip you took. Where did you go? What happened? How did you feel about the trip? What made it interesting?

Narrative Chart

Beginning
- Get the reader's interest.
- Say what you are going to write about.
- Describe the characters.
- Describe the setting (time and place).

↓

Middle
- Tell what happened.
- Use details and descriptions.
- Use dialogue with quotation marks.

↓

End
- How did you feel at the end?
- Did you learn anything?
- Would you take this trip again?

Step 1: Write a draft.

1. Begin with a strong opening. Use a question or some dialogue that will interest the reader.
2. Write a sentence to introduce the topic (what you are going to write about).
3. Put all the events in chronological order. Blend paragraphs into larger chunks of writing. Use transition words like *first, then,* and *next.*
4. Use a dictionary or other reference materials to help you with spelling and meaning.

Step 2: Revise your draft.

Carefully reread your draft and make sure that you did these things.

Content and Organization
1. You thought about your audience and your purpose for writing.
2. You used details to make the story exciting.
3. You used dialogue with quotation marks.
4. You wrote a beginning, a middle, and an end.
5. You wrote a title for your story.

Sentence Construction
6. You wrote clearly and used different kinds of sentences.

Usage
7. You used strong descriptive words and correct grammar.

Step 3: Peer edit.

1. Ask a partner to read your story.
2. Ask your partner how you can make your narrative better.
3. Revise your narrative if necessary. Add, elaborate, delete, combine, or rearrange text to make your story clearer.

Step 4: Proofread and finish.

1. Proofread (carefully read) your story to check for mechanics: correct spelling, punctuation, and capitalization.
2. If possible, type your story on a computer. Check for mechanics using the computer software.
3. If your narrative is more than one page long, number the pages.
4. Make a title page that includes your name and the title.
5. Exchange papers with a partner. Proofread each other's story to be sure that the edits make sense.

Step 5: Publish.

1. If you are writing on a computer, choose a font (kind of type) for your narrative. You can also use a border to decorate your narrative.
2. If you are writing by hand, make a final copy in your best handwriting.
3. You can add pictures or drawings to your narrative if you wish.
4. Create a class collection of the stories. Create a table of contents to organize the stories.
   a. Analyze your classmates' published works as models for writing. Review them for their strengths and weaknesses.
   b. Set your goals as a writer based on your writing and the writing of your classmates.

The Heinle Newbury House Dictionary

Student Handbook

Projects

These projects will help you learn more about the theme of the unit—traditions and cultures. Ask your teacher for help if you need it.

Project 1: Create a Poster About a New Tradition

Create a new tradition based on an important event in your city or town.

1. Learn more about your city or town. Read Internet sites or books you find in the library. Find a fact that tells about an important event in the history of your community. For example, when was it founded?
2. Brainstorm ways to celebrate that event each year. On what date should it be celebrated? List activities people can do to celebrate the tradition.
3. Describe your new tradition on a piece of posterboard. Include the event that will be remembered, the date of the tradition, and special activities to celebrate it.
4. Arrange the information in a way that is easy for people to read. You may include pictures with captions.
5. Use capitalization and punctuation that will clarify and enhance your information.

PUBLIC LIBRARY DAY

Come CELEBRATE our public library's anniversary—75 years!

Poetry readings!

Free cookies and juice!

Wednesday, November 15, from 10–4.

Project 2: Give a Cross-Cultural Presentation

In a group of three, find out about the differences between two cultures.

1. In your group, choose two cultures.
2. Cultures have many different characteristics. Choose three from the list below.

Examples of Characteristics

Food
Holidays
Traditional clothing
How people greet each other
How people feel about family

---

3. Research (find out about) the three characteristics you chose for your two cultures. You can:
   a. Use the Internet. Use the keyword "cultures" or, for example, "Chinese culture."
   b. Use reference books.
   c. Interview people from each of the cultures you chose.
4. As you find information, look for pictures, objects, and other visuals to use in your presentation.
5. Write a report to organize the information you found. List the sources that were used, such as books or websites.
6. Present your results to the class. Explain the differences between the two cultures. Act out what people do. Use visuals.

Further Reading

Here is a list of books about the theme of traditions and cultures. Pick one or more of them. Notice how you read at a different rate or speed depending on the type of text. Write your thoughts and feelings about what you read in your Reading Log. Take notes about your answers to these questions. Then discuss your answers with a partner.

1. What new cultural traditions did you read about?
2. Are the traditions you read about similar to the ones of your family?
3. How are cultures the same? How are they different?

Sadako and the Thousand Paper Cranes

by Eleanor Coerr, Penguin USA, 2002. Sadako is sick with leukemia because of the atom bomb that was dropped on Hiroshima during World War II. A friend reminds Sadako of the Japanese legend that says if a sick person folds one thousand cranes, she will become healthy again.

Native American Games and Stories

by James and Joseph Bruchac, Fulcrum Publishing, 2000. Learn how to play authentic Native American games and the stories of their origins. Instructions are included on how to make the necessary equipment.

Fiesta Femenina: Celebrating Women in Mexican Folktale

by Mary-Joan Gerson, Barefoot Books, Inc., 2001. This book tells eight Mexican folktales from a variety of different cultures. Read folklore from the ancient Maya and Aztec as well as stories of Euro-Mexican origin.

Culture and Customs of Costa Rica

by Chalene Helmuth, Greenwood Publishing Group, Inc., 2000. Take a journey through the history of Costa Rica from its discovery by Christopher Columbus in 1502 to its establishment as one of the most progressive Central American countries.

China: The Culture

by Bobbie Kalman, Crabtree Publishing Co., 2001. This book explores Chinese culture. Read about how a potato print and abacus are used. Discover traditional Chinese performing arts, festivals, and foods.

Texas Traditions: The Culture of the Lone Star State, Vol. 1

by Robyn Montana Turner, Little, Brown & Co., 1996. Texas is truly a multicultural state. This book offers a glimpse into the various cultures that have made Texas the unique place it is today.

Homeless Bird

by Gloria Whelan, HarperCollins Children's Books, 2001. In this book, thirteen-year-old Koly has an arranged marriage, as dictated by Indian custom. She is soon widowed and abandoned by her husband's family. But she discovers the courage to survive on her own.

Companion
Web site

Reading Log

Heinle
Reading Library
The Legend of
Sleepy Hollow

UNIT 2

Environment

Tiger in a Tropical Storm (Surprise!), Henri Rousseau, oil painting. 1891.

View the Picture

1. Describe the environment that you see in this painting.

2. How would you describe the environment where you live?

In this unit, you will read selections about different types of environments and the living things in them. You will read and learn how to recognize a poem, a fable, an interview, a fiction story, and an informational article. You will practice writing each of these forms.

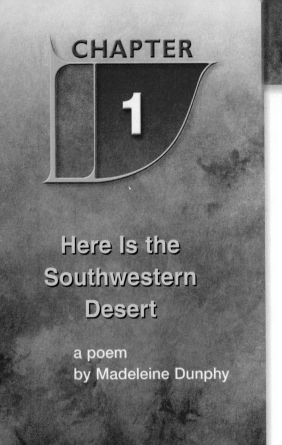

CHAPTER 1

Here Is the Southwestern Desert

a poem
by Madeleine Dunphy

Objectives

Reading Describe images as you read a poem.

Listening and Speaking Act out a poem.

Grammar Identify the simple present tense.

Writing Write a poem about the environment.

Content Science: Learn about types of climate.

Use Prior Knowledge

Describe Images of a Desert

The reading selection in this chapter describes the desert of the southwestern United States. A desert is a dry region with little or no rain.

1. Close your eyes and suppose you are in the desert. What images (pictures) come to your mind? What do you see, hear, smell, taste, and touch in the desert?

2. In the ovals of the web, write words that relate to your images and ideas of the desert. If you wish, you may add extra ovals to the web.

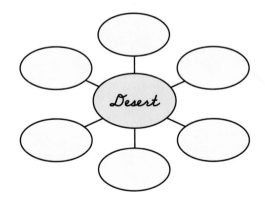

Build Background

The Southwestern Desert

The *southwestern desert* refers to the desert regions in Arizona, New Mexico, Texas, Oklahoma, California, Nevada, and Utah. Some of these deserts extend into Mexico.

Content Connection

Some well-known southwestern deserts are the Mojave, the Sonoran, and the Chihuahuan Deserts.

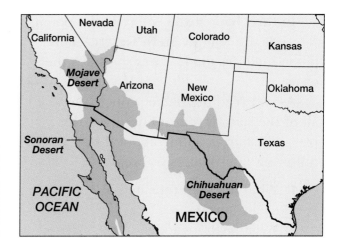

Build Vocabulary

Use Context to Understand Vocabulary

The **context** of a word is the other words around it. You can use the context to help you understand new words.

1. Read the sentences below. The underlined words are from the reading selection.

   a. The bird <u>perches</u> on the tree.
   b. The bird <u>spies</u> on the worm.
   c. The sun <u>blazes</u> on the tree.
   d. The dog <u>unearths</u> the bone.

2. Now read these definitions. Match the definitions with the underlined words in the sentences. Use the context to help you decide which definition is correct.

a. to dig up
b. to land and rest on something
c. to burn strongly
d. to see after looking around

3. Write the words and their definitions in your Personal Dictionary.

Personal Dictionary   The Heinle Newbury House Dictionary   Activity Book *p. 41*   Student CD-ROM

Text Structure

A Poem

In this chapter, you will read the poem "Here Is the Southwestern Desert." This poem includes the features shown in the chart.

As you read the poem, notice how all of the stanzas repeat lines from the previous stanzas. Think about the following questions as you read:

1. What lines are repeated in each stanza?
2. What lines are added to each stanza?

Poem	
Repetition	the repeating of an idea, a phrase, or a sentence
Stanzas	groups of lines used to separate ideas

Student
CD-ROM

Reading Strategy

Describe Images

Writers often use words that help readers create **images** (pictures) in their minds. Poetry often has many images in it.

In "Here Is the Southwestern Desert," the author describes animals, plants, and other parts of the environment. In each stanza, she adds new images.

As you read or listen to the audio recording of the poem, close your eyes from time to time. Describe the images that you see to the class in your own words. Use the images you form to help you understand the meanings of new words.

Listen carefully to the images described by your classmates. What effect do they have on you?

Student
CD-ROM

Here Is the
SOUTHWESTERN DESERT

a poem by Madeleine Dunphy

Audio
CD 1, Tr. 7

1   Here is the southwestern desert.

2   Here is the **cactus**
    that is covered with **spines**
    and can live without rain
    for a very long time.
    Here is the southwestern desert.

3   Here is the **hawk**
    that perches on the cactus
    that is covered with spines
    and can live without rain
    for a very long time.
    Here is the southwestern desert.

4   Here is the **lizard**
    who is spied by the hawk
    that perches on the cactus
    that is covered with spines
    and can live without rain
    for a very long time.
    Here is the southwestern desert.

---

cactus a plant that grows in the desert and has sharp needles

spines sharp, pointy needles on a cactus

hawk a large bird that hunts animals for food

lizard a reptile with four legs

Describe Images

What is your image of the roadrunner and the lizard? Are they running fast or slowly? Is the roadrunner close to the lizard, or are they far apart?

5   Here is the **roadrunner**
    that chases the lizard
    who is spied by the hawk
    that perches on the cactus
    that is covered with spines
    and can live without rain
    for a very long time.
    Here is the southwestern desert.

6   Here is the tree,
    which **shelters** the roadrunner
    that chases the lizard
    who is spied by the hawk
    that perches on the cactus
    that is covered with spines
    and can live without rain
    for a very long time.
    Here is the southwestern desert.

---

roadrunner   a type of bird that can run very quickly
    and lives in the desert

shelters   provides protection

7   Here is the sun
      that **blazes** on the tree,
      which shelters the roadrunner
      that chases the lizard
      who is spied by the hawk
      that perches on the cactus
      that is covered with spines
      and can live without rain
      for a very long time.
      Here is the southwestern desert.

Describe Images

What is your image of the sun and the bobcat? What is the day like? Do you think the bobcat feels good?

8   Here is the **bobcat**
      who **basks** in the sun
      that blazes on the tree,
      which shelters the roadrunner
      that chases the lizard
      who is spied by the hawk
      that perches on the cactus
      that is covered with spines
      and can live without rain
      for a very long time.
      Here is the southwestern desert.

---

blazes burns strongly

bobcat a wild cat that lives in North America and
      has a short tail and brown fur with spots

basks enjoys the sun while sitting or lying down

9 Here is the **badger**
that smells the bobcat
who basks in the sun
that blazes on the tree,
which shelters the roadrunner
that chases the lizard
who is spied by the hawk
that perches on the cactus
that is covered with spines
and can live without rain
for a very long time.
Here is the southwestern desert.

Describe Images

What is your image of the squirrel and the badger? What is the badger doing? Where is the squirrel? Is the squirrel frightened?

10 Here is the squirrel
who is **unearthed** by the badger
that smells the bobcat
who basks in the sun
that blazes on the tree,
which shelters the roadrunner
that chases the lizard
who is spied by the hawk
that perches on the cactus
that is covered with spines
and can live without rain
for a very long time.
Here is the southwestern desert.

---

badger an animal that digs and lives in the ground   **unearthed** uncovered

11

Describe Images

What is your image
of the coyote?
Does it move
quickly or slowly?

Here is the **coyote**
that **pounces** on the squirrel
who is unearthed by the badger
that smells the bobcat
who basks in the sun
that blazes on the tree,
which shelters the roadrunner
that chases the lizard
who is spied by the hawk
that perches on the cactus
that is covered with spines
and can live without rain
for a very long time.
Here is the southwestern desert.

---

coyote   a type of wolf that is similar to a dog and lives
    in parts of North America

pounces   attacks by jumping quickly on something

12 Here is the snake
that **hisses** at the coyote
that pounces on the squirrel
who is unearthed by the badger
that smells the bobcat
who basks in the sun
that blazes on the tree,
which shelters the roadrunner
that chases the lizard
who is spied by the hawk
that perches on the cactus
that is covered with spines
and can live without rain
for a very long time.
Here is the southwestern desert.

---

hisses   makes a low, soft sound

Describe Images

What is your image of the hare? Where is it? Do you think it is frightened?

13   Here is the **hare**
who hears the snake
that hisses at the coyote
that pounces on the squirrel
who is unearthed by the badger
that smells the bobcat
who basks in the sun
that blazes on the tree,
which shelters the roadrunner
that chases the lizard
who is spied by the hawk
that perches on the cactus
that is covered with spines
and can live without rain
for a very long time.
Here is the southwestern desert.

---

hare   an animal like a large rabbit

Describe Images

What is your image of the hare and the cactus? What is the hare doing to the cactus?

14 Here is the cactus
that is food for the hare
who hears the snake
that hisses at the coyote
that pounces on the squirrel
who is unearthed by the badger
that smells the bobcat
who basks in the sun
that blazes on the tree,
which shelters the roadrunner
that chases the lizard
who is spied by the hawk
that perches on the cactus
that is covered with spines
and can live without rain
for a very long time.
Here is the southwestern desert.

About the Author

Madeleine Dunphy (born 1962)

Madeleine Dunphy travels a lot to write her books. She goes to many faraway and interesting places, such as The Democratic Republic of Congo, the Amazon Rain Forest, Peru, Cambodia, and Australia. Dunphy also taught environmental studies in Thailand.

➤ How do you think Madeleine Dunphy's travels and experience helped her write "Here Is the Southwestern Desert"?

Beyond the Reading

Reading Comprehension

Question-Answer Relationships (QAR)

"Right There" Questions

1. **Recall Facts** What plant is covered with spines?
2. **Recall Facts** What animals are named in the poem?
3. **Recall Facts** What plants are named in the poem?

"Think and Search" Questions

4. **Draw Conclusions** What type of weather does the desert *not* have for a long time?
5. **Use Context Clues** What do you think the roadrunner does well?

"Author and You" Questions

6. **Make Inferences** How do you think the animals in the poem get food?

7. **Describe** Based on what you learned from the poem, how would you describe the desert?

"On Your Own" Questions

8. **Compare** How does the desert compare with the environment you live in?
9. **Explain** How do people depend on each other?
10. **Connect Ideas** How does this poem connect to what you learned about the food chain on page 25?

Activity Book
p. 42

Student
CD-ROM

Build Reading Fluency

Echo Read Aloud

Effective readers learn to read with feeling. Echo reading helps you read with feeling and expression. Your teacher reads a line. Then the class reads (echoes) the same line aloud. Turn to page 80.

1. Listen to your teacher read.
2. Read the same line aloud with expression.
3. Continue listening and reading.

Listen, Speak, Interact

Act Out a Poem

The poem "Here Is the Southwestern Desert" includes many action verbs. Work in a small group to act out a part of the poem.

1. Choose a series of lines from the poem.
2. Identify the action that each person in the group will demonstrate.
3. As a group, act out the actions for the class. Do not use words. Use movements only.
4. Ask the class to guess which lines of the poem you are demonstrating.
5. Discuss your presentation. Talk about how acting out part of the poem helped you understand and remember it better.

Elements of Literature

Recognize Free Verse

Poems sometimes have rhyming words at the ends of the lines. Rhyming words end with the same sounds. For example, the words *hill* and *Jill* rhyme in these lines:

Jack and *Jill*
went up the *hill.*

Free verse is a type of poetry that does not use rhyming words. The stanzas of a free verse poem can also be made up of a different number of lines.

With a partner, study how free verse is used in "Here Is the Southwestern Desert."

1. Notice how the number of lines changes in each stanza. Why did the writer add more lines to each stanza?
2. Read a few lines of the poem to your partner. Then listen as your partner reads aloud a few lines.
3. Note how the last words of each line do not rhyme. Discuss why you think the writer didn't use rhyming words. Write your conclusion in your Reading Log.

Reading Log

Activity Book
p. 43

Student
CD-ROM

Word Study

Recognize Word Origins

Many words in English are influenced by other cultures and languages. "Here Is the Southwestern Desert" uses words whose origins are Greek, Old English, and Nahuatl, a Native American language.

1. Reread stanza 13. Find the words *cactus, hare,* and *coyote.*
2. Read the chart to learn what languages these words come from.
3. Do you know of any other English words that come from other cultures and languages? If so, share these with the class.

Word	Language	Root Word
cactus	Greek	kaktos
hare	Old English	hara
coyote	Nahuatl	coyotl

Activity Book
p. 44

Student
CD-ROM

Grammar Focus

Identify the Simple Present Tense

Use the **simple present tense** to say that something happens regularly or that it is generally true. The simple present tense has two forms.

I <u>like</u> to bask in the sun.

The bobcat like**s** to bask in the sun.

When the subject of a simple present tense verb is **third person singular** (*he, she,* or *it*), you must add an *-s* to the verb.

1. Reread stanza 8 of the poem. Find the simple present tense verbs.
2. Write three sentences that tell what you do every day. Capitalize and punctuate each sentence correctly to make its meaning clear.

	Singular (just one)	**Plural (more than one)**
First Person	I <u>like</u> the sun.	We <u>like</u> the sun.
Second Person	You <u>like</u> the sun.	You <u>like</u> the sun.
Third Person	She <u>likes</u> the sun. He <u>likes</u> the sun. It <u>likes</u> the sun.	They <u>like</u> the sun.

Note: When the verb ends in *ss, sh, ch, x,* or *z,* add **-es:** perch—perch**es**

Activity Book
pp. 45–46

Student
Handbook

Student
CD-ROM

From Reading to Writing

Write a Poem About the Environment

"Here Is the Southwestern Desert" is a poem about the environment. Write your own poem about the environment. Use the poetry features you learned.

1. Brainstorm ideas using a web like the one shown.
2. Include at least two stanzas that have different numbers of lines.
3. Repeat at least one line in each stanza.
4. Use the simple present tense.
5. Illustrate your poem.

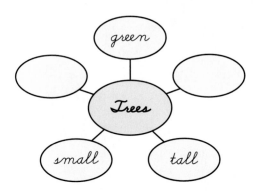

6. Read your poem to the class or to a partner. Speak slowly, clearly, and with expression.

Activity Book
p. 47

Student
Handbook

Across Content Areas

SCIENCE

Learn About Types of Climate

A **climate** is the kind of weather that a place or region has. Here are four types of climates:

A **desert climate** is hot and dry.

In a **tropical climate,** the weather is hot all year. During part of the year, it rains a lot. During the rest of the year, it doesn't rain much.

Regions with **continental climates** usually have four seasons. It can be very hot in the summer and very cold in the winter.

An **arctic climate** has very long, cold winters. Summers are short and not warm.

Work with a partner. Choose the correct words to complete these sentences.

1. Alaska has _____ .
   a. an arctic climate
   b. a continental climate
2. Much of Arizona has _____ .
   a. a desert climate
   b. a continental climate
3. Hawaii has _____ .
   a. a continental climate
   b. a tropical climate

Work with a partner to create a record of temperatures in your community for one week. Organize the record according to days of the week. Revise it as you correct spelling mistakes.

Activity Book
p. 48

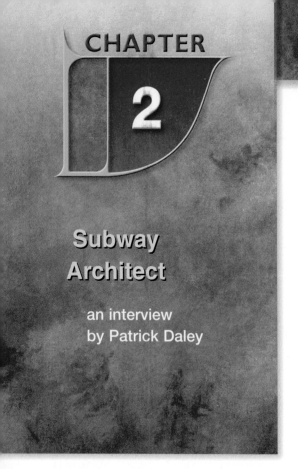

CHAPTER 2

Subway Architect

an interview
by Patrick Daley

Objectives

Reading Distinguish facts from opinions as you read an interview.

Listening and Speaking Role-play an interview.

Grammar Identify and punctuate questions.

Writing Write a personal narrative.

Content The Arts: Design a mural.

Use Prior Knowledge

Identify Different Types of Transportation

A subway is a train system that runs below the ground. Many large cities have a subway. People ride the subway to get from one place in a city to another or to travel to towns near the city. Have you ever ridden on a subway?

1. On a piece of paper, draw a Word Wheel like the one here.
2. Think about the ways you can travel around your city or town.
3. Write your ideas in the wheel.

4. Compare your wheel with a partner's. Which types of transportation do you use? When do you use them?

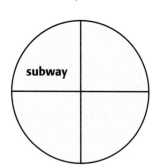

Build Background

New York City

New York City is located in the southeastern part of New York state. It has the largest population of any city in the United States. New York City is made up of five areas called *boroughs*. The five boroughs are: Manhattan, Brooklyn, Queens, the Bronx, and Staten Island.

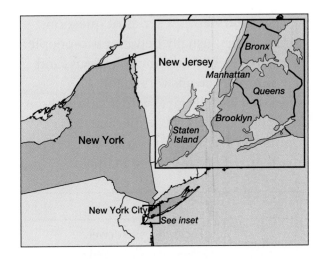

Content Connection

New York City grew quickly in the late 1800s and the streets became very crowded. To solve this problem, the city constructed its first subway system in 1904.

Build Vocabulary

Take Notes as You Read

You can use note cards while reading to **take notes** on words you do not understand.

1. As you read "Subway Architect," identify any words you do not understand as you read the text.
2. Write each word on one side of a note card. Use one card for each word.
3. As you continue to read, you may understand some of the words you wrote down earlier. Write those meanings on the other sides of the note cards.
4. When you finish reading, review your note cards. Ask your teacher or use a dictionary to find the meanings of any words you still do not understand. Write those definitions on the note cards.
5. Exchange note cards with a partner. Test each other as a way to review and memorize words.

The Heinle
Newbury House
Dictionary

Activity Book
p. 49

Student
CD-ROM

Text Structure

Interview

An **interview** is a series of questions and answers, usually between two people. The **interviewer** asks the questions, and the **interviewee** answers them. The interview usually gives information about the interviewee's life, experiences, or opinions. The interview you will read is made up of the following features:

Interview	
Questions	asked by the interviewer Each question is labeled Q.
Answers	information given by the interviewee Each answer is labeled A.

The selection also includes an **introduction.** The introduction explains what the interview is about.

1. Before you read, look at how the interview is organized.
2. Pause after reading the introduction (paragraphs 1–3). What do you think you will learn in this interview?
3. After you have read the interview, write in your Reading Log what you learned about the person interviewed.

Reading Log

Student CD-ROM

Reading Strategy

Distinguish Facts from Opinions

Facts explain information that is true. **Opinions** tell what someone thinks about something. An opinion cannot be proven to be true or false.

Look at the following examples of fact and opinion.

Fact: There is a subway in New York City.

Opinion: The subway is the best way to travel.

1. Look for examples of facts and opinions as you read "Subway Architect."
2. Think about how you can tell the difference between a fact and an opinion. For example, opinions might start with words like "I think . . ."

Student CD-ROM

SUBWAY ARCHITECT

an interview
by Patrick Daley

Audio
CD 1, Tr. 8

1   Do you like to ride trains or subways? Got any ideas for building a better train or subway **station?** Could you handle hanging out underground?

2   If so, you might want to check out Jorge Ramos's job. Jorge spends a lot of time under the streets of New York City. That's because he's fixing part of the subway.

3   A subway is a system of trains that run underground. New York City has one of the busiest subways in the world. Millions of people ride it each day. And it's about 100 years old! So, how do you improve something so big, busy, and old? Let's find out!

> **Distinguish Facts from Opinions**
>
> Name a fact that appears in this paragraph.

---

station   a place where people using the subway arrive and depart

Distinguish Facts from Opinions

What is Jorge Ramos's opinion about riding the subway?

4 **Q:** First, there's one question that I have to ask. . . .

5 **A:** Wait! I know what the question is. And the answer is YES! I do ride the subway. It's fast. It's fun. It's the best way to get around. I love being in a subway train!

6 **Q:** Okay. So what kind of work does an **architect** like you do?

7 **A:** I draw plans for buildings, homes, and even subway stations.

8 **Q:** Have you always liked to draw?

9 **A:** Yes. I grew up in Colombia, in South America. As a boy, I drew pictures of the beautiful buildings in my country. I thought some day I would draw pictures for magazines and books. But when I moved to the United States, I became interested in subway stations.

10 **Q:** Really? Why are you so interested in subway stations?

11 **A:** It's a big **challenge** to design a space that millions of people use each day. It's got to be easy for people to figure out where they're going. And the space must be easy for people to move around in. You don't want them bumping into each other or **plowing** each other down! Also, the space has to look good, and be safe.

---

architect a person who designs buildings and other structures

challenge a situation that tests someone's abilities

plowing crashing into

12 **Q:** Tell me about the **project** you're working on right now.

13 **A:** We are fixing up a subway station in a part of New York City called Queens.

Distinguish Facts from Opinions

In paragraph 14, is the interviewer asking for a fact or an opinion?

14 **Q:** What's the first thing you did to get that project started?

15 **A:** I had a big meeting. I asked people from the neighborhood how they thought their subway station could be improved.

16 **Q:** What was that meeting like?

17 **A:** It was loud! Everyone had an opinion. In fact, you'd be surprised how many opinions there were at that meeting.

18 **Q:** Oh **yeah?** Like what?

19 **A:** Some people wanted a bigger station. Some people thought the station was too big. Some people wanted the station to be cleaner. Some wanted it to be safer. Some people thought that the station needed **murals** and other kinds of art.

---

project a specific task
yeah a slang term for "yes"

murals large paintings done on walls

20 **Q:** Did you start building the station right after the meeting?

21 **A:** No. I began planning *how* to build it. I met with builders. I met with people who work for the subway system. Then I took my plans back to the neighborhood.

22 **Q:** Why would you go back to another meeting? The first one sounded **awful**!

23 **A:** Well, it wasn't really so awful—just noisy and busy. Plus, I really want people in the neighborhood to be a part of the planning. After all, it really is *their* subway station.

24 **Q:** After all of that, the building part must be easy, right?

Distinguish Facts from Opinions

Find one fact and one opinion in paragraph 25.

25 **A:** Are you kidding? Working on a subway station is never easy. Here's why: We can't close the subway station during the day. So we have to work late at night. Also, we can't work in bad weather. So forget about getting much done in the winter.

---

awful very bad

26 Q: What's left to do at the station you're building now?

27 A: I have to make sure that the subway signs are clear and helpful. So I'll test them first. I'll make **a bunch** of paper signs. Then I'll go to the station and tape them up. I'll pretend that I am a visitor. Can I find my way around? Or do I get lost? I'll take a lot of notes about what happens. After that test, I'll make changes to the signs. Then the paper signs will be made into real signs.

28 Q: What else have you done to help visitors in the station?

Distinguish Facts from Opinions

Do you think the first sentence of this answer is a fact or an opinion? Why do you think so?

29 A: There is a law that says we must put **ramps** and elevators in all stations. That way, **elderly** people and people in wheelchairs can ride the subway. Next to the tracks where the trains come, we paint the floor with a special paint. The paint has tiny **bumps** in it. The bumps let blind people know when they are standing too close to the train tracks.

---

a bunch many

ramps walkways that go between two levels of a building or a train

elderly old

bumps rounded, raised pieces of something

30 **Q:** Is there anything else left to do?

31 **A:** Yes. A **sculptor** is making art to hang on the walls. When that's done, the city **inspector** will come. She will decide whether the station is ready for all riders.

32 **Q:** What do you want people to say about the new station?

33 **A:** I want subway **employees** to say, "I'm **proud** I work here." I want visitors to say, "What a nice station." I want people in the neighborhood to say, "I love this station!" Building a good subway station is my gift to the neighborhood.

> **Distinguish Facts from Opinions**
>
> Is Jorge Ramos expressing facts or opinions in paragraph 33?

---

sculptor an artist who shapes objects from stone, metal, or other substances

inspector a person who looks at something closely

employees people who work for a person, business, government, or other organization

proud pleased, satisfied with someone's success

About the Author   Patrick Daley

Patrick Daley has written books for students. One of these books includes debate topics (topics to argue for or against something). Daley used to work as the editor of a magazine. He was also the publisher of a reading program students can use to improve their reading skills.

➤ Why do you think Patrick Daley wrote an interview about a subway architect? To explain? To entertain? To influence?

Beyond the Reading

Reading Comprehension

Question-Answer Relationships (QAR)

"Right There" Questions

1. **Recall Facts** What kinds of things does Jorge Ramos do as an architect?
2. **Recall Facts** What was the first thing Jorge Ramos did to start his project in Queens?
3. **Recall Facts** Why isn't working on a subway station easy, according to Jorge Ramos?

"Think and Search" Question

4. **Identify Steps in a Process** Look at paragraph 21. Name the four steps that Jorge Ramos took to build a subway station.

"Author and You" Question

5. **Recognize Character Traits** Do you think Jorge Ramos is a person who pays attention to other people's opinions? Why?

"On Your Own" Questions

6. **Use Prior Knowledge** What did you know about the subway before reading the interview? What did you learn?
7. **Raise Questions** What unanswered questions do you have after reading the selection? How would you look for the answers to your questions?
8. **Ask Questions** What questions do you have about different jobs? How could you do an interview to find the answers?
9. **Revise Questions** Discuss two of your questions with your teacher. How could you revise your questions to make them clearer?

Activity Book
p. 50

Student
CD-ROM

Build Reading Fluency

Repeated Reading

Repeated reading can help increase your reading rate and build confidence. Each time you reread you improve your reading. Turn to page 98. Your teacher or partner will time your rereading for six minutes.

1. With a partner, one read the questions, the other read the answers aloud.
2. Stop after six minutes.

Listen, Speak, Interact

Role-Play an Interview

With a partner, role-play an interview between Jorge Ramos and the interviewer.

1. Decide who will role-play Jorge Ramos and who will role-play the interviewer.
2. If you are the interviewer:
   a. Make a list of five new questions to ask Jorge Ramos.
   b. Base your questions on what you learned from the selection.
3. If you are Jorge Ramos:
   a. Answer the questions the way Jorge Ramos might answer them.

b. Combine your personal knowledge with what you learned from the text to respond.
4. Perform your role play for the class. Be sure to look at each other as you act out the interview. Speak clearly so that the audience believes you.
5. Evaluate your classmates' role plays for content and delivery. Were your classmates believable?

Elements of Literature

Understand Character Motivation

Characters in literature can be real, like Jorge Ramos, or they can be made up. But all characters have **motivation.** Motivation is the reasons characters act the way they do.

1. Reread paragraphs 8–11.
2. What do you think motivated Jorge Ramos to be an architect? In your Reading Log, write two or three sentences to express your ideas.

3. Choose a character from a reading in Unit 1. Compare and contrast that character's motivation with Jorge Ramos's motivation.
4. Share your ideas with a partner.

Reading Log

Activity Book
p. 51

Student
CD-ROM

Word Study

Learn About the Prefix *Sub-*

A **prefix** is a group of letters added to the beginning of a word. It changes the word's meaning. For example, the word *subway* has the prefix *sub-*. The prefix *sub-* means "below" or "under."

1. Copy the chart in your Personal Dictionary.
2. With a partner, discuss the meaning of the root word. Then try to guess the meanings of the words with *sub-*.
3. Use a dictionary to check your work.

Prefix	Word	New Word	Meaning
sub-	way	subway	train system that runs underground
sub-	freezing	subfreezing	
sub-	marine	submarine	
sub-	title	subtitle	

4. Find other words in the dictionary with the prefix *sub-*. Write two sentences with the words. Be sure to spell the root words and prefix correctly.

Personal Dictionary

The Heinle Newbury House Dictionary

Activity Book *p. 52*

Student CD-ROM

Grammar Focus

Identify and Punctuate Questions

In this chapter you learned that an interview includes **questions.** The questions in the reading selection are easy to find because the letter *Q* is placed before them. However, there are other ways to identify questions.

The punctuation at the end of a question is a **question mark.**

How are you**?**

Many questions begin with **question words:** *Who, What, When, Where, Why,* and *How.*

<u>Where</u> are you going?

<u>What</u> is your name?

1. Reread paragraph 16.
   a. What is the question word?
   b. Identify the punctuation used at the end of the question.
2. Reread paragraphs 22 and 28. Identify the question words.

Activity Book *pp. 53–54*

Student Handbook

Student CD-ROM

From Reading to Writing

Write a Personal Narrative

Jorge Ramos says that he liked to draw when he was a boy. Drawing was his hobby. A hobby is an activity that you enjoy doing often. Write three paragraphs about one of your hobbies.

1. Make notes to help you organize the following information:
   a. Facts: Information about your hobby.
   b. Opinions: Why you enjoy this hobby.
2. Use the information in your notes to help you write your paragraphs.
3. Remember to capitalize the first word of each sentence. Remember to indent your paragraphs.

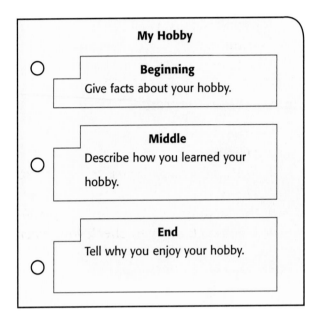

My Hobby

Beginning
Give facts about your hobby.

Middle
Describe how you learned your hobby.

End
Tell why you enjoy your hobby.

Activity Book
p. 55

Student
Handbook

Across Content Areas

Design a Mural

In "Subway Architect," you learned that some subway stations have **murals**—large paintings on walls. Suppose that it is your job to create a mural for a new subway or bus station.

1. Think of a design that shows something about the neighborhood where the station is located.
2. Draw the plan for your mural on a piece of paper. Use colored pencils, markers, or paint.
3. Write an explanation that tells how the mural relates to your neighborhood.
4. Work with a partner to write a news story about your mural. Organize your ideas in a logical order. Revise the story to correct spelling and grammar mistakes. Read your news story to the class.

Activity Book
p. 56

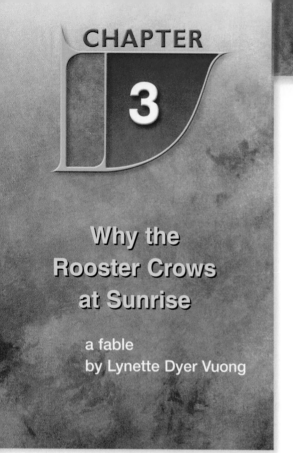

CHAPTER 3

Why the Rooster Crows at Sunrise

a fable
by Lynette Dyer Vuong

Objectives

Reading Identify main idea and details as you read a fable.

Listening and Speaking Perform a skit.

Grammar Identify object pronouns.

Writing Write a fable.

Content Science: Learn about conservation.

Use Prior Knowledge

Talk About the Importance of the Sun

With a partner, talk about the importance of the sun. Think about this question:

How does the sun help us?

1. Make a list of ideas on a piece of paper. For example: The sun gives us heat.
2. Share your ideas with the class.
3. Talk about what the world would be like without the sun.

The Sun

1. *The sun gives us heat.*

Build Background

Oral Tradition

The reading selection in this chapter is a modern version of an old Vietnamese story. Parts of the story have been passed down from parents to children. Telling stories in this way is called the **oral tradition.**

Storytelling is an important tradition in many cultures. The stories often teach children important ideas and values.

SOCIAL STUDIES **Content Connection**

Vietnam is a country in Southeast Asia. It has a tropical climate.

Build Vocabulary

Understand Words in Context

Context is the information that surrounds a word. You can use context to help you understand new words.

We are **starving** to <u>death</u> because we <u>can't</u> see to <u>find food</u>.

1. Read or listen to the selection. Use context to help you learn the meanings of new words.

2. Complete a chart like the one here in your Personal Dictionary.

Word	Context Words	What I Think Word Means	Dictionary Definition
starving	death can't find food	very hungry	to feel pain or die from lack of food

Personal Dictionary

The Heinle Newbury House Dictionary

Activity Book p. 57

Student CD-ROM

Text Structure

Fable

In this chapter you will read or listen to the audio recording of the **fable** "Why the Rooster Crows at Sunrise." A fable is a short narrative that teaches a lesson. The distinguishing features of a fable are listed in the chart. Look for the features as you read or listen to "Why the Rooster Crows at Sunrise."

1. With a partner, talk about a fable you know. What country or region does it come from? Did you learn it by the oral tradition? Does it have a moral? What is it?
2. With a partner, compare and contrast the features of "Why the Rooster Crows at Sunrise" to fables you have heard from other regions and cultures.

Fable	
Personification	the characters are animals that act like humans
Plot	what happens in the story Beginning ↓ Middle ↓ End
Moral	a lesson taught in a fable

Student
CD-ROM

Reading Strategy

Identify Main Idea and Details

When you read a story, it is important to understand the **main idea.** The main idea is the most important idea. **Details**—examples, explanations, and events—tell us more about the main idea.

1. Read paragraph 1 of "Why the Rooster Crows at Sunrise." Find three details about how the people treated the sun.

2. What do you think the main idea of this paragraph is?
3. As you read this fable, look for details that help you identify main ideas.

Student
CD-ROM

Why the Rooster Crows at Sunrise

a fable by Lynette Dyer Vuong

1 Long ago the sun lived close to the earth. She spent her days just above the treetops, shining down on the fields and houses below. But as day followed day, she grew more and more unhappy with her **lot.** The people who owed her their light and warmth neither gave her thanks nor showed her any **respect.** Housewives hung their laundry in front of her face and dumped their garbage right under her nose. Men and women alike burned wood and trash, choking her with the smoke, until one day her father, Ngoc Hoang—Jade **Emperor,** the king of heaven—took **pity** on her and carried her away from the **polluted atmosphere.**

Identify Main Idea and Details

Find the main idea in paragraph 2.

2 "The people don't deserve you," Jade Emperor said as he set her down in a safe place on the other side of the Eastern Sea. "If I had left you there, they would have poisoned you with their **filth.**"

3 Now day was no different from night. People **shivered** in their houses and could not recognize each other even when they stood side by side.

lot condition in life	**polluted** made dirty
respect thoughtful concern about the importance of something	**atmosphere** the air above Earth
Emperor a title for a ruler	**filth** dirt and garbage
pity the feeling of sorrow or sympathy caused by the suffering or hardships of others	**shivered** shook in the body from cold

4   In the forest the animals could not see to hunt, and day by day they grew hungrier. At last they gathered to discuss the situation.

5   The rooster spoke first. "If only we could go to the sun and **appeal** to her in person, perhaps she would take pity on us and give us a little light."

6   The duck nodded. "We could try. If only we knew where to find her."

7   "I've heard she lives across the Eastern Sea," the bluebird **chirped.** "I'd be willing to lead you there if you'd do the talking."

8   "I'd do the talking," the rooster offered, "if I had a way to get there. But you know I can't swim. How could I get across the Eastern Sea?"

9   The duck smiled. "On my back, of course. No one's a better swimmer than I am."

---

appeal   ask for help   **chirped**   made a high, short, sharp sound

10   The three friends set off at once, the bluebird leading the way and the rooster riding on the duck's back. At last they reached the other side of the sea, where they found the sun **taking her ease.**

11   "Please come back, sister sun," they begged as they told her of the **plight** the world was in. "Come back and stay with us the way you did before."

12   But the sun shook her head. "How can you ask me to come back? You know I had to leave for my health's sake. Why, my very life was in danger in that polluted atmosphere."

13   "We are starving to death because we can't see to find food. Won't you take pity on us and give us a little light before we all die?" the rooster **pleaded.**

14   The sun was silent for a long moment. Finally she **sighed.** "I know you must be **desperate,** or you wouldn't have come all this way to see me." She sighed again. "I can't live with you as I used to; but if you'll call me when you need light, I'll come and shine for you for a few hours."

---

taking her ease   relaxing, being comfortable
plight   a difficult situation
pleaded   requested urgently

sighed   let out air from the mouth from emotion or being tired
desperate   in immediate, very strong need

15　The rooster nodded eagerly. "My voice is loud, so I'll do the calling. When you hear me **crowing,** you'll know it's time to wake up and get ready to cross the sea."

16　"I can help too." The bluebird stepped forward. "My voice may not be as loud as brother rooster's; but once he wakes you, you'll be able to hear me, and you'll know it's time to leave your home and start your journey."

17　The sun agreed. And from then on, the sun, the rooster, and the bluebird have kept their **bargain.** When the rooster crows, the sun knows it's time to get ready for her day's work; and just as the birds begin their chirping, she appears over the eastern **horizon.**

> **Identify Main Idea and Details**
>
> What is the main idea of this fable?

---

crowing　making a loud cry
bargain　an agreement

horizon　the place in one's view where the earth's surface forms a line with the sky

About the Author　Lynette Dyer Vuong (born 1938)

Lynette Dyer Vuong grew up in the state of Michigan. When she was seven years old, she discovered her love of writing. She began to write about adventures in ancient lands. After high school, she lived in Vietnam for 13 years. While in Vietnam, Dyer Vuong spent much time in bookstores exploring Vietnamese stories. The fable "Why the Rooster Crows at Sunrise" is a story she adapted from the original. It is included in a collection of other stories from Vietnam.

➤ Why do you think the author wrote "Why the Rooster Crows at Sunrise"? To inform? To entertain? To teach?

Beyond the Reading

Reading Comprehension

Question-Answer Relationships (QAR)

"Right There" Questions

1. **Recall Facts** Where did the sun live long ago?
2. **Recall Facts** Where did the sun's father take her?
3. **Recall Facts** What characters gathered to discuss their problem of not having daylight?

"Think and Search" Questions

4. **Analyze Causes and Effects** Why did the sun's father take her away from the earth?
5. **Summarize** Summarize the bargain that the rooster, the duck, and the bluebird made with the sun.

"Author and You" Questions

6. **Identify the Main Idea** What lesson do you think the characters learned after the sun left?

7. **Draw Conclusions** How do you think life on the earth changed after the sun agreed to shine for a few hours?
8. **Analyze Illustrations** Why do you think illustrations are used with the fable instead of photos? How do the style (look and feel) and elements (parts) of the illustrations add to the effect of the fable?

"On Your Own" Question

9. **Make Inferences** Why do you think people tell fables such as "Why the Rooster Crows at Sunrise"?

Activity Book
p. 58

Student
CD-ROM

Build Reading Fluency

Read Silently

Reading silently is good practice. It helps you learn to read faster. An effective reader reads silently for longer periods of time.

1. Listen to the audio recording of paragraph 1, page 110.
2. Listen to the chunks of words as you follow along.
3. Reread paragraph 1 silently two times.
4. Your teacher will time your second reading.
5. Raise your hand when you are done.
6. Record your timing.

Listen, Speak, Interact

Perform a Skit

Imagine that the sun stopped rising in our world today. Create a three-minute **skit** (a short play) about the world without the sun.

1. With two or three other students, brainstorm an idea.
2. Write your skit. Include speaking roles for everyone in the group.
3. Practice your skit. You may use props or costumes.
4. Present your skit to the class.
5. Evaluate each skit. Could you hear all the speakers? Was the skit believable?

Elements of Literature

Review Personification

In this chapter, you learned that **personification** is one feature of a fable. A writer using personification gives human thoughts, feelings, and actions to animals or things.

1. Review the fable. How is each character like a human?
2. How is each character *not* like a human?
3. Copy the chart in your Reading Log. Choose one character from the fable. In the left column, write how the character is like a human. In the right column, write how the character is not like a human.

Fable Character: _____	
Like a Human	**Not Like a Human**

Reading Log   Activity Book   Student
                 p. 59   CD-ROM

Word Study

Learn About Words with Multiple Meanings

Homonyms are words that are pronounced the same and may be spelled the same, but they have different meanings.

> The duck smiled, "On my **back,** of course."

> "Come **back** and stay with us the way you did before."

1. With a partner, reread paragraphs 1 and 2. Find the words *lot* and *safe.*
2. In a dictionary, find the definition that goes with the word as it is used.

Paragraph	Homonyms	Meanings
9	back	the top of an animal
1	lot	
2	safe	

3. Copy the chart in your Personal Dictionary. Write the meanings.

Personal Dictionary

The Heinle Newbury House Dictionary

Activity Book p. 60

Student CD-ROM

Grammar Focus

Identify Object Pronouns

You know that nouns and pronouns can be used as subjects of sentences. The subject pronouns are *I, you, he, she, it, we,* and *they.*

Noun	Pronoun
The animals went to the sun.	They asked her to come back.

Many sentences also have **objects.** The subject of a sentence does something to the object.

Subject	Object
The people choked the sun with smoke.	

Pronouns can also be used as **objects** in sentences. The object pronouns are *me, you, him, her, it, us,* and *them.*

Subject	Object
The people choked her with smoke.	

Use object pronouns in place of the underlined nouns below. Choose the appropriate pronouns and spell them correctly.

1. Jade Emperor took his daughter away.
2. In the end, the sun helped the animals.

Activity Book pp. 61–62

Student Handbook

Student CD-ROM

From Reading to Writing

Write a Fable

In a small group, write a fable. Your fable should teach a lesson, or a moral; for example, "Studying is important" or "We should take care of Earth."

1. Copy the diagram below to help you get started. Use it to organize your ideas.

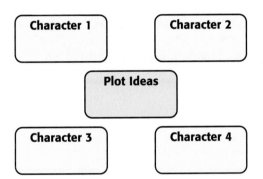

2. Create characters that act like humans. Use pronouns and object pronouns correctly in your fable to tell about your characters.
3. Think of main ideas and give details to explain them.
4. Be sure your fable has a beginning, a middle, and an end.
5. Draw a picture for your fable.
6. Capitalize and punctuate your fable correctly to strengthen its meaning.
7. Review and edit your fable to publish and share with your class and others.

Activity Book   Student
p. 63   Handbook

Across Content Areas

Learn About Conservation

Conservation is the protection of the environment. Look at these words related to *conservation.*

1. To **conserve** the environment is to protect it from pollution.
2. A person who works to conserve the environment is a **conservationist.**
3. **Conservation** is the act of protecting the environment.

Complete these sentences with *conserve, conservationist,* and *conservation.*

People still pollute the environment. A ____ tells people how they can help the environment. For example, people can ____ the environment by not throwing their garbage on the ground. ____ is important because we need a clean, healthy place to live.

Activity Book
p. 64

CHAPTER 4

Gonzalo

an excerpt from a novel
by Paul Fleischman

Objectives

Reading Draw conclusions as you read narrative fiction.

Listening and Speaking Interpret nonverbal communication.

Grammar Recognize and use comparative adjectives.

Writing Write narrative fiction.

Content Science: Learn about plants.

Use Prior Knowledge

Discuss Learning a New Language

In this chapter's reading selection, the main character learns English by watching television. How else can people learn a new language?

1. With a partner, copy the chart on a piece of paper.
2. List your ideas in your chart. Circle the idea that you think is best.
3. Share your ideas with the class.

How to Learn a New Language
1. watch television

Build Background

Guatemala

The characters in "Gonzalo" come from Guatemala, a country in Central America. Spanish is the official language of Guatemala, but native people speak about 20 different languages. Many Guatemalans are farmers. They grow sugarcane, cotton, coffee, corn, and bananas.

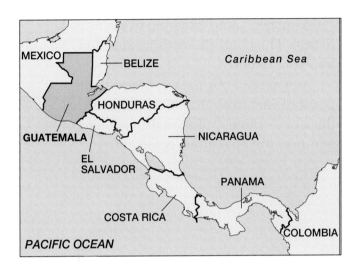

Content Connection

The Mayan people make up about half the population of Guatemala. Their culture is over 1,500 years old.

Build Vocabulary

Use Word Squares to Remember Meanings

Making **word squares** can help you remember the meanings of new words. Look at this example:

Word equation	Symbol $2 + 2 = 4$
Meaning math statement that says two amounts are equal	Sentence I am learning about equations in math.

1. Create two word squares. Fill in the squares for the underlined words in these sentences.
   a. He could not sit out in the plaza.
   b. He was the janitor at my school.
2. Use a dictionary to find the meanings.
3. As you read "Gonzalo," make word squares for other words that you want to remember.

The Heinle Newbury House Dictionary

Activity Book p. 65

Student CD-ROM

Text Structure

Narrative Fiction

"Gonzalo" is an example of **narrative fiction.** The chart shows the features of narrative fiction.

As you read "Gonzalo," identify the point of view. Also, look for and analyze the story's details, plot, main problem, and how the characters resolve it.

Narrative Fiction	
Structure	has a beginning, a middle, and an end
Narrator's Point of View	first person—narrator is a person in the story third person—narrator is not a person in the story
Details	gives information about characters and events to help readers connect with the story
Plot	events in the story
Problem and Solution	tells how characters resolve a problem

Student CD-ROM

Reading Strategy

Draw Conclusions

You **draw conclusions** when you decide that something is true, or not true, after thinking carefully about all the facts. For example:

You read: Guatemala and Belize are the only countries in Central America that have a border with Mexico.

Conclusion: El Salvador does not have a border with Mexico.

Drawing conclusions will help you understand and remember what you read.

As you read or listen to "Gonzalo," use information in the text to draw conclusions about the characters. Compare your conclusions with a partner.

Student CD-ROM

GONZALO

an excerpt from a novel
by Paul Fleischman

Prologue

The narrator of the story is named Gonzalo Garcia. He lives in a Spanish-speaking neighborhood in a city in the United States.

1 The older you are, the younger you get when you move to the United States.

2 They don't teach you that equation in school. Big Brain, Mr. Smoltz, my eighth-grade math teacher, hasn't even heard of it. It's not in *Gateway to Algebra*. It's Garcia's Equation. I'm the Garcia.

3 Two years after my father and I moved here from Guatemala I could speak English. I learned it on the playground and watching lots of TV. Don't believe what people say—cartoons make you *smart*. But my father, he worked all day in a kitchen with **Mexicans** and **Salvadorans.** His English was worse than a **kindergartner's.** He would only buy food at the *bodega* down the block.

Draw Conclusions

Why was the father's English "worse than a kindergartner's"?

---

gateway a passage, something that helps you reach a goal

algebra a form of math

Mexicans people from the country of Mexico

Salvadorans people from the country of El Salvador

kindergartner a four- or five-year-old child in kindergarten, or classes before the first grade of school

bodega a store where the owners speak Spanish

Outside of there he lowered his eyes and tried to get by on **mumbles** and smiles. He didn't want strangers to hear his mistakes. So he used me to make phone calls and to talk to the **landlady** and to buy things in stores where you had to use English. He got younger. I got older.

4   Then my younger brothers and mother and **Tío** Juan, her uncle, came north and joined us. Tío Juan was the oldest man in his **pueblo.** But here he became a little baby. He'd been a farmer, but here he couldn't work. He couldn't sit out in the plaza and talk—there *aren't* any plazas here, and if you sit out in public some gang driving by might use you for **target practice.** He couldn't understand TV. So he **wandered** around the apartment all day, in and out of rooms, talking to himself, just like a kid in **diapers.**

---

mumbles   quiet and unclear words

landlady   a woman who owns a building where people rent apartments

tío   the Spanish word for "uncle"

pueblo   the Spanish word for "village"

target practice   when people practice shooting at something

wandered   walked around without trying to get someplace

diapers   what babies wear to cover the area between the legs

Draw Conclusions

What conclusion can you make about the number of beauty parlors in Tío Juan's pueblo? How do you know?

5   One morning he wandered outside and down the street. My mother **practically fainted.** He doesn't speak Spanish, just an Indian language. I finally found him standing in front of the **beauty parlor,** staring through the glass at a woman with a **drier** over her head. He must have wondered what weird planet he'd moved to. I led him home, holding his hand, the way you would with a three-year-old. Since then I'm supposed to **baby-sit** him after school.

6   One afternoon I was watching TV, getting smart on *The Brady Bunch.* Suddenly I looked up. He was gone. I checked the halls on all five floors of the apartment house. I ran to the street. He wasn't in the *bodega* or the **pawnshop.** I called his name, imagining my mother's face when she found out he'd fallen through a **manhole** or been run over. I turned the corner, looking for the white

---

practically   nearly, almost

fainted   fell over unconscious

beauty parlor   a place to get your hair cut and fingernails polished

drier   a machine that sits over your head and dries your hair

baby-sit   watch a child while the parents are away

The Brady Bunch   a U.S. television show popular in the 1970s

pawnshop   a business that lends people money in exchange for holding their personal valuables for a short time

manhole   a hole in the street used to reach water pipes and telephone wires

straw hat he always wore. Two blocks down I **spotted** it. I **flew** down the sidewalk and found him standing in front of a **vacant** lot, making gestures to a man with a shovel.

7   I took his hand, but he pulled me through the trash and into the lot. I recognized the man with the shovel—he was the janitor at my old school. He had a little garden planted. Different **shades** of green leaves were coming up in rows. Tío Juan was smiling and trying to tell him something. The man couldn't understand him and finally went back to digging. I turned Tío Juan around and led him home.

---

spotted saw
flew ran very quickly
vacant empty

shades colors that are only slightly different from a basic one

8

Why does Gonzalo's mother buy a trowel and seeds? What information in the text helped you draw this conclusion?

That night he told my mother all about it. She was the only one who could understand him. When she got home from work the next day she asked me to take him back there. I did. He studied the sun. Then the soil. He felt it, then smelled it, then actually tasted it. He chose a spot not too far from the sidewalk. Where my mother changed busses she'd gone into a store and bought him a **trowel** and four packets of seeds. I cleared the trash, he **turned the soil.** I wished we were farther from the street and I was praying that none of my friends or girlfriends or **enemies** saw me. Tío Juan didn't even notice people—he was **totally wrapped up** in the work.

---

trowel   a small tool used to dig up soil
turned the soil   plowed

enemies   people who wish you harm
totally wrapped up   completely focused on

9   He showed me exactly how far apart the rows should be
and how deep. He couldn't read the words on the seed
packets, but he knew from the pictures what seeds were
inside. He poured them into his hand and smiled. He
seemed to recognize them, like old friends. Watching him
carefully **sprinkling** them into the **troughs** he'd made, I
realized that I didn't know anything about growing food
and that he knew everything. I stared at his busy fingers,
then his eyes. They were focused, not faraway or confused.
He'd changed from a baby back into a man.

sprinkling   dropping lightly and in small amounts   **troughs**   long and narrow ditches

About the Author

Paul Fleischman (born 1952)

Paul Fleischman lives in Monterey, California. The story you
read is part of the novel *Seedfolks*. Fleischman created the
character Gonzalo from his experience as a volunteer in an
English as a Second Language middle school class. He decided
to write *Seedfolks* after learning that gardening can help people
who feel isolated and lonely. He believes that community
gardening joins people together and gives them a sense of
accomplishment.

➤ If you could ask Paul Fleischman a question about this story,
what would it be?

Beyond the Reading

Reading Comprehension

Question-Answer Relationships (QAR)

"Right There" Questions

1. **Recall Facts** How does Gonzalo say he learned English?
2. **Recall Facts** What was Tío Juan's job in Guatemala?

"Think and Search" Question

3. **Identify the Main Idea** How does Tío Juan grow younger when he comes to the United States?

"Author and You" Questions

4. **Draw Conclusions** Why was Gonzalo's mother so frightened when Tío Juan left the house alone?
5. **Describe** How does Gonzalo's mother solve Tío Juan's problem?
6. **Make Inferences** Why does the author describe the seeds as Tío Juan's "old friends"?

"On Your Own" Questions

7. **Discuss** How might learning to live in a new place make a person "older"?
8. **Identify Mood** What is the mood of the narrator at the beginning of the story? Does the mood change from the beginning to the end of the story? Does it contribute to the effect of the text?
9. **Compare Experiences** Have you or your classmates had similar experiences to Gonzalo's? Describe these experiences.
10. **Connect** How does the theme (the general message) of "Gonzalo" cross cultures? How does it connect cultures?

Activity Book
p. 66

Student
CD-ROM

Build Reading Fluency

Audio CD Reading Practice

Listening to the Audio CD of "Gonzalo" is good reading practice. It helps you to become a fluent reader. Turn to page 122.

1. Listen to the Audio CD for "Gonzalo."
2. Follow along in your student book, page 122.
3. Listen to the phrases, pauses, and expression of the reader.

Listen, Speak, Interact

Interpret Nonverbal Communication

Verbal communication uses words. When people communicate without using words, it is **nonverbal communication.**

In the reading selection, Gonzalo does not speak the same language as Tío Juan. How might a person communicate with someone who speaks another language?

1. With a partner, think of a simple activity that you can express without using words. An example is asking for something to eat.

2. Decide how you will express your activity nonverbally.
3. Present your activity to the class.
4. Ask the class to guess your activity.
5. When you don't understand something, how can you ask the person to help you? What verbal and nonverbal language can you use?

Elements of Literature

Discuss the Theme

The **theme** is the general message that the author wants you to get from the story. A theme is often not stated directly. You figure it out as you read.

Sometimes the theme in a reading is a lesson about life. The characters in the story give you clues (details that help you understand) to the theme through their words and actions.

1. With a partner, reread paragraph 9 of "Gonzalo."
2. What did Gonzalo learn from Tío Juan?
3. What do you think the theme of the story is?

4. Write your interpretation of the theme in your Reading Log. Also write some of the details that helped you understand the theme.
5. Does the theme connect to the reading selections in Chapters 1, 2, and 3? Explain.

Reading Log

Activity Book
p. 67

Student
CD-ROM

Word Study

Using the Dictionary

Look up the word **plaza** (paragraph 4) in a large dictionary. You will find an entry like this:

> **pla•za** /'plɑ-zə, 'plæ-/ *n* [Sp, fr. L *platea* broad street—more at PLACE] (1683) **1a:** a public square in a city or town **b:** an open area usually located near urban buildings and often featuring walkways, trees and shrubs, places to sit, and sometimes shops **2:** a place on a thoroughfare (as a turnpike) at which all traffic must temporarily stop (as to pay tolls) **3:** an area adjacent to an expressway which has service facilities (as a restaurant, service station, and rest rooms) **4:** SHOPPING CENTER

1. What do the first symbols mean? Use them to pronounce the word. Your teacher will help you.
2. Where did the word come from (word origin)? Do you know what the word means in its original language?
3. How many meanings does the word have? Which meaning fits the use of **plaza** in paragraph 4?
4. Do the same activity with the following words from the reading.
   a. equation (paragraph 2)
   b. kindergartner (paragraph 3)
   c. weird (paragraph 5)

Activity Book   Student
p. 68   CD-ROM

Grammar Focus

Recognize and Use Comparative Adjectives

Adjectives describe nouns—people, places, and things.

Tío Juan is an <u>old</u> man.

Sometimes authors use adjectives to compare people, places, or things. This makes their writing more vivid.

Tío Juan is 70. My grandfather is 75. My grandfather is old**er** than Tío Juan.

Older is the **comparative form** of the adjective *old*. Add *-er* to a short adjective to make a comparative form.

Tío Juan's garden is beautiful. It is **more beautiful** than my garden.

Use *more* for long adjectives like *beautiful*.

1. Find two examples of comparative adjectives in "Gonzalo." Look in paragraph 1.
2. Write two sentences using the comparative form of adjectives.

Activity Book   Student   Student
pp. 69–70   Handbook   CD-ROM

From Reading to Writing

Write Narrative Fiction

In "Gonzalo," the main character learns English after moving to the United States. Write a story about a fictional character (someone you make up) who needs to learn how to do something.

1. Choose a title for your story.
2. Make sure your story has a beginning, a middle, and an end.
3. Include details that tell how the person resolves his or her problem about how to do something.
4. Use comparative adjectives to show how the person changes.

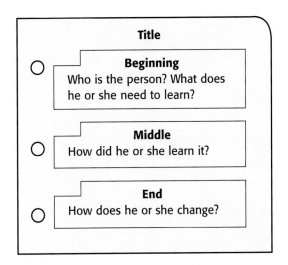

Title

○ **Beginning**
Who is the person? What does he or she need to learn?

○ **Middle**
How did he or she learn it?

○ **End**
How does he or she change?

Activity Book
p. 71

Student Handbook

Across Content Areas

Learn about Plants

Three main parts of plants are the **roots, leaves,** and **stems.**

Roots go down into the soil. They take water and **nutrients** (things that make the plant grow) from the soil.

Leaves have many shapes. They are usually, but not always, green. Leaves make energy for the plant.

Stems hold up the leaves.

On a piece of paper, complete the labels. Write one of these words:

roots	stem	leaf

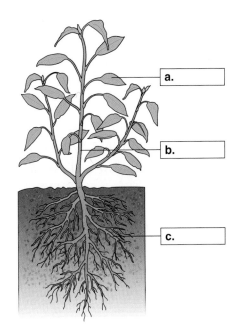

a.

b.

c.

Activity Book
p. 72

CHAPTER 5

Rain Forest Creatures

an excerpt from a
nonfiction book
by Will Osborne
and Mary Pope Osborne

Objectives

Reading Outline information to understand reading as you read an informational text.

Listening and Speaking Recall details.

Grammar Identify the subject and verb of a sentence.

Writing Write an informational report.

Content Social Studies: Read pie charts.

Use Prior Knowledge

Describe Your Image of a Rain Forest

A forest is an area covered by trees. In a rain forest, it rains a lot. There are often very large rivers. Rain forests are the home of millions of different kinds of plants and animals.

1. You are taking a walk in a rain forest. What do you see? What do you hear? What do you feel? What can you smell?
2. Fill in the chart with some ideas and then describe your images to your partner.

3. Are your ideas of what you will find in a rain forest correct? Use the Internet to check your answers. (Search for the words *rain forest.*)

A Walk in a Rain Forest				
	See	**Hear**	**Feel**	**Smell**
Animals	*snakes*			
Plants				*flowers*
Other things in nature			*It's hot!*	

Build Background

The Amazon Rain Forest

The Amazon Rain Forest is the largest rain forest in the world. It is located in South America and covers about 25 percent of the continent—about 2.3 million square miles. Most of the rain forest is located in the country of Brazil. Scientists are constantly discovering new species in this huge natural environment.

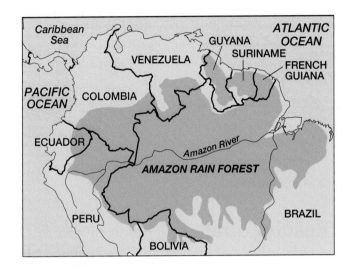

SCIENCE

Content Connection

A rain forest is a type of **biome.** A biome is a very large environment that has a specific climate as well as certain plants and animals.

Build Vocabulary

Use Text Features

Some nonfiction texts include **text features** that help the reader identify vocabulary words. Look at the following vocabulary words. In the selection, they appear in italics, a different kind of type in which the letters slant to the right. *This sentence is in italics.*

> *predators*
> *camouflage*
> *prey*
> *nocturnal*

1. Write the four words in your Personal Dictionary.
2. As you read, stop when you find each of these words.
3. Write the definition that you find in the text next to the word listed in your Personal Dictionary.
4. Write your own sentences using these vocabulary words.

Personal Dictionary

The Heinle Newbury House Dictionary

Activity Book *p. 73*

Student CD-ROM

Text Structure

Informational Text

The reading in this chapter is an **informational text.** Informational texts explain and give information about a topic. In an informational text, authors call our attention to information in a few ways.

As you read each section of "Rain Forest Creatures," look at the headings and captions.

Informational Text	
Headings	titles for separate sections of text; printed in large, bold type
Captions	words that explain a picture

Student
CD-ROM

Reading Strategy

Outline Information to Understand Reading

Making an **outline** of an informational text helps you remember what you read. Look at the outline here.

1. Copy the outline and complete it as you read or listen to the audio recording of "Rain Forest Creatures."
2. Use the headings in the text as the main topics. Then add details. This outline goes to paragraph 9. Finish it on your own.

Student
CD-ROM

The title of the reading

Rain Forest Creatures

Main topic- **I.** Predators and Protection

Subtopic—— **A.** Predators

First detail———— **1.** Predators kill other
for subtopic   animals

Second———— **2.** Prey—killed and eaten
detail for
subtopic   **B.** _____

         1. Camouflage—colors
           help animals blend in
         2. Staying still
         3. _____

   II. _____

         A. Definition: A nocturnal
           creature that comes out
           only at night
         B. Examples
           1. Bats
           2. _____
           3. _____

Rain Forest Creatures

an excerpt from a nonfiction book by
Will Osborne and Mary Pope Osborne

1 　They **creep** and **crawl**! They **flit** and fly! They **growl** and **howl**! The world's rain forests are alive with millions of animals, bugs, and birds.

Predators and Protection

2 　Most rain forest animals depend on other animals for food. Animals that kill and eat other animals are called *predators*. The animals that predators kill are called their *prey*.

3 　Many rain forest **creatures** have special ways of protecting themselves from predators. Some have colors that help them blend with their natural surroundings. This kind of protection is called *camouflage* (KAM-uh-flahzh).

4 　Some creatures fool predators by looking like plants. If they stay very still, predators will leave them alone— because they won't see them!

> **Outline Information to Understand Reading**
>
> What is the heading for this section? Where is it on your outline?

Audio
CD 1, Tr. 11

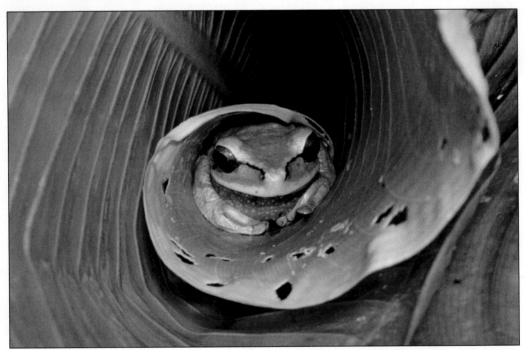

Tree frog in leaf

---

creep move slowly
crawl move slowly and close to the ground
flit move quickly

growl make a low sound in anger
howl cry loudly
creatures living beings

Night monkeys

5   Some creatures scare predators away by looking bigger and scarier than they really are. Many moths and butterflies have marks on their wings that look like big eyes. When these creatures open their wings, predators think the eyes belong to a creature that might eat *them!*

> ### Outline Information to Understand Reading
>
> The detail in this paragraph is "scare predators away." Write this detail in your outline.

Night Creatures

6   The rain forest is just as alive at night as it is during the day. Many creatures come out only after the sun has gone down. They are called ***nocturnal*** (nok-TUR-nul) creatures.

7   Many nocturnal creatures have very large eyes. Their big eyes let in more light and help them see in the **moonlit** forest.

---

nocturnal   active at night   **moonlit**   given light from the moon

Crocodile

8   Bats are common nocturnal creatures. There are hundreds of different kinds of bats in the world's rain forests. Many bats have a strong sense of smell that helps them find fruits and flowers in the dark. Others use sound to find and capture insects and to find their way in the night.

9   At night, rain forest trees **twinkle** with fireflies and click beetles. Scientists think insects like these "talk" to each other with their flashing lights.

> **Outline Information to Understand Reading**
>
> Add the creatures mentioned in paragraph 9 to your outline.

Water Creatures

10   Rivers run through most of the rain forests of the world. Thousands of different kinds of fish live in these rivers. Snakes, crocodiles, and lizards **slither** and sleep on the banks.

Army Ants

11   Army ants have painful **stingers.** They **raid** the rain forest floor in large **swarms,** searching for food.

---

twinkle   shine
slither   move by sliding and turning
stingers   pointed body parts that are used to stab

raid   attack suddenly
swarms   large numbers of insects that move in groups

12   A swarm of marching army ants travels a **foot** every minute. Sometimes there are more than a million ants in the swarm!

Outline Information to Understand Reading

Which details about army ants will you include in your outline?

foot   12 inches, or about 30.5 centimeters

13   Army ants catch and kill spiders and insects. Sometimes they also kill small animals that can't get out of their way.

14   Army ants don't eat people. But you still wouldn't want to be in their path. A sting from an army ant really hurts!

About the Authors   Mary Pope Osborne and Will Osborne

Mary Pope Osborne has lived a life of adventure. She grew up in a military family and moved frequently. She enjoyed living in many different places. Pope Osborne continued to love change as an adult. After graduating from college, she held a variety of jobs that included working as an actress, a waitress, a travel consultant, a medical assistant, and a children's book editor. She met her husband, the coauthor of "Rain Forest Creatures," at a play in which he performed.

➤ Why do you think the authors wrote about the rain forest? Was it to entertain, to influence, or to express an opinion?

Beyond the Reading

Reading Comprehension

Question-Answer Relationships (QAR)

"Right There" Questions

1. **Recall Facts** What does *camouflage* mean?
2. **Recall Facts** When do nocturnal creatures come out?
3. **Recall Facts** What animals do army ants eat for food?

"Think and Search" Questions

4. **Describe** How does the word *army* describe what army ants are like?
5. **Compare and Contrast** Choose two animals described in the article and tell how they are similar and different.

"Author and You" Questions

6. **Draw Conclusions** Do you think bats have good eyesight? Explain your answer.

7. **Make Inferences** The writers explain that rain forest creatures have colors that help them blend with their natural surroundings. What do you think some of these colors are? Why?

"On Your Own" Questions

8. **Explain** If you could be a rain forest creature, which one would you like to be? Explain your answer.
9. **Understand Author's Purpose** What do the authors want you to learn in this article?
10. **Discuss** Do you think that it is important to protect the rain forest? Why or why not?

Activity Book
p. 74

Student
CD-ROM

Build Reading Fluency

Adjust Your Reading Rate to Scan

When you scan, you adjust your reading rate to read fast. **Scanning** means looking quickly at the text for key words to help you answer a question. Work with a partner. Read aloud key words as you look for information. Write your answers on a piece of paper.

1. What is a predator?
2. What size eyes do nocturnal creatures have?
3. Name two creatures that live on the water banks.
4. What creatures make the rain forest trees twinkle?
5. Why do army ants kill?

Listen, Speak, Interact

Recall Details

Play a game where the goal is to remember the most details and content from the reading vocabulary.

1. First, write seven questions and answers for "Rain Forest Creatures." An example is, "What rain forest creature has a strong sense of smell?" (Answer: a bat)
2. Write each question and answer on a note card. Make sure to use vocabulary from the selection.

3. Then, meet with a partner. Take turns asking each other questions. Do not look in your books.
4. Keep score by giving one point for each correct answer. If you and your partner both wrote the same question and answer, you both automatically get one point.
5. When you finish, add up the points to find out who won the game.

Elements of Literature

Examine Visual Features

In this chapter, you learned that the purpose of an informational text is to explain something. This type of writing often includes **visuals** with **captions** to help the reader understand the text.

1. Look at the pictures on each page of the selection.
2. Read each caption. Think about how the captions help you understand the picture as well as the text.
3. Think of two more pictures that you would like to add to the selection.
4. Draw a diagram like this one. Write the page number for each picture. Draw the pictures in the boxes.
5. Write a caption that explains each picture and supports the text.

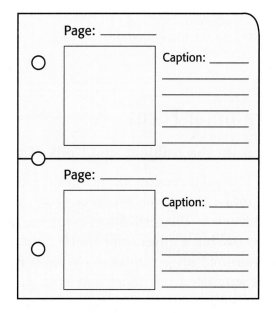

Activity Book
p. 75

Student
CD-ROM

Word Study

Learn Word Origins

Many English words come from other languages and cultures. For example, the word *camouflage* is a French word that has become a part of the English language.

English has been borrowing words from French for over a thousand years. Sometimes the spelling in English has changed a little from the original French word.

1. In your Personal Dictionary, copy the list of other English words that come from French.
2. Match each word with the correct definition listed in the right-hand column. Use a dictionary to help you.

English Words from French

collage
group
dialogue
role
souvenir
genre

Definitions

a. an object that is bought to remember a place
b. people that have something in common
c. type of writing
d. different pictures placed together
e. a talk between two people
f. the part one has in a group

Personal Dictionary   The Heinle Newbury House Dictionary   Activity Book p. 76   Student CD-ROM

Grammar Focus

Identify the Subject and Verb of a Sentence

The **subject** of a sentence is the word or phrase that performs the action indicated by the **verb.** Every complete sentence has a subject and a verb. Note the underlined subject and the circled verb in this sentence from paragraph 9:

At night, rain forest trees (twinkle) with fireflies and click beetles.

1. Write five sentences from the selection on a piece of paper.

2. Underline the subject of the sentence. Then circle the verb.
3. Decide if the following sentences are complete or not. If not, add a subject or a verb to make them complete.
   a. Many animals in the rain forest.
   b. Is hot and rainy there.
   c. Bats are nocturnal creatures.

Activity Book pp. 77–78   Student Handbook   Student CD-ROM

From Reading to Writing

Write an Informational Report

Write an informational report that explains something about a place in your community.

1. Write the report in the third person (use the pronouns *he, she, it,* and *they,* not *I* and *we*) and the present tense. Remember that a sentence must have a subject and a verb.
2. Include two or more separate sections. Write a heading for each section. The headings should provide clues about the main idea of each section.
3. Draw one or two pictures for the report. Add captions that explain what the pictures show.

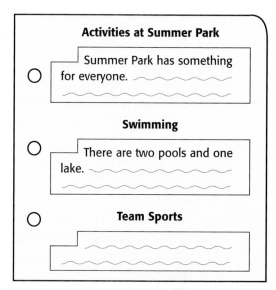

Activities at Summer Park

Summer Park has something for everyone.

Swimming

There are two pools and one lake.

Team Sports

Activity Book
p. 79

Student
Handbook

Across Content Areas

Read Pie Charts

Earth's rain forests are disappearing. The **pie charts** here show the change from 1950 to 2002. Each circle represents Earth's land surface.

1. Which color shows the rain forests?
2. Which color shows other kinds of land on Earth?
3. Which statement is true, **a** or **b**?
   a. The rain forests were bigger in 1950 than in 2002.
   b. The rain forests were smaller in 1950 than in 2002.

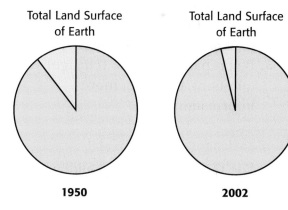

Total Land Surface of Earth

Total Land Surface of Earth

1950

2002

☐ Rain Forests

☐ Other Land

Activity Book
p. 80

Listening and Speaking Workshop

Perform an Interview

> **Topic**
>
> In Unit 2, you read selections about environments in a desert, a large city, and a rain forest. With a partner, write an interview and perform it in class.

Step 1: Prepare for your interview.

1. Decide who will be the interviewer—the one who asks questions—and who will be the interviewee—the one who answers the questions.
2. Make a list of questions and answers. Use what you learned from the readings in the unit to help you brainstorm. For example:
   a. What is your name?
   b. Where do you live?
   c. What's good about the environment where you live?
   d. What can you do to make it better?
3. Be prepared to revise (change) your questions as you get more information.

Step 2: Practice.

1. Use the "Interviewer's Guidelines."
2. If possible, record your interview so you can evaluate your work.
3. Speak clearly and look at each other.
4. Sit up straight and listen to the other person.

> **Interviewer's Guidelines**
>
> 1. Listen for important words and phrases.
> 2. If the interviewee has difficulty answering a question, consider changing it.
> 3. Be polite.
>   a. Don't interrupt the interviewee.
>   b. Thank the interviewee for doing the interview with you.

5. If you don't understand or need to revise your questions:
   Interviewer: Ask politely for more details.
   Interviewee: Ask the interviewer to repeat a question or to restate it (say it in different words).
6. After the interview:
   a. The interviewer summarizes (states in his or her own words) the interviewee's answers.
   b. The interviewee checks the interviewer's summary. If you made a recording, use it to help you check.

Step 3: Present your interview to the class or another audience.

1. Tell the interview topic.
2. Conduct your interview using the questions and answers that you practiced above.

Step 4: Evaluate your classmates' interviews.

1. Use the Active Listening Checklist to evaluate your classmates' interviews.
2. Create other items to add to the Active Listening Checklist.

Student Handbook

> **Active Listening Checklist**
>
> 1. I liked ____ because ____ .
> 2. I want to know more about ____ .
> 3. I understood the major ideas of your interview. Yes / No
> 4. The interviewer spoke confidently and knew the subject well. Yes / No
> 5. I understood the purpose of the interview. Yes / No

Viewing Workshop

View, Compare, and Contrast

Respond to Media

In Unit 2 you read the poem "Here Is the Southwestern Desert." Compare this poem with a rhyming tale entitled "Bringing the Rain to Kapiti Plain."

1. Rent a video of "Bringing the Rain to Kapiti Plain" or borrow one from your school library.
2. Watch the video with a partner.
3. Discuss with your partner how the video and the poem "Here Is the Southwestern Desert" are similar and different.
4. Use a chart like the one shown to record your responses.
5. Discuss with your class how reading the poem affects how you feel about deserts. Discuss how viewing the video affects how you feel about Kapiti Plain.

Here Is the Southwestern Desert Bringing the Rain to Kapiti Plain	
Alike:	*Different:*

6. Discuss with the class which media form (print or video) is more influential and informative.
   a. Explain with examples what you liked or disliked about each.
   b. Explain if you think the purpose of both versions is to inform, entertain, or persuade.

Further Viewing

Watch the *Visions* CNN Video for Unit 2. Do the Video Worksheet.

CNN Video

Writer's Workshop

Write Rules

Prompt

Following rules about safety can make your neighborhood a better place to live. Write a guide that tells about rules that would help a person in your neighborhood.

Step 1: Get ideas for your rules.

1. With a partner, brainstorm ideas for rules. Use the Cluster Map.
2. Use resources to help you find rules. Go to the library to research information about safety rules, or look on the Internet (search word: *safety*).
3. Use graphic features, such as pictures and signs, to help you locate information. Also, use headings. They often tell about important ideas.

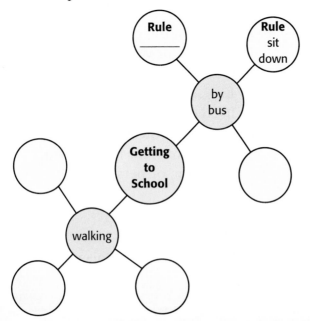

Step 2: Organize your rules.

1. Evaluate your research. Make sure the information you found is useful.
2. Summarize information about the rules you found on a piece of paper. Use your own words.
3. Choose three of the most important rules. Organize them in order, with the most important one first.
4. Use the three rules to complete the outline in the model below. This outline in the next step will also help you to summarize and organize information.

Step 3: Write a draft of your guide.

1. Think of a title for your rules.
2. Write a paragraph that explains why you are writing this list of rules. This is the introduction.
3. Write a heading for your rules.
4. Write your three rules in a numbered list (1, 2, 3). Start each rule on a new line.

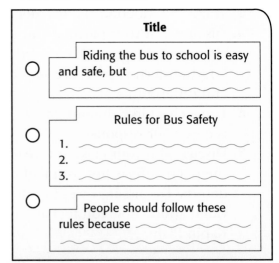

5. You can explain a rule if you think your audience needs more information.

6. After your list of rules, write a final paragraph to explain why following these rules are good for people. This is the conclusion.

7. Use reference sources, such as a dictionary or grammar guide, to help you clearly write your paragraph.

Step 4: Revise the draft of your guide.

Carefully reread your draft and make sure you did the following:

1. You thought about your audience and your purpose for writing.

2. You wrote a paragraph of introduction and a paragraph of conclusion.

3. You used a heading for your rules. You put them in a numbered list.

4. You used reference sources to help you clarify ideas and revise text.

5. You used a resource, such as your Student Handbook, to help you revise your guide.

Step 5: Get peer editing.

1. Ask a partner to read your guide.

2. Ask your partner how you can make your guide better.

3. Revise your guide if necessary.

Step 6: Proofread and finish.

1. Use reference sources to proofread your guide. Check for mechanics: correct spelling, punctuation, and grammar.

2. If possible, type your story on a computer and check for mechanics.

3. Review your guide to make sure the rules are clearly written.

Step 7: Publish your guide.

1. Add visuals and captions that will help your audience understand.

2. If you wrote your guide on a computer, choose a font that you like. You can choose one font for your opening and closing paragraphs, and another one for your rules.

3. If you are writing by hand, make a final copy in your best handwriting.

4. With other students, post your guides on a bulletin board in the classroom or in the school so that other people can read them. If possible, post them on the Internet.

5. Take your guide home and share it with your family members.

The Heinle Newbury House Dictionary

Student Handbook

Projects

The following projects will help you expand what you learned about environments.

Project 1: Make a Poster of a Special Environment

Research an environment made by people.

1. Think of some special environments not in nature where people might live or work; for example, a submarine, a spacecraft, and a zoo.
2. Choose one special environment to learn more about. Make a list of questions about the place:
   a. What happens in the environment?
   b. What does a person (or animal) need to live there?
   c. What are the good and bad things about the environment?
   d. How can it be better?
3. Use your school library to research information about the environment. Record the answers to your questions and other facts on note cards. Write the answers in complete sentences.
4. Use headings, tables of contents, and graphic features (maps, pictures, charts). Use these text features to locate and organize information.
5. Ask your teacher or librarian to help you interpret information in the graphic features.
6. Revise your questions as you get information. Ask your school librarian to help you find the answers to additional questions.

7. Present the results of your research on a poster. Include pictures that relate to the environment. Include lists and charts to organize and summarize facts you learned about the environment.

Project 2: Prepare and Present a News Report

What is your community doing to protect the environment? Prepare a news report to discuss this issue.

1. Work with a partner to create questions to research. Ask your teacher or the librarian to help you.
2. Use multiple resources, such as newspapers and the Internet, to find answers to your questions.
3. If possible, interview the mayor or someone in charge of protecting the community's resources.
4. Organize your research and compose a news report.
5. Be sure to clarify and support your ideas with evidence, elaborations, and examples.
6. Edit your report and revise it to make it accurate.
7. Use a computer to write your report.
8. Pretend that you are speaking on television or on radio. Think about your audience. Adjust your word choice, diction (way of speaking), style, and usage to your audience.
9. Practice your news report.
10. Present your news report to the class or as a school announcement.

Further Reading

The following is a list of books that examine the theme of the environment. Chose one or more of them. Write your thoughts and feelings about what you read in your Reading Log. Answer the following questions:

1. How do humans affect the environment? How can humans protect the environment?
2. How are the environments you read about the same or different from the one you live in?
3. Can you connect the issues in the books you read to those of the reading selections in this unit?

Seedfolks
by Paul Fleischman, HarperCollins Children's Books, 1997. In this book by award-winning author Paul Fleischman, a story is told by thirteen different characters about a vacant lot in Cleveland, Ohio, that the community turns into a garden.

Lostman's River
by Cynthia C. DeFelice, William Morrow & Co., 1995. In 1906, Tyler and his family move from New York City to the Florida Everglades. Once there, Tyler discovers hunters who threaten the ecosystem of the Everglades. He fights to protect the Everglades and the animals that live there.

John Muir: Young Naturalist
by Montrew Dunham and Al Fiorentino, Simon & Schuster Children's, 1998. This is the biography of the "father of the conservation movement" in the United States. John Muir worked with President Theodore Roosevelt to establish the National Parks Service and create Yosemite National Park.

How Cities Work: Open Your Eyes to the Wonders of the Urban Environment
by Preston Gralla, DIANE Publishing Co., 1999. This book explains how the water, gas, and electric systems operate to keep cities functioning.

Environments of the Western Hemisphere
by John C. Gold, Twenty-First Century Books, 1997. This books discusses the different environments of North and South America. The book highlights the successes and failures of the people who have settled the land in the Western Hemisphere.

Song of the Trees, Vol. 1
by Mildred D. Taylor, Dial Books for Young Readers, 1976. Award-winning author Mildred Taylor writes about an African-American family in the southern United States during the Great Depression. The family tries to save the forest on their land from being cut down.

Weather and Sky: Explore the Extreme Forces of the Earth and Harsh Environment of Space
by Tim Walker and Chris Oxlade, Advantage Publishers Group, 2000. This book discusses the mysteries of natural disasters and space. Explore the planets and comets. Read about the devastation caused by typhoons and tornadoes.

Companion Web site

Reading Log

Heinle Reading Library Aesop's Fables

Conflict and Cooperation

Martin Luther King Jr. memorial, in Selma, Alabama.

View the Picture

1. Describe what you see.
2. Why do you think someone made a statue of Martin Luther King Jr.?

In this unit, you will read about conflict and cooperation. You will explore this theme by reading a song, a diary entry, a play, an excerpt from a personal narrative, and an informational text. You will also practice writing these forms.

151

CHAPTER 1

Into the Reading

We Shall Overcome

a traditional song

Objectives

Reading Make inferences as you read song lyrics.

Listening and Speaking Practice intonation.

Grammar Talk about the future using *will* and *shall*.

Writing Write lyrics for a song about the future.

Content The Arts: Learn about types of songs.

Use Prior Knowledge

Share and Compare Traditional Songs

Traditional songs are songs that are passed down from generation to generation. People usually learn traditional songs in school or from their families.

1. With a partner, talk about or sing some traditional songs that you know from your culture or region.
   a. What is the title, or name, of the song?
   b. What is the song about?
   c. How does the language in the song reflect the culture or region?

Name of Student	Title of Song	What Song Is About
Julio	Mi Escuelita	a school

2. Copy the chart on a piece of paper. Write information about the songs.
3. Share your chart with the rest of the class.

Build Background

The Civil Rights Movement

African-Americans did not always have the same rights as other Americans. For example, in many places, African-Americans had to sit in the back of public buses or trains. In the 1950s and 1960s, many people worked to get equal rights for all Americans. This is called the Civil Rights movement. People participated in marches, or long walks, to protest and push for change. During the marches, they sang songs about freedom. Freedom means that you can speak and act without being stopped. One famous freedom song is "We Shall Overcome."

Content Connection

SOCIAL STUDIES

In 1965, about 25,000 people marched into Montgomery, Alabama, to show they wanted equal rights for all Americans.

Build Vocabulary

Learn Words About Freedom

"We Shall Overcome" uses words that help you understand freedom.

We shall live in <u>peace</u>.

Peace is a part of freedom. Peace is a time without war.

1. Copy the chart in your Personal Dictionary.
2. With a partner, read the definitions.
3. Complete the chart with the words listed below.

Word	Definition
	a type of government where people vote for the representatives who make laws
	carrying out and applying laws in a way that is fair
	freedom or permission to do something by law

justice	right	democracy

Personal Dictionary

The Heinle Newbury House Dictionary

Activity Book
p. 81

Student CD-ROM

Text Structure

Song Lyrics

The reading selection in this chapter is a **song.** A song has words called **lyrics** that are set to music. The chart shows some features of lyrics that are used in "We Shall Overcome."

As you read, listen to, or sing "We Shall Overcome," look for these features.

♫ Song Lyrics ♫	
Verses	groups of lines
Refrain	lines repeated at the end of each verse
Direction	a word or words that tell how to sing the song

Student
CD-ROM

Reading Strategy

Make Inferences

When you **make inferences,** you use information in the text and what you already know to make a guess. For example, you hear a song about a person who wants to live in the mountains. You might make the inference that the person likes the mountains.

Writers do not always say everything directly. If you make inferences as you read, you will understand more of what the writer is saying.

1. As you read or listen to "We Shall Overcome," make inferences about the people who sing the song. Write your inferences on a piece of paper.
2. Compare your inferences with a partner. Did you both hear the same message?

Student
CD-ROM

WE SHALL OVERCOME

OVERCOME

a traditional song

Audio
CD 1, Tr. 12

Prologue

"We **Shall Overcome**" is a song about peace and justice. The words come from a song that was written in 1901. The song has gone through many changes.

People sang "We Shall Overcome" during marches of the **Civil Rights** movement in the 1960s in the United States. Now people all over the world sing it when they are fighting for their civil rights.

Make Inferences

What do the people singing the song want to overcome?

---

shall will

overcome fight against something successfully

civil rights the rights of each citizen

dignity pride in oneself

2 **We'll** walk hand in hand,
   We'll walk hand in hand,
   We'll walk hand in hand someday.
   Oh, deep in my heart I do believe
   we'll walk hand in hand someday.

3 We shall live in peace,
   We shall live in peace,
   We shall live in peace someday.
   Oh, deep in my heart I do believe
   we shall live in peace someday.

4 We shall all be free,
   We shall all be free,
   We shall all be free someday.
   Oh, deep in my heart I do believe
   we shall all be free someday.

Make Inferences

Why do the people who are singing say they are not alone? Explain your answer.

5 We are not alone,
   We are not alone,
   We are not alone someday.
   Oh, deep in my heart I do believe
   we are not alone someday.

We'll We will

Beyond the Reading

Reading Comprehension

Question-Answer Relationships (QAR)

"Right There" Questions

1. **Recall Facts** What is the title of the song?
2. **Recall Facts** When was the song written?
3. **Recall Facts** According to the song, how will people walk someday?

"Think and Search" Questions

4. **Make Inferences** Why is there a direction to sing the song "with dignity"?
5. **Make Inferences** Are the people singing the song living in peace?

"Author and You" Question

6. **Understand Features** List three features that tell you the reading selection is a song.

"On Your Own" Questions

7. **Describe Effects** What effect did listening to the song and lyrics have on you?
8. **Explain** Do you think singing a song like this helps people reach their goals? Explain your answer.

Activity Book
p. 82

Student
CD-ROM

Build Reading Fluency

Adjust Your Reading Rate to Memorize

One purpose of reading is to memorize. You must adjust your reading rate to read slowly. You need to read, think, and reread to remember. Reading a song can give you excellent practice in reading to memorize.

1. Listen to the audio recording of "We Shall Overcome."
2. In small groups, read or sing each line slowly on pages 156–157.
3. Practice memorizing the song.
4. In small groups, present the song to the class.

Listen, Speak, Interact

Practice Intonation

When you sing a song, your voice goes up and down. When you speak, your voice also goes up and down. This is called **intonation.**

In English, statements have intonation like this. Listen as your teacher demonstrates how this intonation sounds:

We shall overcome.

1. Work with a partner. Take turns reading a verse from "We Shall Overcome." Follow the intonation for statements as you read.
2. Compare your intonation with your partner's. Did your voices go up and down on the same words?
3. Compare your reading of the lyrics with the way they are sung on the audio recording.

Elements of Literature

Recognize Repetition

"We Shall Overcome" uses **repetition.** Repetition is saying the same thing more than once. You repeat something when you want to say it more strongly. Repetition helps the people singing the song show that they feel strongly about the song's message.

1. Copy this chart in your Reading Log.
2. Reread "We Shall Overcome," or listen to the audio recording again.
3. In your chart, write the line from each verse that is repeated.
4. Think about why the people singing these verses might feel strongly about the lines that are repeated.
5. Compare the lyrics of the song to the poems you read in Unit 1. How are they the same? How are they different?

Verse	Repeated Line
Verse 1	We shall overcome
Verse 2	
Verse 3	
Verse 4	
Verse 5	

Reading Log Activity Book p. 83 Student CD-ROM

Word Study

Recognize Homographs

The English language contains some words that are spelled the same but have different pronunciations and meanings. These words are called **homographs.** Look at these examples of homographs:

We shall <u>live</u> in peace. (verse 3)

We heard a <u>live</u> concert on the radio.

In the first sentence, the word *live* means "to be alive." This word is pronounced with a short *i* as in *sit*.

In the second sentence, the word *live* means "a performance that is heard as it is happening." This word is pronounced with a long *i* as in *line*.

1. Copy these homographs in your Personal Dictionary.

bass/bass	tear/tear	lead/lead

2. Use a dictionary to check the pronunciations and meanings of the words.

3. With a partner, practice pronouncing the words.

4. Write the definitions in your Personal Dictionary.

Personal Dictionary   The Heinle Newbury House Dictionary   Activity Book *p. 84*   Student CD-ROM

Grammar Focus

Talk About the Future Using *Will* and *Shall*

The **future tense** tells about things that are going to happen. The words *will* and *shall* show future tense.

Will is used more often. It describes an activity that you predict or promise to do in the future.

We **will** go to the zoo tomorrow.

Will can be made into a contraction (shortened words).

We'**ll** go to the zoo tomorrow.

Shall is rarely used today to talk about the future, but it can be used to make a suggestion.

Shall we leave now?

Reread verse 2 of "We Shall Overcome." On a piece of paper, write a sentence that uses *will*.

Activity Book *pp. 85–86*   Student Handbook   Student CD-ROM

From Reading to Writing

Write Lyrics for a Song About the Future

Write lyrics for a song about what you will do in the future.

1. Choose a topic to write about.
2. Give your song a title.
3. Follow the structure of a song. Give a direction about how to sing the song. Write one verse. Use repetition.
4. Use *will* to tell about what you think will happen to you.
5. You can think of a song that you know and match your lyrics to the music and intonation of that song.
6. Choose a style (how the song is written) and a voice (how the song sounds) that best fit your topic and audience.

We Will Laugh	
direction:	happily
verse:	I will laugh with my family,
	I will laugh with my friends,
	I will laugh with my neighbors.
	Oh, we will all laugh together.

7. Perform your song. As you listen to your classmates, recognize the structure and intonation of their song.

Activity Book
p. 87

Student Handbook

Across Content Areas

Learn About Types of Songs

Here are some types of songs:

lullaby a song that you sing to a child to help him or her fall asleep

anthem a song that shows admiration or respect for something

ballad a song that tells a story

hymn a religious song

Complete each of the following sentences with the correct type of song.

1. The old man sang a ____ about how a famous princess saved her country.
2. We looked at the flag as we sang the national ____ .
3. We sang a ____ at church.
4. The baby cried and cried until his mother sang a ____ .

In a small group, write a letter to a favorite songwriter. Tell this person why you like his or her songs. Organize your letter into paragraphs. Revise it for spelling and grammar.

Activity Book
p. 88

Zlata's Diary

an excerpt from a diary
by Zlata Filipović

Objectives

Reading Recognize sequence of events as you read an excerpt from a diary.

Listening and Speaking Role-play a persuasive conversation.

Grammar Use verbs with infinitives.

Writing Write your opinion.

Content Social Studies: Learn the points of the compass.

Use Prior Knowledge

Discuss Your Feelings About Experiences

Think about experiences in your life that made you feel happy, sad, scared, or angry.

1. On a piece of paper, make a chart like the one here. Write some of your experiences in the chart. How did each experience make you feel?
2. Share your chart with a partner.

Experience	How I Felt
I moved to a new city.	sad

Examples of Experiences	**Examples of Feelings**	
I got an A in math.	happy	hopeful
My cat ran away.	sad	brave
I broke my arm.	scared	angry

Build Background

Bosnia and Herzegovina

Bosnia and Herzegovina is a country in Eastern Europe. Its capital city is Sarajevo. Bosnia and Herzegovina was once part of the country of Yugoslavia. In 1992, Bosnia and Herzegovina broke away from Yugoslavia to form a new country. This began years of war between different groups of people in the area.

In 1995, the groups agreed to stop fighting. Today, the government of the country is working to make it strong.

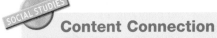

Content Connection

Bosnia and Herzegovina is on the Balkan Peninsula in southeastern Europe. A **peninsula** is a body of land surrounded by water on three sides.

Build Vocabulary

Find Antonyms in a Thesaurus

Antonyms are words that have opposite meanings; for example, *night/day, happy/sad, good/bad.*

Read the words and definitions. Match each word with its antonym. Check your answers in a dictionary or a **thesaurus.** A thesaurus is a book that gives synonyms and antonyms. You can also find a thesaurus on the Internet. Do a search for *thesaurus.*

Words and Definitions	Antonyms
war fighting	create
destroy ruin	combine
separate move apart	wonderful
terrible very bad	peace

The Heinle Newbury House Dictionary

Activity Book p. 89

Student CD-ROM

Text Structure

Diary

"Zlata's Diary" is an excerpt from the **diary** of Zlata Filipović, a 12-year-old girl. A diary is a book with blank pages in which you write your experiences and thoughts every day. As you read, look for the features of a diary.

Student
CD-ROM

Diary	
Structure	A diary is divided into sections called entries. There is an entry for each day the author writes. Each entry includes the date and important events.
Personal Experiences	A diary includes the most important events, feelings, and thoughts of each day. A diary entry can be very personal because the diary is not meant to be read by anyone else.
Direct Address	Many writers "speak" to their diary. They give their diary a name and use the pronoun *you.* Zlata names her diary *Mimmy.*
Informal Writing	A diary sometimes uses everyday language that may not be grammatically correct, such as incomplete sentences.

Reading Strategy

Recognize Sequence of Events

The **sequence of events** is the order in which events happen. It can help you remember what you read. It can also help you find information in a text. This timeline lists a sequence of events.

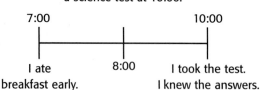

I remembered that I had a science test at 10:00.

7:00   10:00

I ate breakfast early.   8:00   I took the test. I knew the answers.

1. As you read or listen to the audio recording of "Zlata's Diary," identify the dates of each diary entry.
2. Transition words and phrases such as *today* and *right now* can help you understand the order of events.
3. Organize the ideas on a timeline. Show the sequence of events for one of the diary entries in the selection.

Student
CD-ROM

Zlata's Diary

an excerpt from a diary
by Zlata Filipović

Prologue

When Zlata Filipović began her diary, she was living in Sarajevo, the capital city of Bosnia and Herzegovina. As Zlata writes, enemy armies are surrounding Sarajevo and attacking the city from the hills with bombs and guns.

Zlata named her diary "Mimmy," which was the name of a pet fish she once had. Keka, Braco, Mirna, Bojana, Verica, Oga, Martina, Matea, and Dejan are the names of her friends and family members.

Zlata and her father walk through the streets of Sarajevo.

1

Sunday, April 12, 1992

Dear Mimmy,

The new sections of town—Dobrinja, Mojmilo,Vojničko polje—are being badly **shelled.** Everything is being destroyed, burned, the people are in **shelters.** Here in the middle of town, where we live, it's different. It's quiet. People go out. It was a nice warm spring day today. We went out too. Vaso Miškin Street was full of people, children. It looked like a **peace march.** People came out to be together, they don't want war. They want to live and enjoy themselves the way they used to. That's only **natural,** isn't it? Who likes or wants war, when it's the worst thing in the world?

2

I keep thinking about the march I joined today. It's bigger and stronger than war. That's why it will win. The people must be the ones to win, not the war, because war has nothing to do with **humanity.** War is something **inhuman.**

Zlata

Recognize Sequence of Events

On what date did Zlata join the peace march? How do you know?

---

shelled   shot at by bullets and bombs

shelters   rooms or buildings where people hide from attacks

peace march   when a group of people walk together and demand peace

natural   normal

humanity   human beings as a group

inhuman   cruel; without kindness for other people

Zlata puts her arms around her parents.

Recognize Sequence of Events

Name two events that happened on April 14 before Zlata began writing.

3

Tuesday, April 14, 1992

Dear Mimmy,

People are leaving Sarajevo. The airport, train and bus stations are **packed.** I saw sad pictures on TV of people **parting.** Families, friends separating. Some are leaving, others staying. It's so sad. Why? These people and children aren't **guilty** of anything. Keka and Braco came early this morning. They're in the kitchen with Mommy and Daddy, **whispering.** Keka and Mommy are crying. I don't think they know what to do—whether to stay or to go. Neither way is good.

Zlata

---

packed crowded, or filled, with people
parting leaving

guilty having done something wrong
whispering speaking in a soft, quiet voice

Wednesday, April 15, 1992

4

Dear Mimmy,

There has been **terrible gunfire** in Mokjmilo [a part of Sarajevo]. Mirna spent a whole forty-eight hours in the shelter. I talked to her on the phone, but not for long because she had to go back down to the shelter. I **feel sorry for** her.

5

Bojana and Verica are going to England. Oga is going to Italy. And worst of all, Martina and Matea have already left. They went to Ohrid [a lakeside town in Macedonia]. Keka is crying, Braco is crying and Mommy is crying. She's on the phone right now, and she's crying. And "those boys" up there in the hills keep shooting at us. I just heard that Dejan had left too.

OOOHHHHH! Why war?!

Love you, Mimmy,
Zlata

Recognize Sequence of Events

List these events in the order that they happened: Mommy is crying, Mirna spent forty-eight hours in the shelter, Zlata spoke to Mirna on the phone.

Zlata writes about her hopes and fears in her diary.

---

terrible   very bad, very frightening
gunfire   a shooting of guns

feel sorry for   pity, feel bad for someone

Thursday, April 16, 1992

Recognize Sequence of Events

What does Zlata learn about Martina, Matea, and Dejan on April 16? How is this information different from what she learned on April 15?

Dear Mimmy,

Martina, Matea and Dejan didn't leave, after all. That's really not fair! Yes, of course it is, they mustn't go. But it isn't fair because we all **cried our eyes out** and in the end they didn't leave. There are not enough buses, trains or planes for all the people that want to get out of here.

Love you,
Zlata

7

Saturday, April 18, 1992

Dear Mimmy,

There's shooting, **shells** are falling. This really is WAR. Mommy and Daddy are worried, they sit up until late at night, talking. They're **wondering** what to do, but it's hard to know. Whether to leave and split up, or stay here together. Keka wants to take me to Ohrid. Mommy can't make up her mind—she's **constantly in tears.** She tries to hide it from me, but I see everything. I see that things aren't good here. There's no peace. War has suddenly entered our town, our homes, our thoughts, our lives. It's terrible.

It's also terrible that Mommy has **packed** my suitcase.

Love,
Zlata

---

cried our eyes out cried for a long time
shells bullets
wondering wishing to know

constantly happening all the time
in tears crying
packed put objects in a container in order to move them

8

Monday, April 20, 1992

Dear Mimmy,

War is no joke, it seems. It destroys, kills, burns, separates, brings **unhappiness.** Terrible shells fell today on Baščaršija, the old town center. Terrible **explosions.** We went down into the **cellar,** the cold, dark, **revolting** cellar. And ours isn't even all that safe. Mommy, Daddy and I just stood there, holding on to one another in a corner that looked safe. Standing there in the dark, in the warmth of my parents' arms, I thought about leaving Sarajevo. Everybody is thinking about it, and so am I. I couldn't **bear** to go alone, to leave behind Mommy and Daddy, Grandma and Granddad. And going with just Mommy isn't any good either. The best would be for all three of us to go. But Daddy can't. So I've decided we should stay here together. Tomorrow I'll tell Keka that you have to be brave and stay with those you love and those who love you. I can't leave my parents, and I don't like the other idea of leaving my father behind alone either.

Your Zlata

> **Recognize Sequence of Events**
>
> According to Zlata, what event will happen tomorrow?

Zlata must carry jugs of water home because there is no running water.

---

unhappiness sadness
explosions blasts from bombs
cellar the space below ground level under a building

revolting making someone feel sick; unpleasant; disgusting
bear deal with without suffering or complaining

About the Author | Zlata Filipović (born 1980)

Zlata Filipović began writing her diary in 1991, when Sarajevo was still at peace. Zlata's life and her diary changed when the war began. Instead of writing about friends, sports, music, and school, she began to write about daily life during war. She could no longer go to school, there was very little to eat, and a group of her friends was killed in a park. In 1993, Zlata's diary was published, and the world learned about the young girl's fears and hopes. That same year, Zlata and her parents moved to Paris, France. After she moved, Zlata worked to help other children affected by war.

➤ Why do you think Zlata Filipović continued to write in her diary after the war began? What challenges did she face?

Beyond the Reading

Reading Comprehension

Question-Answer Relationships (QAR)

"Right There" Questions
1. **Recall Facts** Where does Zlata live?
2. **Recall Facts** What does Zlata learn from watching TV?
3. **Recall Facts** Why do Zlata's parents stay up late?
4. **Recall Facts** What does Zlata's family do when there are explosions near where they live?

"Think and Search" Questions
5. **Summarize** How does Keka want to help Zlata? What does Zlata finally decide about Keka's plan?
6. **Analyze Cause and Effect** Why does the "peace march" on April 12 make Zlata feel hopeful?
7. **Compare and Contrast** Why is the part of Sarajevo where Zlata lives safer on April 12 than it is on April 20?

"Author and You" Questions
8. **Draw Conclusions** Why do you think Zlata's mother tries to hide how she feels from Zlata?
9. **Make Judgments** Do you think Zlata makes the right decision about staying in Sarajevo? Why or why not?

"On Your Own" Questions
10. **Respond** If you were Zlata's friend, what advice would you give her to help her feel brave? How do you stay brave when you are scared?
11. **Compare Your Experiences** Have you had any experiences that made you feel the way Zlata does in these diary entries? Tell about them.
12. **Reflect** What do you think you would do if you were in Zlata's situation?

Activity Book
p. 90

Student
CD-ROM

Build Reading Fluency

Reading Silently

Reading silently for longer periods of time helps you become a better reader. It helps you learn to read faster.

1. Listen to the audio recording of "Zlata's Diary."
2. Listen to the chunks of words as you follow along.
3. Reread the diary entry on page 167 silently two times.
4. Your teacher will time your second reading.
5. Raise your hand when you are finished.
6. Record your timing.

Listen, Speak, Interact

Role-Play a Persuasive Conversation

When you want someone to do something, you can talk to the person and give reasons why it's a good idea to do it. A conversation like this is a **persuasive conversation.**

Keka wants to take Zlata away from Sarajevo, but Zlata decides to stay.

1. With a partner, reread paragraph 8. List Zlata's reasons for wanting to stay in Sarajevo.

2. Brainstorm a list of reasons why Zlata should leave Sarajevo.

3. One of you is Zlata, and the other is Keka. Role-play a conversation. Keka will try to persuade Zlata to leave Sarajevo. Zlata will explain why she wants to stay. How does your conversation end?

4. Share your role play with the class.

Elements of Literature

Identify Tone

Tone is the writer's attitude (way of thinking and feeling) toward the subject and characters. An author's tone may be hopeful, sad, angry, scared, confident, or brave. A text may have more than one tone.

Words and phrases show an author's tone. For example, Zlata writes, "Families, friends separating. Some are leaving, others staying." Her tone here is sad—people who love each other are separating.

1. With a partner, read these sentences from "Zlata's Diary":
   a. I keep thinking about the march . . . It's bigger and stronger than war. That's why it will win.
   b. OOOHHHHH! Why war?!

   c. War has suddenly entered our town . . . It's terrible.
   d. Tomorrow I'll tell Keka that you have to be brave and stay with those you love . . .

2. Talk to a partner about the tone that the sentences show. Sometimes more than one tone is possible.

3. Discuss your answers with another pair of students. Are your answers the same?

Activity Book
p. 91

Student
CD-ROM

Word Study

Form Contractions

We use **contractions** to put two words together to make a shorter word. A contraction always includes an **apostrophe** ('). Here are some common contractions:

First Word	Second Word	Contraction
I +	am ⇒	I'm
they +	are ⇒	they're
you +	are ⇒	you're
it +	is ⇒	it's
does +	not ⇒	doesn't

People often use contractions when they speak English and when they write informally. "Zlata's Diary" contains many contractions because it is written as if Zlata were speaking to a friend.

1. Copy the chart in your Personal Dictionary. Add other contractions as you learn them.
2. Read these sentences.
   a. <u>They are</u> in the kitchen with Mommy and Daddy.
   b. <u>She is</u> on the phone right now.
3. On a piece of paper, rewrite the sentences. Use contractions for the underlined words.

Personal Dictionary   The Heinle Newbury House Dictionary   Activity Book p. 92   Student CD-ROM

Grammar Focus

Use Verbs with Infinitives

An **infinitive** is made up of the word *to* plus the simple form of a verb. For example, *to go* and *to be* are infinitives.

Many verbs can be followed by an infinitive. Look at this example:

I want <u>to eat</u> dinner.

Want is the verb. *To eat* is the infinitive.

1. Copy the following sentences on a piece of paper.
   a. They want to live.
   b. She had to go back down.
   c. She tried to hide it.
   d. You have to be brave.
2. Circle each verb. Underline each infinitive.
3. Write three sentences of your own that include a verb and an infinitive. Choose from these verbs: *try, want, decide, begin, hope.* Write your own infinitives.

Activity Book pp. 93–94   Student Handbook   Student CD-ROM

From Reading to Writing

Write Your Opinion

Your opinion is what you believe about something. Study the writings and details of "Zlata's Diary." Write a paragraph that explains your opinion of the diary.

1. What is your opinion? Do you think "Zlata's Diary" gives readers a good idea of life during a war? Use this as the first sentence in your paragraph.
2. Support your opinion with details from the text. For example, Zlata tells about "terrible gunfire." This detail shows that many people are in danger during a war.
3. Indent your paragraph.

I think "Zlata's Diary"

Zlata Filipović writes about _____

This detail shows _____

4. Use contractions to make shorter words in your paragraph. Be sure to include the apostrophe in each contraction.

Activity Book   Student
p. 95   Handbook

Across Content Areas SOCIAL STUDIES

Learn the Points of the Compass

Look at this map. Find the **compass rose.** The compass rose tells you the directions.

N = north   NW = northwest
S = south   SW = southwest
E = east   NE = northeast
W = west   SW = southeast

With a partner, make up five sentences like this: *Romania is north of Bulgaria.* Read your sentences to another pair of students.

Activity Book
p. 96

CHAPTER 3

The Peach Boy

a play
by Suzanne Barchers

Objectives

Reading Analyze cause and effect as you read a play.

Listening and Speaking Talk about values.

Grammar Use compound sentences with *and*.

Writing Write a summary.

Content Science: Classify fruits and vegetables.

Use Prior Knowledge

Discuss Cooperation

A goal is something that you want for the future; for example, to go to college is a goal. Cooperation is working together to reach a goal.

1. Work with a partner. Make a chart like the one here on a piece of paper.

2. Read the goals in the chart. Discuss with your partner how you can cooperate with other people to reach each goal.

3. Write your ideas in the chart.

My Goals	How Cooperating with Other People Can Help Me Reach My Goals
I want to get a good grade on my test.	I can ask my teacher questions. I can study with a partner.
I want to learn another language.	
I want to do something to improve my community.	

Build Background

Japanese Folktales

"The Peach Boy" is a play based on a popular **folktale** from Japan. A folktale is a story that is passed down from generation to generation. Folktales often tell about things that are important to a certain culture.

The main character in "The Peach Boy" is a Japanese hero named Momotaro. Many Japanese folktales tell about Momotaro's exciting adventures. In these adventures, Momotaro often fights monsters or people who do wrong.

Content Connection

The name *Momotaro* contains the Japanese word *Momo*. *Momo* means "peach." A peach is a type of fruit. In Japanese folktales, eating peaches allows people to live forever.

Build Vocabulary

Define Words Related to Nature

The reading selection includes words related to things in nature. Some of these things are types of land, bodies of water, or plants. Look at these words from the selection:

stream	mountains	forest
peach	river	pine tree

1. Copy the chart in your Personal Dictionary.
2. Write the correct nature word for each definition. Use the nature words from the list.
3. Use a dictionary to look up any words you do not know.

Nature Word	Meaning
river	a large body of water that moves in one direction
	a juicy, round fruit with a large seed inside it
	a tall, straight tree with sharp leaves called needles
	a small flowing body of water
	an area of land with many trees
	tall forms of land and rock higher than hills

Personal Dictionary

The Heinle Newbury House Dictionary

Activity Book p. 97

Student CD-ROM

Text Structure

Play

"The Peach Boy" is a **play.** In a play, actors speak in front of an audience. They pretend to be characters in the play. Look at the features of a play listed in the chart.

As you read "The Peach Boy," find out who the characters are. Pay attention to their actions. How do the characters cooperate in the play?

Play	
Characters	people in a drama
Narrator	a person who tells about the characters and events (not all plays have narrators)
Dialogue	the words each character says

Student
CD-ROM

Reading Strategy

Analyze Cause and Effect

Authors sometimes use **cause and effect** to organize their story. A **cause** is the reason why an event happens. An **effect** is an event that happens as a result of a cause. Readers analyze cause and effect to understand why events happen in a story. Look at this example:

> The strong winds <u>caused</u> the tree to fall over.

> **Cause:** There were strong winds.
> **Effect:** The tree fell over.

1. Read the pairs of sentences in the chart. One shows a cause, and one shows an effect.
2. For each pair, decide which sentence shows the cause and which shows the effect.

a.	Saleem got an "A" on the test. Saleem studied for the test.
b.	Monica forgot to put gas in the car. The car ran out of gas.
c.	The traffic got very bad. Many people moved to the town.

3. Look for causes and effects as you read "The Peach Boy."
4. With a partner, perform a scene that contains one of the causes and effects that you found in the play.

Student
CD-ROM

The PEACH BOY

a play by Suzanne Barchers

Audio
CD 1, Tr. 14

1 **Narrator:** Long ago there lived an old man and old woman in a village in Japan. They were **fine** people, but they had no children. One day they were eating their breakfast.

2 **Man:** What are you doing today, my wife?

3 **Woman:** I am going to the stream to **scrub** clothes. What are you going to do, my husband?

4 **Man:** I am off to the mountains to cut some **firewood** for the stove.

5 **Narrator:** The man went to the mountains and the woman went to the stream. When the woman began to scrub her clothes, she noticed something strange **floating** in the river. A big, ripe peach was floating right to her.

6 **Woman:** This is my lucky day! I'll pull the peach to me with this stick. What a fine big peach this is! Wait until my husband sees it.

Analyze Cause and Effect

What caused the woman to say, "This is my lucky day!"?

---

fine   excellent
scrub   wash by rubbing hard

firewood   wood used to start a fire or to keep it burning
floating   resting or moving on the top of water or other liquid

7 **Narrator:** The old woman could hardly wait for her husband to come home.

8 **Woman:** Husband, come quickly. Come see what I have found!

9 **Man:** What is it, wife? Is something the matter?

10 **Woman:** Look at this peach! Isn't it the finest you have ever seen?

11 **Man:** How did you buy a peach like this?

12 **Narrator:** The old woman told him how it came floating down the stream.

13 **Man:** This is a **fine piece of fortune.** I have worked hard today. This will make a wonderful dinner for me.

14 **Narrator:** Just as the old man was about to cut the peach with his knife, he heard a voice.

15 **Momotaro:** Please don't cut me.

16 **Man: My goodness!** What is this I hear?

17 **Narrator:** Suddenly the peach split in half, and a little boy jumped out.

18 **Man and Woman: Goodness gracious!**

Analyze Cause and Effect

What caused the little boy to jump out of the peach?

---

fine piece of fortune   good luck
My goodness!   a phrase that shows surprise

Goodness gracious!   a phrase that shows surprise

19 **Narrator:** The little boy ate one half of the peach and then ate the other half. The old man and woman decided to call him Momotaro, meaning Boy of the Peach. They were **delighted** to have a child and took great care of him. He quickly grew into a fine young man. One day he asked his mother for a **favor.**

20 **Momotaro:** Mother, please make me some cakes.

21 **Woman:** Why, my son?

22 **Momotaro:** You have been very good to me. It is time I did some good of my own. I need the cakes for my **journey.**

23 **Woman:** But son, where are you going?

Analyze Cause and Effect

What effects does Momotaro think his journey will have?

24 **Momotaro:** To the **Island** of the **Ogres.** They have stolen from many people. I hope to free the land of those creatures and return the **belongings** to the people. Then they can live without fear.

25 **Man:** That is a fine idea. I wish you well.

26 **Narrator:** Momotaro's mother made him the cakes. Soon he was ready to leave.

27 **Man and Woman:** Good-bye, son. **Take care.**

28 **Momotaro:** Don't worry, my dear parents. I will be back soon.

---

delighted   very happy
favor   a helpful act
journey   a long trip
island   a piece of land completely surrounded by water

ogres   giants in folktales who eat people
belongings   things people own
take care   an expression that means "be careful"

29 **Narrator:** Momotaro **hurried** away. He was **anxious** to get to the Island of the Ogres. He was walking through the forest when he began to feel hungry. He sat under a pine tree and **unwrapped** his cakes. Suddenly he saw a huge dog **slinking** toward him. The dog spoke to him.

30 **Dog:** Momotaro, what do you have that smells so good?

31 **Momotaro:** I have a cake my mother made for me this morning.

32 **Dog:** If you give me one of your cakes, I will come with you to the Island of the Ogres. I can help you there.

33 **Momotaro:** You are **welcome** to the cake. I **appreciate** your offer of help.

Analyze Cause and Effect

The dog says he will go with Momotaro. Is this a cause or an effect?

---

hurried   moved quickly
anxious   wanting to do something, impatient
unwrapped   took the cover off of, opened

slinking   walking as if afraid or guilty
welcome   given permission
appreciate   be thankful for

34 **Narrator:** Momotaro and the dog continued on their way. Suddenly something jumped in front of Momotaro. It was a monkey.

35 **Monkey:** Momotaro! I hear you are going to the Island of the Ogres. I would like to go with you to help.

36 **Dog:** Who needs a monkey? I am going to help Momotaro!

37 **Momotaro:** There is no need to argue. You may both come. Here is a cake for you, monkey friend.

Analyze Cause and Effect

What do you think caused Momotaro to give cakes to the monkey and the pheasant? Look in the next paragraph and find the effect.

38 **Narrator:** The three continued on their journey. Suddenly they were stopped by a large **pheasant.** The dog **leaped** at it, but the pheasant fought back. Momotaro stopped the fight. He gave the pheasant a cake.

39 **Pheasant:** Thank you, Momotaro. I would like to go with you to the Island of the Ogres. I think I can be of help to you.

40 **Narrator:** The four of them continued down the path, **chatting** and becoming friends. Soon they came to the sea. Momotaro found a boat, and they climbed in it. They came to the island, where the ogres' **castle** was surrounded by high walls and a big gate. Momotaro studied the castle and explained his plan to his friends.

---

pheasant a large, colorful bird with a long tail
leaped jumped

chatting talking in a friendly way
castle a large building with thick walls to guard against attack

41 **Momotaro:** Pheasant, you fly over the castle gate and **peck** at the ogres. Monkey, climb over the wall and **pinch** the ogres. The dog and I will break the bars and come to help when possible.

42 **Narrator:** The pheasant flew over the gate and pecked at the ogres. The monkey climbed over the wall and pinched the ogres. Momotaro and the dog broke the bars and fought hard and long. Soon all the ogres were either dead or taken prisoner.

43 **Momotaro:** Now, my friends. Let us look at their **treasures.**

44 **Narrator:** There were many jewels and fine **goods.** Momotaro returned the stolen goods to the owners and told the people they need never fear the ogres again. There were many riches left for Momotaro and his friends. He returned home to the old man and woman. They were very happy to see him, and they all lived happily for many years.

Analyze Cause and Effect

What was the effect of Momotaro's plan?

---

peck   hit with a sharp object, such as a bird's beak
pinch   squeeze between the finger and thumb

treasures   riches
goods   items that can be bought and sold

About the Author

Suzanne Barchers (born 1946)

Suzanne Barchers has worked as a teacher, a writer, and an editor. She has written books about teaching language arts. Barchers has also written many books for young people about history and folktales.

➤ Why do you think Suzanne Barchers wanted to retell this story about Momotaro? To entertain, to inform, or to persuade?

Beyond the Reading

Reading Comprehension

Question-Answer Relationships (QAR)

"Right There" Questions

1. **Recall Facts** Where do the old man and the old woman live?
2. **Explain** What does "Momotaro" mean?
3. **Recall Facts** Who goes with Momotaro to the Island of the Ogres?

"Think and Search" Question

4. **Recognize Sequence of Events** Which character is the first to join Momotaro on his journey?

"Author and You" Questions

5. **Understand Character Motivation** Why do you think Momotaro allows the three animals to join him on his journey?

6. **Make an Inference** Why do you think the dog, the pheasant, and the monkey want to help Momotaro fight the ogres?

"On Your Own" Questions

7. **Relate Your Experiences** Can you remember a time when your friends or family helped you to reach a goal? What happened?
8. **Present an Opinion** Do you think Momotaro would have been able to fight the ogres if the dog, the pheasant, and the monkey had not helped him? Why or why not?

Activity Book
p. 98

Student
CD-ROM

Build Reading Fluency

Read Aloud to Engage Listeners

Practicing reading aloud helps increase your fluency and expression. Learning to read with expression makes others want to listen to you.

1. Listen to the audio recording of "The Peach Boy."
2. Turn to page 180 and follow along.
3. Pay attention to phrasing and expression.
4. With a partner, read aloud the paragraphs three times.
5. Select your favorite paragraph.
6. Read in front of the class with expression.

Listen, Speak, Interact

Talk About Values

In Build Background you learned that "The Peach Boy" is based on a folktale from Japan. Folktales often show a culture's values—things that are important to people. For example, a value of the culture in the United States is being able to take care of yourself.

1. With a partner, talk about the values you think the selection shows.
2. Use details from the selection to help you. For example, Momotaro's parents are very happy when he becomes their son. This detail shows that family is probably important in Japanese culture.
3. Write your ideas on a piece of paper.
4. Share your notes with the class. Listen carefully as your classmates also share their ideas. What evidence do your classmates share to support their opinions?
5. With your partner, perform a scene in "The Peach Boy" that illustrates your ideas.

Elements of Literature

Recognize Problems and Resolutions

A play often includes **problems and resolutions**—ways that problems are corrected. Authors use problems and resolutions to create interesting stories in their plays. Look at this problem and resolution from the reading selection:

Problem: Momotaro needs food for his journey.

Resolution: His mother makes some cakes for him.

1. Read the problems from the selection listed in the chart. Copy the chart in your Reading Log.
2. With a partner, talk about the author's resolution for each problem.

Problem	Author's Resolution
The ogres have stolen from many people.	
The dog and the pheasant fight each other.	
It is difficult to get into the ogres' castle. It has high walls and a big gate.	

3. Write each resolution in your chart.
4. Perform a dramatic interpretation of your resolution to the class.

Reading Log

Activity Book
p. 99

Student
CD-ROM

Word Study

Identify Homophones

Some words in the English language sound the same but have different spellings and meanings. These words are called **homophones.** Look at these examples of homophones from the selection:

> Come <u>see</u> what I have found! (paragraph 8)

> Soon they came to the <u>sea</u>. (paragraph 40)

See and *sea* are homophones. They are pronounced the same, but they mean different things. *See* means "look at," and *sea* means "a large body of water." The two words also have different spellings.

Look at the homophones and definitions below. Match the homophones with the correct set of definitions. Ask another student or your teacher if you need help.

1. flour / flower
2. ant / aunt
3. ate / eight

a. an insect / a mother's sister
b. the past tense of eat / a number
c. grain used for baking / a plant

The Heinle Newbury House Dictionary   Activity Book p. 100   Student CD-ROM

Grammar Focus

Use Compound Sentences With *and*

A **compound sentence** is two complete sentences joined by a conjunction such as *and.* Conjunctions are words that join parts of sentences.

When you join two complete sentences with *and*, use a comma before *and*.

Two Sentences	The man went to the mountains. The woman went to the stream.
Compound Sentence	The man went to the mountains, **and** the woman went to the stream.

1. Find two more compound sentences with *and* in the reading. Look in paragraphs 17 and 40.
2. On a piece of paper, combine the sentences below using *and.* Don't forget to use a comma before *and.*
   a. The dog asked for a cake. Momotaro gave him one.
   b. The pheasant flew over the gate. The monkey climbed over the wall.

Activity Book pp. 101–102   Student Handbook   Student CD-ROM

From Reading to Writing

Write a Summary

A **summary** gives the most important information of a reading. Write a short summary of "The Peach Boy" that is only one paragraph long.

1. Reread or listen to the audio recording of "The Peach Boy" to summarize.
2. Begin your summary by stating in one sentence what "The Peach Boy" is about. This sentence tells the **theme** (main idea) of the reading.

3. Then write sentences that explain the most important ideas of the beginning, the middle, and the end of the play. Write one or two sentences for each part of the play.
4. Make sure each sentence has a subject and a verb. Each verb must agree with its subject.

Activity Book
p. 103

Student
Handbook

Across Content Areas

Classify Fruits and Vegetables

Sometimes, everyday language is different from language used in science. Here are the scientific definitions of *fruits* and *vegetables*.

Fruits are plants and have seeds inside. A fruit may contain one or more seeds. For example, a peach contains one large seed. An orange has many seeds.

Vegetables are also plants, but they do not have seeds inside them. Many foods that people call vegetables are called fruits in scientific language. For example, some people call a cucumber a vegetable. However, there are seeds inside a cucumber, so in science it is a fruit.

1. Look at these fruits and vegetables:

apple	spinach	tomato
carrot	watermelon	broccoli

2. Copy the chart below.

Fruits	Vegetables

3. Write each word from the list above in the correct column of your chart. Use the scientific definitions.

Activity Book
p. 104

Talking in the New Land

an excerpt from
a personal narrative
by Edite Cunhã

Objectives

Reading Summarize to recall ideas as you read a personal narrative.

Listening and Speaking Summarize and paraphrase.

Grammar Use *could* and *couldn't*.

Writing Write to solve a problem.

Content Language Arts: Learn about graphic features.

Use Prior Knowledge

Share Feelings About Speaking in Different Situations

In the reading selection, the main character's father does not speak English. The character must speak English for him.

1. Suppose you had to do the things listed below because a family member did not speak English.
   a. Talk to a doctor about giving medicine to your brother.
   b. Tell a man that your father doesn't want to talk to him.
   c. Thank a woman for helping your mother.
   d. Talk to a man about a car that your mother is buying.

2. Make a chart like the one here.
3. Think about how you would feel about doing each thing listed.
4. Write each situation from the list in the chart. Write the sentence in the column that tells how you would feel.

Happy ☺	Scared 😨	Angry ☹

Build Background

Portugal

Portugal is a country in southwestern Europe. It is on the Atlantic Ocean, and some people there fish for a living. Many people work in factories, making things like clothing and paper products. Others grow crops such as grapes, olives, and tomatoes. People in Portugal speak Portuguese.

Content Connection

During the 1400s and 1500s, Portuguese explorers traveled to many parts of the world. These explorers were some of the first Europeans to visit Africa, Asia, and South America.

Build Vocabulary

Use Synonyms to Find Meaning

A **synonym** is a word that has a similar meaning to another word.

I could see a <u>slim</u>, <u>slender</u> lady dressed in brown.

Slim and *slender* are synonyms. *Slim* means "thin." *Slender* also means "thin."

1. Read these sentences. The two synonyms in each sentence are underlined.
   a. The lawn is covered with a <u>thick</u>, <u>dense</u> row of tall bushes.
   b. I hid in the <u>fragrant</u>, <u>sweet-smelling</u> shade of the bushes.

2. Decide which word to use in these sentences, *dense* or *sweet-smelling*. Use context clues in the sentences in #1.
   a. The crowd of students in the gym was _____ .
   b. The rose was _____ .

3. Check your answers in a dictionary or synonym finder.

The Heinle Newbury House Dictionary

Activity Book p. 105

Student CD-ROM

Text Structure

Personal Narrative

"Talking in the New Land" is a **personal narrative.** A personal narrative is a story about real events that happened to the author. Look at the features of a personal narrative in the chart.

As you read, think about the events and problems in the selection. Have you had similar experiences?

Personal Narrative	
Characters	real people in the author's life
Events and Problems	events and problems in the author's life
First-Person Point of View	the pronouns *I, me, we,* and *us*

Student
CD-ROM

Reading Strategy

Summarize to Recall Ideas

When you **summarize** a reading selection or part of a reading selection, you give only the most important events or ideas. Writing summaries can help you recall the ideas in a selection. Read this paragraph and its summary.

> Pablo's family members don't speak much English, but Pablo does. They often ask him to translate for them. He often goes to the mall with his mother to help her shop. He makes telephone calls for his father. Once his grandfather got into a car accident, and Pablo had to explain it to the police.

Summary: Pablo translates often for his parents.

As you read or listen to the audio recording of "Talking in the New Land," summarize the paragraphs.

Student
CD-ROM

Talking in the New Land

an excerpt from a personal narrative
by Edite Cunhã

Audio
CD 1, Tr. 15

Prologue

Edite Cunhã was born in Portugal. She moved to Massachusetts when she was seven years old. She began learning English in her new school. When this selection begins, Edite can speak English very well.

Summarize to Recall Ideas

Summarize paragraph 1 in writing.

1   When I was nine, **Pai** went to an **auction** and bought a big house on Tremont Street. We moved in the spring. The lawn at the side of the house dipped downward in a gentle slope and was covered with a thick, dense row of tall lilac bushes. I soon discovered that I could crawl between the bushes and hide from my brothers in the fragrant, sweet-smelling shade. It was **paradise.**

2   I was mostly wild and joyful on Tremont Street. But **now and then** there was a **shadow** that fell over my days.

3   "Oh, *Ediiiite! Ediiiite!*" Since Pai didn't speak English very well, he always called me, without the least bit of warning, to be his voice. He expected me to drop whatever I was doing to take care of something. Pai never called my brother, Carlos. No, Carlos never had to do anything but

play! Recently, I'd had to talk on the telephone to a woman who wanted some old dishes. The dishes, along with a lot of old furniture and junk, had been in the house when we moved in. They were in the **cellar,** stacked in cardboard boxes and covered with dust. The woman called many times, wanting to speak with Pai.

Pai   Portuguese for *Pa,* an informal word for *father*

auction   a sale in which items are sold to the person who offers the most money

paradise   a place where everything is beautiful and peaceful

now and then   sometimes, once in a while

shadow   the dark shape formed when something blocks the sun or other light

cellar   the space below ground level under a building

4   "My father can't speak English," I would say. "He says to tell you that the dishes are in our house and they belong to us." But she did not seem to understand. Every few days she would call.

Summarize to Recall Ideas

Summarize paragraph 5 orally.

5   "Oh, *Ediiiite!*" Pai's voice **echoed** through the empty rooms. I wanted to pretend I had not heard it when it had that tone. But I couldn't **escape.** I couldn't disappear into thin air as I wished to do at such times.

6   "*Ediiiite!*" Yes, that tone was certainly there. Pai was calling me to do something only I could do. What was it now? Did I have to talk to the **insurance company**? They were always using words I couldn't understand: **premium** and **dividend.** That made me nervous.

7   "Please wait. I call my daughter," Pai was saying. He was talking to someone, someone in the house. Who could it be?

8   "Oh, *Ediiiite!*"

9   "*Que éééé?*"

10   "*Come over here and talk to this lady.*" *

* Words in italic type are translations of words spoken in Portuguese.

---

echoed   repeated because sounds bounced off walls or hard surfaces

escape   get away

insurance company   a company that will pay for a loss or an accident in exchange for regular payments

premium   the regular payment for an insurance policy

dividend   money that an insurance company makes and gives to a person who has an insurance policy

Que éééé?   "What iiiis (is) it?" in Portuguese

Summarize to Recall Ideas

Summarize paragraph 11 in writing.

11   **Reluctantly,** I walked through the empty rooms toward the kitchen. Through the kitchen door I could see a slim lady dressed in brown standing at the top of the stairs. She had on high-heeled shoes and was holding a brown purse. As soon as Pai saw me he said to me, "*See what she wants.*"

12   The lady had dark hair that was very smooth. The ends of it flipped up in a way that I liked.

13   "Hello. I'm the lady who called about the dishes."

14   I stared at her without a word. My stomach **turned over.**

15   "*What did she say?*" Pai wanted to know.

16   "*She says she's the lady who wants the dishes.*"

17   Pai's face **hardened** some.

18   "*Tell her she's wasting her time. We're not giving them to her. Didn't you already tell her that on the telephone?*"

19   I nodded, standing **helplessly** between them.

---

reluctantly with hesitation
turned over felt funny

hardened looked hard
helplessly in an unprotected way

20   *"Well, tell her again."* Pai was getting angry. I wanted to **disappear.**

21   "My father says he can't give you the dishes," I said to the lady. She **clutched** her purse and leaned a little forward.

22   "Yes, you told me that on the phone. But I wanted to come **in person** and speak with your father because it's very important to me that—"

23   "My father can't speak English," I **interrupted** her. Why didn't she just go away?

24   "Yes, I understand that. But I wanted to see him." She looked at Pai, who was standing in the doorway to the kitchen holding his **hammer.** The kitchen was up one step from the porch. Pai was a small man, but he looked kind of scary staring down at us like that.

25   *"What is she saying?"*

26   *"She says she wanted to talk to you about getting her dishes."*

Summarize to Recall Ideas

Summarize paragraph 24 in writing.

---

disappear   go out of sight

clutched   held tightly with the hands

in person   physically present, face-to-face

interrupted   started talking in the middle of someone else talking

hammer   a tool with a handle and a metal head used for pounding

Summarize to Recall Ideas

Summarize paragraph 27 orally.

27 *"Tell her the dishes are ours. They were in the house. We bought the house and everything in it. Tell her the lawyer said so."*

28 The lady was looking at me **hopefully.**

29 "My father says the dishes are ours because we bought the house and the lawyer said everything in the house is ours now."

30 "Yes, I know that, but I was away when the house was being sold. I didn't know . . ."

31 There were **footsteps** on the stairs behind her. It was **Mãe** coming up from the second floor to find out what was going on. The lady moved away from the door to let Mãe in.

32 *"This is my wife,"* Pai said to the lady. The lady said hello to Mãe, who smiled and nodded her head. She looked at me, then at Pai in a **questioning** way.

---

hopefully   in a way that shows hope
footsteps   sounds of feet moving on a surface

Mãe   Portuguese for *Ma,* an informal word for *mother*
questioning   looking as if you have a question

33   "*It's the lady who wants our dishes,*" Pai explained.

34   Mãe looked at her again and smiled, but I could tell she was a little **worried.**

35   We stood there in kind of a funny circle; the lady looked at each of us **in turn** and took a deep breath.

36   "I didn't know," she continued, "that the dishes were in the house. I was away. They are very important to me. They **belonged** to my grandmother. I'd really like to get them back." She spoke this while looking back and forth between Mãe and Pai. Then she looked down at me, leaning forward again. "Will you tell your parents, please?"

37   I spoke in a hurry to get the words out.

38   "*She said she didn't know the dishes were in the house because she was away. They were her grandmother's dishes, and she wants them back.*" I felt deep **sorrow** at the thought of the lady returning home to find her grandmother's dishes sold.

39   "*We don't need all those dishes. Let's give them to her,*" Mãe said in her calm way. I felt **relieved.** We could give the lady the dishes and she would go away. But Pai got angry.

Summarize to Recall Ideas

Summarize paragraphs 38 and 39.

---

worried   feeling that something bad might happen
in turn   in order
belonged   were the property of; were owned by

sorrow   sadness
relieved   freed from bad feelings or worry

Summarize to Recall Ideas

Summarize paragraphs 41 and 42 in writing.

40   *"I already said what I had to say. The dishes are ours. That is all."*

41   *"Pai, she said she didn't know. They were her grandmother's dishes. She needs to have them."* I was speaking wildly and loud now. The lady looked at me questioningly, but I didn't want to speak to her again.

42   *"She's only saying that to trick us. If she wanted those dishes she should have taken them out before the house was sold. Tell her we are not **fools**. Tell her to forget it. She can go away. Tell her not to call or come here again."*

43   "What is he saying?" The lady was looking at me again.

44   I **ignored** her. I felt sorry for Pai for always feeling that people were trying to trick him. I wanted him to **trust** people. I wanted the lady to have her grandmother's dishes. I closed my eyes and **willed** myself away.

---

fools people who make silly mistakes
ignored paid no attention to; did not listen to
trust believe, feel that someone is honest

willed tried to control something by using the power of your mind

45 *"Tell her what I said!"* Pai yelled.

46 *"Pai, just give her the dishes! They were her grandmother's dishes!"* My voice **cracked** as I yelled back at him. Tears were rising in my eyes.

Summarize to Recall Ideas

Summarize paragraph 47.

47 I hated Pai for being so **stubborn.** I hated the lady for not taking the dishes before the house was sold. And I hated myself for having learned English.

---

cracked   sounded uneven

stubborn   not wanting to change one's mind

About the Author   Edite Cunhã (born 1953)

Edite Cunhã started writing as a young teenager. She writes poetry and fiction. She now works as a teacher, an artist, and a writer. Cunhã says, "Writing for me is essential. It is like breath. It does not matter if my work is published or not. I must do it to feel alive at home in the world."

➤What questions would you ask Edite Cunhã? How does her experience compare to that of Gonzalo in Unit 2, Chapter 4?

Beyond the Reading

Reading Comprehension

Question-Answer Relationships (QAR)

"Right There" Questions

1. **Recall Facts** On which street does Edite live?
2. **Recall Facts** What is Edite's brother's name?

"Think and Search" Questions

3. **Identify Theme** What does Edite often have to do for her father?
4. **Understand Plot** Why does the lady dressed in brown go to Edite's home?
5. **Explain** What does Edite's mother say they should do with the dishes?

"Author and You" Questions

6. **Recognize Character Traits** Do you think Edite's father is being fair to the lady? Why or why not?

7. **Make Inferences** Do you think Edite's mother feels bad for the lady? Explain.
8. **Make Inferences** Why do you think Edite's father wants to keep the dishes? Because he really likes them? Or is there another reason?

"On Your Own" Questions

9. **Predict** Do you think the lady will get her dishes back? Why do you think so?
10. **Connect Themes** Connect the theme of "Talking in the New Land" to "Gonzalo" (Unit 2, Chapter 4). How are the readings the same? How are they different?

Activity Book
p. 106

Student
CD-ROM

Build Reading Fluency

Rapid Word Recognition

Rapidly recognizing words helps increase your reading rate. It is an important characteristic of effective readers.

1. Review the words in the box.
2. Read the words aloud for one minute. Your teacher will time you.

3. Count how many words you read.
4. Record your results.

bought	thick	gentle	lawn	gentle	bought
house	lawn	thick	gentle	lawn	gentle
lawn	slope	house	bought	slope	house
gentle	gentle	lawn	house	bought	slope

Listen, Speak, Interact

Summarize and Paraphrase

Notice the difference between a **summary** and a **paraphrase:**

Summary	Paraphrase
You give only the most important information.	You say in your own words what another person says.

1. With a partner, reread paragraphs 13, 15, and 16 aloud.
2. Paraphrase each paragraph. Say what Edite said *in your own words.*
3. Choose a paragraph in the reading selection that you like. Summarize it in writing and give it to your partner.
4. Ask your partner: Did I include the most important information?

Elements of Literature

Analyze Characters

In "Talking in the New Land," Edite Cunhã describes the characters' **traits, motivations,** and **points of view.**

1. Read the meanings of the terms and then answer the questions to analyze the characters.

Term	Definition
trait	how characters look and behave
motivation	why characters do things
point of view	the characters' opinions and beliefs, likes, and dislikes

a. Reread paragraphs 18, 39, and 47. What do you learn about Pai's character traits?
b. In paragraph 36, what is the lady's point of view about the dishes?
c. Reread paragraph 39. What is Mãe's point of view about the lady and her dishes?
d. In paragraph 42, what is Pai's motivation for being so angry?
2. Share your answers with the class.

Activity Book
p. 107

Student
CD-ROM

Word Study

Learn the Prefix *Dis-*

A **prefix** is a group of letters added to the beginning of a word. A prefix changes the meaning of the word. The prefix *dis-* often changes a word to its opposite.

appear be seen

disappear stop being seen

1. Read the words in the first box. Notice the prefix and the root word.
2. Match each word with the correct definition.
3. Write a sentence for each word. Be sure to spell the prefix correctly.

Words	Definitions
disagree	a feeling of not being comfortable
disbelieve	have a different idea about
discomfort	not believe someone or something

The Heinle Newbury House Dictionary

Activity Book p. 108

Student CD-ROM

Grammar Focus

Use *Could* and *Couldn't*

Could is the past form of *can*. We use *could* to describe past abilities (things you were able to do). If you were able to do something yesterday, then you *could* do it. If you were not able to do something yesterday, then you *could not* do it.

Sometimes writers join *could* and *not* into a contraction. A contraction is a word formed by joining two words. The contraction for *could not* is *couldn't*. Notice that the apostrophe takes the place of the "o" in *not*.

I <u>could</u> answer the question because I read the book.

I <u>couldn't</u> answer the question because I did not read the book.

1. Reread paragraph 1 of the selection. Find a sentence that uses *could* to show something a character was able to do.
2. Reread paragraph 5. Write a sentence that uses *couldn't* to show something a character was not able to do.
3. Write two sentences of your own—one with *could*, one with *couldn't*.

Activity Book pp. 109–110

Student Handbook

Student CD-ROM

From Reading to Writing

Write to Solve a Problem

Write an ending to solve Edite's problem. Write one paragraph.

1. Choose one of these endings.
   a. Edite tells the lady that she cannot have her dishes.
   b. Edite tells the lady that she can have her dishes.
2. Give two reasons why Edite says this.

3. As you write, picture that you are Edite. Use first-person pronouns (*I, me, we,* and *us*).
4. Make sure you use correct capitalization and punctuation to strengthen your ending.

Activity Book   Student
p. 111   Handbook

Across Content Areas

Learn About Graphic Features

Reread paragraph 10 on page 195, and the footnote at the bottom of the page. The footnote explains the use of italic type— type that is slanted *like this.* Italic type is one **graphic feature.** There are others.

Graphic Feature	Example	Why Used
font	This is one font. *This is another font.*	to give readers different feelings
boldface	**This sentence is in boldface.**	to call attention to important words
bullets	• There is a bullet before this sentence.	to make lists easier to read

1. Read the following sentences. Decide which graphic feature is shown.
   a. Scientists look at **cells** to learn about our bodies.
   b. Make these changes to the report:
      • Indent paragraphs.
      • Fix spelling mistakes.
   c. *You are invited to my party!*
2. Work with a partner. Suppose you have a business where you make cards. Create an order form with graphic features.
3. Organize your form to include features and examples. Use a computer to help you.
4. Revise the form for clarity and neatness.

Activity Book
p. 112

Plain Talk About Handling Stress

an informational text
by Louis E. Kopolow, M.D.

Objectives

Reading Identify main idea and details as you read an informational text.

Listening and Speaking Talk about dealing with stress.

Grammar Recognize complex sentences with *if*.

Writing Write an informational text.

Content Language Arts: Learn different meanings of *conflict*.

Use Prior Knowledge

Identify Ideas About Stress

Most people feel stress sometime in their lives. Stress is a feeling of difficulty. For example, you might feel stress when you have too much homework. What do you know about stress?

1. Write these statements on a piece of paper. Write *T* if you think the statement is true. Write *F* if you think the statement is false. There are no right or wrong answers.
   _____ **a.** Stress is always bad.
   _____ **b.** Some stress can be good.
   _____ **c.** Stress can make you ill.
   _____ **d.** Stress can help you get work done.

2. Compare your answers with a partner's.
3. Talk about your answers with the class.

Build Background

Stress and the Body

Too much stress can affect how people feel and think. For example, it can make people feel angry or sad. Too much stress can also affect the body. When people feel stress, their hearts often beat faster. Their muscles can become tense (tight). Many people get headaches from stress. They may not be able to concentrate (focus). Too much stress can cause people to get sick more often.

Content Connection

People can talk to friends, their family, or psychologists to deal with stress. Psychologists are trained to help people with problems.

Build Vocabulary

Learn Words Related to Stress in Context

The selection includes words related to stress. Here are some of these words:

Words Related to Stress	Meaning
challenge	a difficult job
mental	related to the mind
tension	a state of stress or nervousness
distress	emotional pain or suffering
physical	related to the body

Work with a partner. Copy the chart in your Personal Dictionary. Then complete the following sentences with words from the chart. Take turns reading the sentences aloud.

1. Running and playing tennis are ____ activities.
2. Learning to play the guitar is a ____ . It can be difficult.
3. Juan is very smart. He has strong ____ abilities.
4. Kim felt ____ because her dog died.
5. Today is the big test. The students feel a lot of ____ .

Personal Dictionary

Activity Book
p. 113

Student CD-ROM

Text Structure

Informational Text

An **informational text** gives facts and examples about a topic. "Plain Talk about Handling Stress" gives information about stress. Look at the features of an informational text in the chart.

As you read, notice how facts and examples help you understand the selection.

Informational Text	
Topic	what the text is about
Headings	titles used to organize information
Facts and Examples	details about the topic

Student
CD-ROM

Reading Strategy

Identify Main Idea and Details

The **main idea** is the most important idea in a reading. The **details** include all the information that helps you understand the main idea. Read this paragraph:

Exciting Mexico!

Mexico is an exciting place to live or visit. You can see different plants and animals. You can also see historic buildings.

Main Idea	Details
Mexico is an exciting place to live or visit.	You can see different plants and animals. You can also see historic buildings.

The details explain why Mexico is exciting.

Follow these tips to find the main idea and details in the selection:

1. Read each heading. Then read the first and last sentences of each paragraph. The main idea is usually found in one of these places.
2. The middle sentences are usually details. Ask yourself, "How do the details help me understand the main idea?"

Student
CD-ROM

Plain Talk About

Handling STRESS

an informational text
by Louis E. Kopolow, M.D.

1   You need stress in your life! Does that surprise you? Perhaps so, but it is quite true. Without stress, life would be **dull** and unexciting. Stress adds **flavor,** challenge, and **opportunity** to life. Too much stress, however, can seriously affect your physical and mental **well-being.** A major challenge in this stress-filled world of today is to learn how to **cope** with stress so that it does not become too much.

2   What kinds of things can cause too much stress in our lives? We often think of major **crises** such as natural disasters, war, and death as main sources of stress. These are, of course, stressful events. However, according to psychologist Wayne Weiten, on a day-to-day basis, it is the small things that cause stress: waiting in line, having car trouble, getting stuck in a **traffic jam,** having too many things to do in a **limited** time.

> ### Identify Main Idea and Details
>
> What is the main idea of paragraph 2?

Audio
CD 1, Tr. 16

---

dull   boring

flavor   an exciting quality

opportunity   a chance to advance or meet a goal

well-being   the condition of your body and mind

cope   face difficulties and try to overcome them

crises   emergencies

traffic jam   cars and trucks blocking the road and causing delays

limited   having only a certain amount of something

3 Reacting to Stress

While you can't live completely free of stress and distress, you can **prevent** some distress as well as **minimize** its **impact.** By recognizing the early signs of distress and then doing something about them, you can **improve** the quality of your life and perhaps even live longer.

Helping Yourself 4

When stress does occur, it is important to recognize and deal with it. Here are some suggestions for ways to handle stress. As you begin to understand more about how stress affects you as an individual, you will come up with your own ideas of helping to **ease** the tensions.

> **Identify Main Idea and Details**
>
> What is the main idea of paragraph 3?

---

prevent   stop from happening
minimize   lessen
impact   effect

improve   make better
ease   make less difficult

Try physical activity.

When you are nervous, angry, or upset, **release** the **pressure** through exercise or physical activity. Running, walking, playing tennis, or working in your garden are just some of the activities you might try. Physical exercise will relieve that "up tight" feeling, **relax** you, and turn the **frowns** into smiles. Remember, your body and your mind work together.

> **Identify Main Idea and Details**
>
> Here is the main idea of paragraph 5: Physical activity can help lower stress. What details support this main idea?

Share your stress.

It helps to talk to someone about your concerns and worries. Perhaps a friend, family member, teacher, or **counselor** can help you see your problem in a different light. If you feel your problem is serious, you might seek **professional** help from a psychologist, **psychiatrist, social worker,** or mental health counselor. Knowing when to ask for help may **avoid** more serious problems later.

---

release   let something go

pressure   tension; a feeling of being pushed to
    do things

relax   stop being nervous, tense, or angry

frowns   when you pull the eyebrows down and make
    your mouth tight; usually shows anger or sadness

counselor   someone who gives advice

professional   related to a job

psychiatrist   a doctor who treats mental problems

social worker   a person who works with others to help
    make their lives better

avoid   stay away from

Know your limits.

If a problem is beyond your control and cannot be changed at the moment, don't fight the situation. Learn to accept what it is—for now—until such time when you can change it.

> **Identify Main Idea and Details**
>
> How does the section heading of this paragraph relate to the main idea?

8

Take care of yourself.

You are special. Get enough rest and eat well. If you are **irritable** and **tense** from **lack** of sleep or if you are not eating correctly, you will have less ability to deal with stressful situations. If stress **repeatedly** keeps you from sleeping, you should ask your doctor for help.

---

irritable easily bothered by things
tense nervous, jumpy

lack not enough of something
repeatedly over and over again

Make time for fun.

9   **Schedule** time for both work and **recreation.** Play can be just as important to your well-being as work; you need a **break** from your daily **routine** to just relax and have fun.

Be a participant.

10   One way to keep from getting bored, sad, and lonely is to go where it's all happening. Sitting alone can make you feel **frustrated.** Instead of feeling sorry for yourself, get involved and become a participant. Offer your services in neighborhood or **volunteer** organizations. Help yourself by helping other people. Get involved in the world and the people around you, and you'll find they will be **attracted** to you. You will be on your way to making new friends and enjoying new activities.

> ### Identify Main Idea and Details
>
> What is the main idea of paragraph 10? How does the section heading help you identify the main idea?

---

schedule   plan activities by date and time
recreation   fun things to do
break   a change from something usual
routine   a series of things someone does regularly

participant   a person who takes part in something
frustrated   feeling bothered by something
volunteer   when people help other people for no pay
attracted   interested in

11

Check off your tasks.

Trying to take care of everything at once can seem **overwhelming,** and, as a result, you may not **accomplish** anything. Instead, make a list of what tasks you have to do, then do one at a time, **checking them off** as they're completed. Give **priority** to the most important ones and do those first.

Identify Main Idea and Details

What is the main idea of paragraph 11?

12

Must you always be right?

Do other people upset you—particularly when they don't do things your way? Try **cooperation** instead of **confrontation;** it's better than fighting and always being "right." A little **give and take** on both sides will **reduce** the **strain** and make you both feel more comfortable.

Things To Do Today
1. *Finish homework.* ✓
2. *Go to baseball practice.* ✓
3. *Clean room.*
4. *Do my laundry.*
5. *Help with dinner.*

---

overwhelming   too much for you to deal with

accomplish   finish, complete

checking them off   putting a check next to the tasks with a pen or pencil

priority   the tasks that are the most important and require attention

cooperation   the act of working with someone toward the same goal

confrontation   the act of facing something difficult or dangerous

give and take   when people on both sides of a conflict listen to each other and accept some of each other's ideas

reduce   lessen

strain   difficulty

13   **It's OK to cry.**

A good cry can be a healthy way to bring **relief** to your **anxiety,** and it might even prevent a headache or other physical **consequence.** Take some deep breaths; they also release tension.

14   **Create a quiet scene.**

You can't always run away, but you can "dream the **impossible** dream." A quiet country scene painted mentally, or on a **canvas,** can take you out of the **turmoil** of a stressful situation. Change the scene by reading a good book or playing beautiful music to create a sense of peace and **tranquility.**

> **Identify Main Idea and Details**
>
> What is the main idea of paragraph 14? Which details support the main idea?

---

relief   the taking away or lessening of pain

anxiety   worry, nervous fear about what will happen in the future

consequence   result

impossible   not able to be done

canvas   cloth stretched over a wooden frame for painting pictures

turmoil   disorder, chaos, often with mental suffering

tranquility   peace, calmness

15 **The Art of Relaxation**

The best strategy for avoiding stress is to learn how to relax. Unfortunately, many people try to relax at the same **pace** that they lead the rest of their lives. For a while, **tune out** your worries about time, **productivity,** and "doing right." You will find **satisfaction** in just *being*, without **striving.** Find activities that give you pleasure and that are good for your mental and physical well-being. Forget about always winning. Focus on relaxation, enjoyment, and health. Whatever method works for you, be good to yourself. If you don't let stress get **out of hand,** you can actually make it work for you instead of against you.

> **Identify Main Idea and Details**
>
> What is the main idea of paragraph 15? Which details support the main idea?

---

pace speed of an activity

tune out ignore, not pay attention to

productivity how much a person can do in a certain time

satisfaction pleasure because of having enough

striving working hard for something

out of hand out of control

About the Author — **Louis E. Kopolow, M.D.**

Louis E. Kopolow is a psychiatrist. He is also a college teacher. He teaches others who want to be psychiatrists. Kopolow also runs counseling centers for men in Washington, D.C. These centers help men deal with questions, stress, and problems in their lives.

➤ Why do you think Louis E. Kopolow wrote "Plain Talk About Handling Stress"? To teach you how to handle stress? To teach you how to avoid stress? Explain.

Beyond the Reading

Reading Comprehension

Question-Answer Relationships (QAR)

"Right There" Questions

1. **Recall Facts** According to the author, do we need some stress in our lives?
2. **Recall Facts** What does the author say is the best strategy for avoiding stress?

"Think and Search" Questions

3. **Identify** Name two ways that stress can be good for you.
4. **Identify** Name three things that can cause stress on a day-to-day basis.
5. **Identify Steps in a Process** The author tells how to deal with having too many tasks. What steps does the author suggest?

"Author and You" Questions

6. **Identify the Main Idea** Which of these sentences is the main idea of the selection?

   a. Crying can help you release tension.
   b. Dealing with stress can help you have a better life.
   c. All stress is bad.

7. **Paraphrase** Explain one of the author's suggestions for handling stress. Use your own words.

"On Your Own" Questions

8. **Connect to Your Experiences** How do you handle stress in your life?
9. **Find Similarities and Differences Across Texts** Look up "Turkish Delight" in the table of contents of this book. Reread that selection. How is its text structure the same as or different from this chapter?

Activity Book
p. 114

Student
CD-ROM

Build Reading Fluency

Adjust Your Reading Rate to Scan

When you scan, you adjust your reading rate to read fast. Scanning means glancing at the text for key words to help you answer questions. Work with a partner. Read aloud key words as you look for information. Write your answers on a piece of paper.

1. What is one way to handle stress?
2. Who are three people you can share your stress with?
3. What is one way you can take care of yourself?
4. What is the title of the paragraph on "fun"?
5. What is the title of the paragraph about priorities?

Listen, Speak, Interact

Talk About Dealing with Stress

The selection suggests ways to deal with stress. How can you use these suggestions in a real-life situation?

1. Work with a small group.
2. Choose a stressful situation that you have experienced.
3. List ways that you could deal with the stressful situation. Use paragraphs 5–14 of the selection to help you.

Examples of Stressful Situations
You have too many things that you have to do.
You have just had an argument with your best friend.
You are waiting in a very long line at the store.

4. Think of ways you could act out dramatically the stressful situation and ways to deal with it.
5. Share your presentation with the class. Make sure to use words from the selection in your presentation.

Elements of Literature

Use Headings to Find Information

Informational texts often have **headings**—titles that come before a section or paragraph. Headings tell readers where to find information in a text.

"Plain Talk About Handling Stress" has two kinds of headings. One kind is general and appears before a group of paragraphs. The other kind is more specific and appears before one paragraph. Both kinds are in boldface.

Helping Yourself (page 211)

Try physical activity. (page 212)

On a piece of paper, match the information with the head that you would use to find it.

Information You Want to Find

1. How can I help others?
2. How can I lower my stress?
3. How can I relax?
4. Who can I talk to about stress?

Heads

a. **Helping Yourself**
b. **The Art of Relaxation**
c. **Be a participant.**
d. **Share your stress.**

Activity Book
p. 115

Student
CD-ROM

Word Study

Locate Meanings, Pronunciations, and Origins of Words

A large dictionary gives information about words. It gives the **meaning,** the **pronunciation,** and the **origin**—the languages that a word comes from. Read these dictionary entries.

psy•chi•a•try /səˈkaɪətri/ the branch of medicine that cures mental diseases [Greek *psukhē,* soul]

phys•i•cal /ˈfɪzɪkəl/ of or related to the body [Greek *phusikē,* of nature]

1. Copy and complete the chart in your Personal Dictionary.

Word	The First Sound	Meaning	Derivation
psychiatry	s		Greek
physical		of or related to the body	

2. Write a sentence for each word. Check to make sure you spell every syllable in the word correctly.

Personal Dictionary

Activity Book
p. 116

Student CD-ROM

Grammar Focus

Recognize Complex Sentences with *If*

A clause is a group of words with a subject and a verb. **Complex sentences** have two types of **clauses.**

1. An independent clause can stand on its own as a sentence.

2. A dependent clause cannot stand on its own as a sentence. It must be used with an independent clause.

Dependent Clause	Independent Clause
If you are irritable,	you will have less ability to deal with stressful situations.

This sentence is a **conditional sentence.** Conditional sentences have a dependent clause that begins with *if* and ends with a comma.

1. Look at paragraphs 6, 8, and 15 of the selection. Find and copy three conditional sentences.

2. Underline the dependent clauses. Circle the independent clauses.

3. Write your own conditional sentence with *if.* Use correct punctuation.

Activity Book
pp. 117–118

Student Handbook

Student CD-ROM

From Reading to Writing

Write an Informational Text

Write three paragraphs to solve how to deal with a stressful situation.

1. Paragraph 1: Include a **thesis statement.** (Tell readers what the text is about.)
2. Paragraph 2: Include details that support your thesis statement.
3. Paragraph 3: Write a conclusion. Tell how your ideas can help readers.
4. Use the pronoun *you* to speak directly to your readers.

5. Use a dictionary and grammar guide to help with your writing.
6. Use resources, like the Internet or library books on your topic, to help you gather information. Be sure to cite your resources.

Activity Book
p. 119

Student
Handbook

Across Content Areas

Learn Different Meanings of *Conflict*

Stressful situations often involve a conflict. The word *conflict* can mean different things. Look at these definitions:

> **con•flict** /ˈkɑnˌflɪkt/ *n.* [Latin: *conflictus* collision] **1** a difference, disagreement *There is a conflict between what you are saying and what the contract says.* **2** an argument *The two men had a conflict over who would run the company.* **3** a war *World War I was an armed conflict among many nations of the world.*

1. Use the dictionary entry to pronounce *conflict.*
2. What is the origin of the word *conflict?*

3. Copy the following sentences. Match each one with the correct definition of *conflict*. Write *Definition 1, Definition 2,* or *Definition 3.*
   a. Giselle and Ali had a conflict over who would wash the car.
   b. Many people were killed in the conflict between the two armies.
   c. There was a conflict between the report in the newspaper and the report on the radio.

Activity Book
p. 120

Listening and Speaking Workshop

Literary Response: Report Your Favorite Selection

Topic

Choose the reading selection that you enjoyed the most in this unit. Prepare a report to share with the class that explains why you liked the selection.

Step 1: Choose your favorite selection.

1. List information about the selection on a note card like the one here. Include the title, the author, the genre, and the topic. The genre tells what type of literature the selection is. The topic tells what the selection is about.
2. If you do not remember the genre of the selection, look at the Table of Contents for Unit 3 on page 150. The genre is listed below the title.

> *My Favorite Selection*
>
> Title: *The Peach Boy* _____
>
> Author: _____
>
> Genre: _____
>
> Topic: _____
>
> _____

Step 2: Brainstorm a list.

List reasons why you liked the selection. Use the following questions to help you.

1. Did the selection include an exciting or interesting plot?
2. As you read, did you see pictures in your mind?
3. Did the reading make you think about your own experiences?
4. Did you learn something that you did not know before?

Step 3: Prepare your report.

Choose three of the reasons from Step 2 to present. Make a note card about each one. Write an example to support your reason.

> *Reason #1*
>
> *The plot was funny.*
>
> *Ex: Momotaro jumped out of a peach!*

Step 4: Practice your report.

Practice your report with a friend or family member.

1. Use your note cards to help you remember what to say.
2. Begin by telling the title, author, genre, and topic of the selection.
3. Ask your friend or family member to evaluate your report by using the Active Listening Checklist.

Student
Handbook

Active Listening Checklist

1. The report made me want to read _____ because _____.

2. The report did not make me want to read _____ because _____.

3. I want to know more about _____.

4. I understood the main ideas of your report. Yes / No

Speaking Checklist

1. Did I speak too fast, too slow, or just right?

2. Did I speak loud enough for the class to hear me?

3. Did I look at the class as I spoke?

4. Did I use examples from the selection to support my reasons?

Step 5: Present your report to the class.

1. Use the responses to the Active Listening Checklist to revise your report.

2. Present your report to the class.

3. When you are finished, use the Speaking Checklist to evaluate your report.

Viewing Workshop

View, Compare, and Contrast

Learn About the Civil Rights Movement

In Unit 3, you read the lyrics to the song "We Shall Overcome." You learned that many people sang this song at civil rights meetings.

1. Borrow two videos of documentaries about the Civil Rights movement from the library. A documentary is a film or television program based on facts or events in history.

2. Compare and contrast the documentaries. Look for ways the makers of the documentaries represent the Civil Rights movement. How are the points of view and ideas alike? How are they different? Use a Venn Diagram to organize your ideas.

3. Is "We Shall Overcome" played or sung during either documentary? How did learning more about the Civil Rights movement help you understand why people often sang this song? Do you think the purpose of this video was to inform, entertain, or persuade?

4. How do the makers of these documentaries represent the meaning of the Civil Rights movement?

Further Viewing

Watch the *Visions* CNN Video for Unit 3. Do the Video Worksheet.

CNN Video

Writer's Workshop

Response to Literature: Write a Review of Literature

Writing Prompt

The editor of the school newspaper has asked students to send in reviews of literature. A review tells about the strengths (good things) and weaknesses (bad things) of a reading. Choose a selection from this unit and write a review to send to the newspaper.

Step 1: Evaluate a selection.

Decide which selection from this unit you will review.

1. Reread the selection in your book. Write a short summary of the selection on a piece of paper.
2. Use a chart like the one here to list the strengths and weaknesses of the selection. Think about why the selection is (or is not) a good piece of literature. Then think about how the selection might be improved.

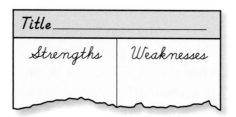

Step 2: Write a draft.

Your review should be three paragraphs long. Include an introduction, a body, and a conclusion. Write your review on a computer, if possible. Use reference materials to help you correctly write your review.

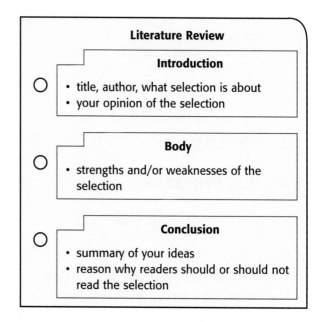

Literature Review

Introduction
- title, author, what selection is about
- your opinion of the selection

Body
- strengths and/or weaknesses of the selection

Conclusion
- summary of your ideas
- reason why readers should or should not read the selection

Step 3: Revise your work.

1. Reread your draft. Revise your work using your responses to these questions:
   a. Did I state my opinion clearly?
   b. Did I support my opinion by listing the strengths and weaknesses of the selection?
   c. Did I clearly summarize why people should or should not read the selection?
   d. Did I indent my paragraphs?

2. Make sure your ideas are clear.

   a. Elaborate (explain) any difficult words or phrases.

   b. Delete (remove) any text that is repeated.

   c. Rearrange sentences so that your ideas follow a logical order.

   d. Combine sentences with words like *and, but, because, if,* or *when.*

3. With a partner, read each other's work. Then discuss how your reviews can be improved. Use what you learned to make revisions.

Step 4: Edit and proofread.

1. Read your review carefully to make sure that you have used correct spelling, punctuation, and grammar. Choose appropriate reference materials to help you.

   a. Use a dictionary to check the spelling of words.

   b. If you wrote your review on a computer, run the checks for spelling, punctuation, and grammar.

2. Use your Student Handbook as a resource to check your writing.

Step 5: Publish.

Prepare your review to send to the editor of the school newspaper.

1. If you wrote your review on a computer, choose a font that is easy to read. A font is a style of type. If you wrote the review by hand, make sure your handwriting is neat and clear.

2. Put your review in an envelope. Address the review to: Editor of the School Newspaper. Add the name and address of your school.

3. Write your name and address in the upper left corner of the envelope.

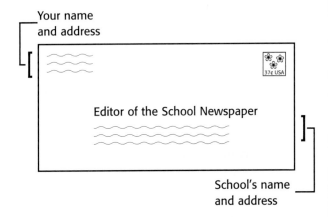

Your name and address

Editor of the School Newspaper

37¢ USA

School's name and address

4. Make a bulletin board to publish the reviews written by the class. Put reviews of the same reading together. Analyze the reviews by comparing and contrasting them. Evaluate them for their strengths and weaknesses.

5. Set goals as a writer based on your writing and the writing of your classmates.

The Heinle Newbury House Dictionary

Student Handbook

Projects

Project 1: Create a Storyboard

In Unit 3, you learned about different conflicts people can have. Create a storyboard. Show a conflict you know about and a solution for the conflict.

1. Choose a conflict from the unit or make one up.
2. On a piece of paper, draw four boxes like the ones shown. Number them in order.
3. In the first box, draw a conflict between two people. You may include dialogue, if you wish.
4. In the remaining boxes, show how the people solve their problems.

Project 2: Present a Radio Program

In this unit, you learned about stress. A person in a stressful situation may ask for help about how to handle it. There are radio programs that talk about how to handle stress. People telephone the radio station to ask for help with stress.

1. Work with a partner. List three stressful situations.
2. Brainstorm ways to handle the stressful situation. Refer to Chapter 5 if you need to.
3. Complete a chart like the one shown.
4. Take turns role-playing a situation in which one person calls a radio station to ask for help with a stressful situation. Another person should role-play the part of the radio station worker who helps the caller handle the stress.
5. Share your role play with others in the class.

Stressful Situation	Ways to Handle Stress

Further Reading

Here is a list of books about the themes of conflict and cooperation. Read one or more of them. Write your thoughts and feelings about what you read in your Reading Log. Take notes about your answers to these questions:

1. What kinds of conflicts are presented in the books you read?
2. How do the characters deal with the conflicts they are faced with?
3. What did you learn about handling conflicts from what you read?

Zlata's Diary: A Child's Life in Sarajevo
by Zlata Filipović, Christina Pribichevich-Zoric (translator), and Janine Di Giovanni (introduction), Penguin USA, 1995. Zlata's world changes from that of a normal teenager to one where she is dealing with the reality of war. She writes about her feelings and the hardships that her family experiences because of the war in Sarajevo.

Conflict Resolution: Communication, Cooperation, Compromise
by Robert Wandberg, Capstone Press, 2000. This book talks about the types, causes, and results of conflicts in the life of teenagers. It also discusses how to resolve the various types of conflicts.

Hoops
by Walter Dean Myers, Laurel Leaf, 1983. At 17, Lonnie Jackson is on his way to becoming a professional basketball player. His coach tries to teach Lonnie how to deal with the pressures of being a great player.

Soldier's Heart: Being the Story of the Enlistment and Due Service of the Boy Charley Goddard in the First Minnesota Volunteers
by Gary Paulsen, Delacorte Press, 1998. Charley Goddard lies about his age to enlist as a soldier during the Civil War. Fighting in the war turns out not to be the adventure he thought it would be.

Over the Wall
by John H. Ritter, Penguin Putnam Books for Young Readers, 2000. Tyler does not know how to control his temper. During the summer, he spends time with his cousins in New York where he learns how to use his love of baseball to better deal with his anger.

Breaking the Chains of the Ancient Warriors: Tests of Wisdom for Young Martial Artists
by Terrence Webster-Doyle, Atrium Society Education for Peace Publications, 1996. This is a collection of stories about the tests of wisdom. The tests of wisdom include humility, peaceful conflict resolution, love, strength, and honor.

Companion
Web site

Reading Log

Heinle
Reading Library
Dr. Jekyll
and Mr. Hyde

UNIT 4

Heroes

The Life Line, Winslow Homer, oil on canvas. 1884.

View the Picture

1. Do you think the person in this picture is a hero? Use details from the picture to explain.
2. Who in your life do you think is a hero? Why?

In this unit, you will read a legend, two biographies, a speech, and two poems about heroes. You will learn about the different ways that people can be heroes. You will also learn the elements of these writing forms and how to write them yourself.

CHAPTER 1

The Ballad of Mulan

a legend

Into the Reading

Objectives

Reading Make predictions as you read a legend.

Listening and Speaking Develop a character.

Grammar Use prepositional phrases.

Writing Write a legend.

Content Social Studies: Use map features to read a map.

Use Prior Knowledge

Discuss Heroes

A hero is a person who is very brave or who does something great. For example, a firefighter who saves people from a burning building is a hero.

1. Think of two people who you think are heroes.
2. With a group, discuss what you think makes someone a hero. Think about different ways that a person can be a hero.
3. On a piece of paper, write your ideas in a web like this one.
4. Draw a picture of a hero performing an act. Tell the class why the person is a hero.

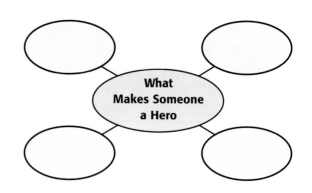

What Makes Someone a Hero

Build Background

Early China

"The Ballad of Mulan" takes place in China at some time between the years 386 and 534. During this time, China's rulers fought wars against armies from nearby lands. There were also many wars among the Chinese people.

"The Ballad of Mulan" describes the brave actions of a Chinese girl named Mulan. A ballad tells a story that is often sung. People in China have told stories about Mulan for more than a thousand years. People are not sure whether she was a real person in history, but many people think that some events in "The Ballad of Mulan" are based on real events.

SOCIAL STUDIES

Content Connection

For thousands of years, China was ruled by different groups of families known as dynasties. The leaders of these Chinese dynasties were called emperors.

Build Vocabulary

Evaluate Your Understanding of Words

You can use a dictionary to find the meanings and pronunciations of new words. Look at this dictionary entry.

bal•lad /ˈbæləd/ *n. frml.* a poem or song that tells a story with simple words

1. Write these words in your Personal Dictionary.

ballad	sorrowful	troops
emperor	invaders	endure

2. Write the meanings of the words you know.
3. After you read "The Ballad of Mulan," write the meanings of the words you learned.
4. Use a dictionary to look up the meanings and pronunciations of the words you did not understand. Write down the definitions.

Personal Dictionary

The Heinle Newbury House Dictionary

Activity Book p. 121

Student CD-ROM

Text Structure

Legend

"The Ballad of Mulan" is a **legend.** A legend is a made-up story that has been passed down from generation to generation. A generation is a group of people that are about the same age.

As you read or listen to "The Ballad of Mulan," note how Mulan's actions show that caring for your parents is an important value.

Student
CD-ROM

Legend	
Main Character	The legend is usually about a hero, who was often a real person in history.
Events	The legend's events are usually based on real events in history, but parts of the story are often made up.
Exaggeration	The qualities and actions of the hero are often exaggerated (shown as greater than they really were). This is done to show, for example, how strong, honest, or good the hero was.
Values	Legends teach values (ideas about what is important and right).

Reading Strategy

Make Predictions

When you **make predictions,** you use information or pictures in a text to guess what might happen next. As you continue to read, you may need to change your predictions.

1. Read the title of the selection on page 233. Then look at the pictures on pages 234–237. What predictions can you make about what the selection is about? Who is the most important character? What clues helped you make your predictions? Write your answers on a piece of paper.

2. As you read each paragraph of "The Ballad of Mulan," ask yourself, "What do I think will happen next?" After you read new clues, check if your prediction is correct.

3. As you continue to read, write down predictions about how the story will end. When you finish reading, compare your predictions with what really happened.

Reading Log

Student
CD-ROM

THE BALLAD OF

Mulan

a legend

Audio
CD 2, Tr. 1

1 Long ago, in a village in northern China, there lived a girl named Mulan. One day, she sat at her **loom** weaving cloth. *Click-clack! Click-clack!* went the loom.

2 Suddenly, the sound of weaving changed to **sorrowful** sighs. "What troubles you?" her mother asked.

3 "Nothing, Mother," Mulan softly replied.

4 Her mother asked her again and again, until Mulan finally said, "There is news of war."

5 "**Invaders** are attacking. The Emperor is calling for **troops.** Last night, I saw the **draft** poster and twelve **scrolls** of names in the market. Father's name is on every one."

Make Predictions

How do you think Mulan will try to help her father?

6 "But Father is old and **frail**," Mulan sighed. "How can he fight? He has no grown son and I have no elder brother."

7 "I will go to the markets. I shall buy a saddle and a horse. I must fight in Father's place."

8 From the eastern market Mulan bought a horse, and from the western market, a saddle. From the southern market she bought a **bridle,** and from the northern market, a whip.

---

loom   a machine for weaving thread into cloth
sorrowful   very sad
invaders   people who enter a place by force
troops   groups of soldiers
draft   a call to fight in the military

scrolls   rolls of paper or other material on which to write
frail   weak
bridle   straps on a horse's head to control it

9   At dawn Mulan dressed in her **armor** and bid a sad **farewell** to her father, mother, sister, and brother. Then she **mounted** her horse and rode off with the soldiers.

10   By nightfall she was camped by the bank of the Yellow River. She thought she heard her mother calling her name.

11   But it was only the sound of the river crying.

12   At sunrise Mulan took leave of the Yellow River. At **dusk** she reached the **peak** of Black Mountain.

13   In the darkness she longed to hear her father's voice but heard only the **neighing** of enemy horses far away.

14   Mulan rode ten thousand miles to fight a hundred battles. She crossed peaks and **passes** like a bird in flight.

15   Nights at the camp were **harsh** and cold, but Mulan endured every hardship. Knowing her father was safe warmed her heart.

16   The war dragged on. **Fierce** battles **ravaged** the land. One after another, noble generals lost their lives.

Make Predictions

Do you think Mulan will be a good soldier? Which text clues helped you make your prediction?

---

armor   covering worn by soldiers to protect the body

farewell   good-bye

mounted   climbed on

dusk   the time after the sun sets and before the dark of night

peak   the pointed top of a mountain

neighing   loud, high sounds made by horses

passes   openings that you can travel through

harsh   unpleasant, rough

fierce   violent, wild

ravaged   destroyed, ruined

17   Mulan's skill and courage won her respect and **rank.**
After ten years, she returned as a great general, **triumphant**
and **victorious!**

18   The Emperor **summoned** Mulan to the High Palace.
He praised her for her bravery and leadership in battle.

19   The Court would **bestow** many great **titles** upon her.
Mulan would be **showered** with gifts of gold.

20   "Worthy General, you may have your heart's desire,"
the Emperor said.

21   "I have no need for honors or gold," Mulan replied.

22   "All I ask for is a swift camel to take me back home."
The Emperor sent a troop to **escort** Mulan on her trip.

23   In town, the news of Mulan's return created great
excitement. Holding each other, her proud parents walked
to the village gate to welcome her.

Make Predictions

What do you think Mulan will ask the Emperor to give her? Why do you think this?

---

rank   a high position in the army
triumphant   having won victory or success
victorious   triumphant
summoned   called or sent for

bestow   give formally
titles   high social positions
showered   gave a lot of something
escort   lead, guide

24   Waiting at home, Mulan's sister **beautified** herself. Her brother sharpened his knife to prepare a pig and sheep for the feast in Mulan's honor.

25   Home at last! Mulan threw open her bedroom door and smiled. She removed her armor and changed into one of her favorite dresses.

26   What a surprise it was when Mulan appeared at the door! Her **comrades** were **astonished** and amazed. "How is this possible?" they asked.

27   "How could we have fought side by side with you for ten years and not known you were a woman!"

28   Mulan replied, "They say the male rabbit likes to hop and leap, while the female rabbit prefers to sit still. But in times of danger, when the two rabbits **scurry** by, who can tell male from female?"

29   Mulan's **glory** spread through the land. And to this day, we sing of this brave woman who loved her family and served her country, asking for nothing in return.

Make Predictions

What do you think amazes the soldiers?

---

beautified   made pretty
comrades   close friends or people who work with you
astonished   very surprised

scurry   run quickly, often in fear
glory   great honor or fame

Beyond the Reading

Reading Comprehension

Question-Answer Relationships (QAR)

"Right There" Questions

1. **Recall Facts** Who is Mulan?
2. **Recall Facts** Why does Mulan take her father's place in the army?
3. **Recall Facts** Where does Mulan buy what she needs to fight in her father's place?
4. **Recall Facts** How long is Mulan away from her home?

"Think and Search" Questions

5. **Evaluate Evidence** How does Mulan feel about leaving her home?
6. **Summarize** How does Mulan's family feel about her coming home?

"Author and You" Questions

7. **Analyze Characters** Why do you think Mulan refused the honors and gold that the Emperor offered her?

8. **Make Inferences** Why do you think Mulan changed into one of her favorite dresses when she returned home?

"On Your Own" Questions

9. **Describe Character** What three words would you use to describe Mulan? Why did you choose these words?
10. **Understand Genre Features** Why do you think people still tell legends about Mulan?
11. **Compare Oral Traditions** What other legends or ballads do you know? What regions or cultures are they from? Compare them to "The Ballad of Mulan."

Activity Book
p. 122

Student
CD-ROM

Build Reading Fluency

Repeating Reading

Repeated reading helps increase your reading rate and builds confidence. Each time you reread you improve your reading fluency.

1. Turn to page 234.
2. Your teacher or partner will time you for six minutes.
3. With a partner, take turns reading each paragraph aloud.
4. Stop after six minutes.

Listen, Speak, Interact

Develop a Character

You learned earlier that characters in legends are often based on real people. Many of these real people did something great or had great qualities.

1. Work with a partner to think of a new character for a legend. Base your character on a real person. This real person can be someone who lived long ago or someone who is alive today.

2. Discuss what your character did and his or her important qualities—honesty and strength, for example.

3. Write down your ideas on a piece of paper. Then draw a picture of your character or create a song about your character.

4. Tell or sing your legend for the class.

Elements of Literature

Determine Main and Minor Characters

The **main character** is the most important character in a story. Most of a story is about what the main character feels and does.

Minor characters are less important characters. They often speak with the main character and take part in some events in the story.

1. In your Reading Log, complete a chart like the one shown.

2. Write the names of the main character and three minor characters.

3. Describe one event for each character.

Character	Event
Main Character	
Minor Character: The Emperor	He sends a troop to help Mulan return home.
Minor Character	
Minor Character	

Reading Log   Activity Book p. 123   Student CD-ROM

Word Study

Use the Suffix -ly to Form Adverbs

A **suffix** is a group of letters that is added to the end of a word. A suffix changes the meaning of a word.

The suffix -ly means "in a certain manner." The word *suddenly* in paragraph 2 of the selection means "in a sudden, or unexpected, manner." *Suddenly* is an adverb. Adverbs usually tell how, when, or where something happens.

1. In your Personal Dictionary, complete a chart like the one here.
2. Write the root word and the suffix for each -ly word. Then write what you think each -ly word means.
3. Use a dictionary to check your definitions.

Root Word	Suffix	-ly Word	Definition
sudden +	-ly ⇒	suddenly	in a sudden manner
		softly	
		quietly	

4. Write a sentence of your own for each -ly word in the chart. Be sure to spell the root words and suffix correctly.

Personal Dictionary

The Heinle Newbury House Dictionary

Activity Book p. 124

Student CD-ROM

Grammar Focus

Use Prepositional Phrases

Prepositions are words like *in, at, on, over, by, under, through, over, with*. A **prepositional phrase** is a group of words that starts with a preposition and contains a noun or a pronoun as its object. Look at these prepositional phrases. The prepositions are in bold type, and the objects are underlined.

in a <u>village</u>   **at** her <u>loom</u>

Prepositional phrases can answer the questions "Where?" or "When?" Writers often use them to describe settings.

1. Find the prepositional phrases in paragraphs 7, 15, 23, and 24. Write them on a piece of paper. Circle the prepositions and underline the objects.
2. Share your work with a partner.
3. Together, write three prepositional phrases that describe the setting of your classroom, for example: "There is a map on the wall."

Activity Book pp. 125–126

Student Handbook

Student CD-ROM

From Reading to Writing

Write a Legend

"The Ballad of Mulan" teaches several important values. One of them is that people should love and care for their parents.

Write a short legend that teaches a value that is important to you. Base your legend on a real person from history who did something great. Parts of your legend may be made up.

1. Think of a hero from history who did something great. This hero will be your main character.

2. Decide what value this hero's actions show, such as honesty or working hard to reach a goal. You can exaggerate the hero's actions.

3. Write your legend with a clear beginning, a middle, and an end. Use transition words like *then*, *next*, *soon*, and *finally* to organize your ideas.

4. Use prepositional phrases to make your writing clear.

Activity Book
p. 127

Student
Handbook

Across Content Areas

Use Map Features to Read a Map

Maps often include features to help you read them. One of these features is a **compass rose**, which shows **direction.** Another feature is a chart to show **distance** (how far apart things are). Maps may also include charts that explain map **symbols.** Map symbols, such as stars and lines, may stand for capital cities and rivers.

Use the map of China to answer the questions.

1. What is the capital city of China?
2. Name the rivers shown on the map.
3. About how many miles is the city of Lanzhou from the city of Beijing?

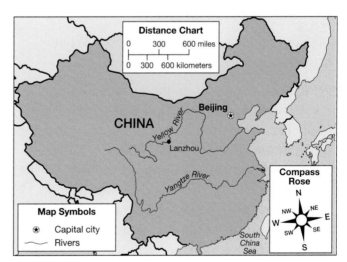

Activity Book
p. 128

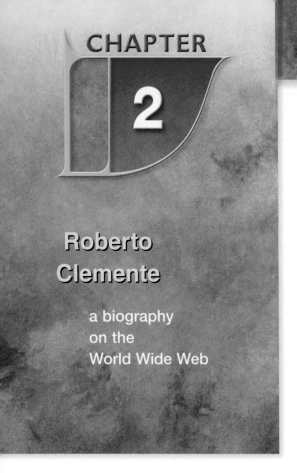

Roberto
Clemente

a biography
on the
World Wide Web

Objectives

Reading Use chronological order to recall and locate information in a biography.

Listening and Speaking Discuss learning from a person's example.

Grammar Identify prepositional phrases of time.

Writing Write a biography.

Content Science: Learn about earthquakes.

Use Prior Knowledge

Discuss Sports Heroes

Sports heroes are great athletes. What do you know about sports heroes?

1. With a partner, make a chart like the one here.
2. List the names of two or three sports heroes that you know about.
3. List what you know about each sports hero. For example, list the sports hero's team, what sport the person plays, or what awards the person has won.
4. Compare your list with other groups' lists. Which sports heroes are listed most often?

Sports Heroes	Facts I Know
Michael Jordan	He used to play basketball for the Chicago Bulls.

Build Background

Puerto Rico

Puerto Rico is an island in the Caribbean Sea, southeast of Florida. Puerto Rico is part of the United States, but it is not a state. It is a commonwealth. Puerto Ricans are United States citizens.

This means that they are free to move to and from the United States. Spanish is the main language of Puerto Rico.

Content Connection

There are many islands in the Caribbean. Most are independent countries, like Haiti, The Dominican Republic, Cuba, and Antigua. Some of the languages spoken are Spanish, French, Dutch, and Creole.

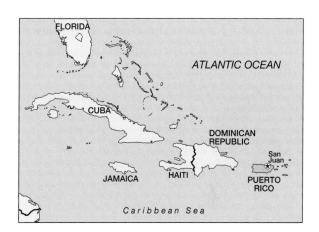

Build Vocabulary

Recognize Baseball Terms

"Roberto Clemente" includes many baseball terms that may be unfamiliar to you.

1. Use this chart as you read the selection.
2. Copy the words and meanings that interest you in your Personal Dictionary.

Personal
Dictionary

The Heinle
Newbury House
Dictionary

Activity Book
p. 129

Student
CD-ROM

Baseball Terms	
Term	**Meaning**
Major League Baseball	professional baseball in the United States
National League	a group of teams that are part of Major League Baseball
American League	a group of teams that are part of Major League Baseball
World Series	games played between the best National League and American League teams
MVP	Most Valuable Player; an award

Text Structure

Biography

"Roberto Clemente" is a **biography.** A biography is the true story of someone's life written by another person.

As you read, look for the features of a biography listed in the chart. Think about the events in Roberto Clemente's life. Do you admire what he did?

Biography	
Dates	important dates in the person's life
Events	important things that happened in the person's life
Other People	people who were important in the person's life
Order of Events	usually begins with events that happened early in the person's life; usually ends with events that happened at the end of the person's life

Student
CD-ROM

Reading Strategy

Use Chronological Order to Recall and Locate Information

Chronological order is the order in which events happen. Knowing when an event happened can help you find it in a text. It can also help you remember what you have read.

1. As you read "Roberto Clemente," take notes on important events and dates. Look for key words such as *first, next, then,* and *today* that help you keep track of the chronology.

2. When you finish the selection, use your notes to complete a chart like the one here. Write the events in the order in which they happened. Write the date next to the event if a date is given.

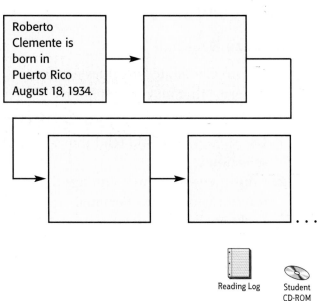

Reading Log

Student
CD-ROM

Roberto Clemente

a biography on the
World Wide Web

1   Roberto Clemente Walker was born in Puerto Rico on August 18, 1934. He was the youngest of four children. Roberto excelled in many sports, but his real love was baseball. He first played baseball in Puerto Rico. Then he signed with the **Brooklyn Dodgers.**

2   Roberto joined the **Pittsburgh Pirates** in 1955. He played his entire eighteen-year Major League Baseball career with them. He played in two World Series. He was the **National League Batting Champion** four times. He was awarded twelve **Gold Gloves.** He was selected National League MVP in 1966. He was chosen MVP in the 1971 World Series.

3   On November 14, 1964, he married Vera Cristina Zabala in Puerto Rico. They had three sons: Roberto Jr., Luis Roberto, and Roberto Enrique. All three sons were born in Puerto Rico because Roberto was proud of his **heritage.**

> ### Use Chronology to Recall and Locate Information
>
> What important event happened in 1955?

Audio
CD 2, Tr. 2

National League stars Roberto Clemente, Willie Mays, and Hank Aaron stand together for a victory portrait after the All-Star Game of 1961 in San Francisco.

Brooklyn Dodgers   a professional baseball team that now plays in Los Angeles

Pittsburgh Pirates   a professional baseball team

National League Batting Champion   the National League player who hits the most balls in a season

Gold Glove   an award given to the best players who play in the field and catch the ball

heritage   beliefs, history, and traditions

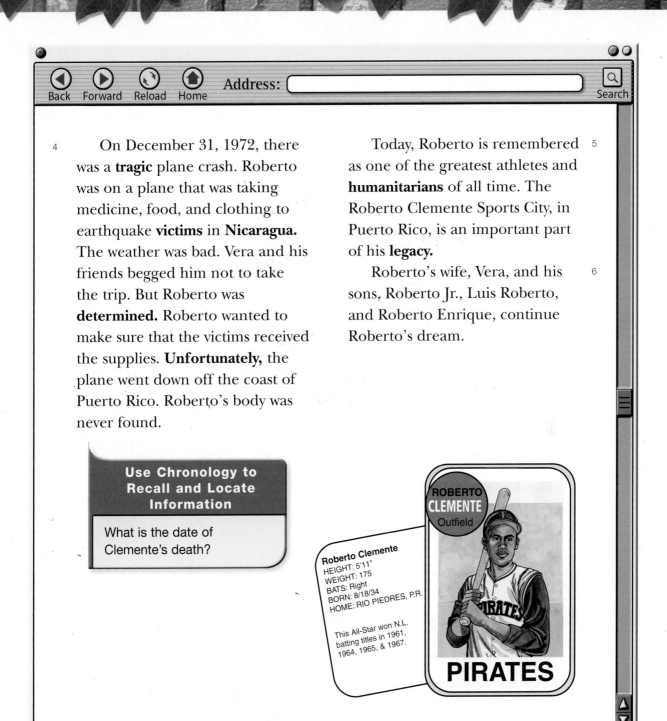

4   On December 31, 1972, there was a **tragic** plane crash. Roberto was on a plane that was taking medicine, food, and clothing to earthquake **victims** in **Nicaragua.** The weather was bad. Vera and his friends begged him not to take the trip. But Roberto was **determined.** Roberto wanted to make sure that the victims received the supplies. **Unfortunately,** the plane went down off the coast of Puerto Rico. Roberto's body was never found.

5   Today, Roberto is remembered as one of the greatest athletes and **humanitarians** of all time. The Roberto Clemente Sports City, in Puerto Rico, is an important part of his **legacy.**

6   Roberto's wife, Vera, and his sons, Roberto Jr., Luis Roberto, and Roberto Enrique, continue Roberto's dream.

Use Chronology to Recall and Locate Information

What is the date of Clemente's death?

ROBERTO CLEMENTE
Outfield

Roberto Clemente
HEIGHT: 5'11"
WEIGHT: 175
BATS: Right
BORN: 8/18/34
HOME: RIO PIEDRES, P.R.

This All-Star won N.L. batting titles in 1961, 1964, 1965, & 1967.

PIRATES

---

tragic   very sad, having to do with a disaster
victims   people who have been harmed or hurt
Nicaragua   a country in Central America
determined   really wanted to (do something)

unfortunately   sadly
humanitarians   people who do good for others
legacy   something passed on to another generation

Beyond the Reading

Reading Comprehension

Question-Answer Relationships (QAR)

"Right There" Questions

1. Recall Facts How many Gold Gloves did Clemente win?

2. Recall Facts Where was Clemente going when his plane crashed?

"Think and Search" Questions

3. Understand Sequence of Events Which U.S. baseball team did Clemente join first?

4. Identify Which awards did Clemente receive for his skills in baseball?

5. Recognize Character Traits Why is Clemente thought of as a great athlete?

6. Recognize Character Traits Why is Clemente thought of as a great humanitarian?

7. Use Chronology to Recall Information Did Clemente get married before or after joining the Pittsburgh Pirates? Use your knowledge of the chronology to find the answer.

"Author and You" Questions

8. Describe What three words would you use to describe Clemente?

9. Draw Conclusions Why do you think Clemente's wife and friends did not want him to fly to Nicaragua?

"On Your Own" Question

10. Support Opinions Do you think that it is important for sports stars to help people in need? Explain your answer.

Activity Book
p. 130

Build Reading Fluency

Reading Chunks of Words

Reading chunks or phrases of words is an important characteristic of fluent readers. It helps you stop reading word by word.

1. With a partner, take turns reading aloud the underlined chunks of words.

2. Read aloud two times each.

> On December 31, 1972, there was
> a tragic plane crash. Roberto was on a plane
> that was taking medicine, food, and clothing
> to earthquake victims in Nicaragua. The weather
> was bad. Vera and his friends begged him
> not to take the trip. But Roberto
> was determined.

Listen, Speak, Interact

Discuss Learning from a Person's Example

When you learn from a person's example, you try to act like that person.

1. With a small group, list reasons why Roberto Clemente is a hero. Ask these questions:
   a. Which of his actions make him a sports hero?
   b. Which other actions, besides his sports skills, make him a hero?

2. Discuss how people could learn from Clemente's example. List your answers to the following questions:
   a. Which of his actions do you think people should imitate (copy)?
   b. Why do you think so?
   c. What can people do to help others in need?

3. Present your answers to the class.

Elements of Literature

Recognize Third-Person Point of View

Point of view is the relationship of a narrator to a story. Biographies are usually told from the **third-person point of view.** This means that the writer describes the actions and feelings of other people, not his or her own actions and feelings.

Look back at the following readings. Are they told from first-person or third-person point of view? Talk about your ideas with a partner.

1. "Coyote," page 18
2. "Thanksgiving," page 30
3. "Sadako and the Thousand Paper Cranes," page 58
4. "Gonzalo," page 122

Point of View		
	First Person	**Third Person**
Who Is the Narrator?	someone in the story	someone not in the story
Pronouns Used	I, me, we, us	he, him, she, her, it, they, them
What the Narrator Describes	his or her own actions and feelings	other people's actions and feelings
Examples	I played baseball.	He played in two World Series.

Activity Book
p. 131

Student
CD-ROM

Word Study

Understand the Prefix *un-*

A **prefix** is a group of letters that is added to the beginning of a word. A prefix changes the meaning of a word.

> Unfortunately, the plane went down off the coast of Puerto Rico.

The word *unfortunately* has the prefix *un-*. In this word, *un-* means "not." This prefix is added to the word *fortunately*, which means "happily." ***Un****fortunately* means "not happily," or "sadly."

1. Copy the chart in your Personal Dictionary.

New Word	Meaning
unsafe	
uncooked	
unhappy	

2. Write these words in the correct box.

raw	sad	dangerous

3. Write a sentence for each new word. Be sure to spell the prefix correctly.

Personal Dictionary

The Heinle Newbury House Dictionary

Activity Book p. 132

Student CD-ROM

Grammar Focus

Identify Prepositional Phrases of Time

Some prepositional phrases answer the question "When?"

> I was born on January 1, 1992.

The prepositional phrase *on January 1, 1992* tells *when* I was born.

Look at the chart to see how the author uses prepositions to show time.

1. Find prepositional phrases of time in paragraphs 2–4 of the selection.
2. Write two original sentences that have these prepositions.

Prepositional Phrases of Time		
	When to Use	**Example**
on	when describing an event on a day of the week or a date that includes a month, day, and year	The game was <u>on</u> Saturday. Clemente was born <u>on</u> August 18, 1934.
in	when describing an event that happened in a certain year or month	Roberto joined the Pittsburgh Pirates <u>in</u> 1955. He got married <u>in</u> November.

Activity Book pp. 133–134

Student Handbook

Student CD-ROM

From Reading to Writing

Write a Biography

Write a biography of someone you know, such as a friend or family member. Write three to five paragraphs.

1. Ask the person these questions to write your biography.
   a. When were you born? Where were you born?
   b. Name two important events that happened in your life. When did each of these events happen?
   c. Name two things that you like to do today.
2. Use the dates to organize events in the order that they happened. Use prepositional phrases of time.
3. Write in the third-person point of view.
4. Use possessive nouns when telling about something the person owns.

Activity Book
p. 135

Student
Handbook

Across Content Areas

Learn About Earthquakes

Earthquakes happen when huge rocks move or break deep inside Earth. During an earthquake, the ground shakes. This shaking is caused by **seismic waves.** Seismic waves are the energy that is released from the breaking of rocks.

A scientist who studies earthquakes is called a **seismologist.** Seismologists use a **seismograph**—a machine that notes how much the ground moves during an earthquake. A number based on a scale called the **Richter Scale** tells how strong an earthquake is.

1. On a piece of paper, write *T* if you think a statement is true. Write *F* if you think a statement is false.
   a. To learn about earthquakes, you could speak with a seismologist.

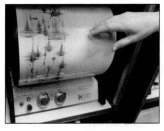

Seismograph

   b. Seismographs cause earthquakes.
   c. Seismic waves form before rocks break inside Earth.
2. Write a record of three earthquakes that have happened. Use references to research the information. Organize your record to show dates and location. Revise your record for spelling.

Activity Book
p. 136

CHAPTER 3

Nelson Mandela

an excerpt from a biography
by Jack L. Roberts

The Inaugural Address, May 10, 1994

an excerpt from a speech
by Nelson Mandela

Objectives

Reading Draw inferences as you read a biography and a speech.

Listening and Speaking Create and present dialogue.

Grammar Recognize commands with *let*.

Writing Write a persuasive speech.

Content Social Studies: Read a timeline.

Use Prior Knowledge

Discuss Freedom

When people have freedom, they are able to do or say certain things without being afraid. For example, people in the United States have freedom of speech—they can say or write what they want. What other examples of freedom can people have?

1. With a partner, complete a web like the one here on a piece of paper.
2. Brainstorm examples of freedom that you have. List these in your web. You may add more circles if needed.

3. With another pair of students, discuss what your lives would be like if someone took your freedom away.

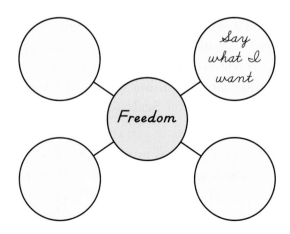

Build Background

Apartheid

For many years, the government of South Africa practiced **apartheid.** This kept white people and black people separate from each other. Under apartheid, black South Africans had few freedoms. They could not go to the same schools as white South Africans. They could not live in the same neighborhoods. They were not allowed to vote or take part in government.

Nelson Mandela worked for many years to end apartheid. Apartheid finally ended in 1991. In 1994, all people in South Africa were able to vote for the president of the country. They chose Nelson Mandela as their president.

Content Connection

The country of South Africa is located at the southern tip of Africa.

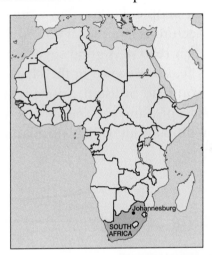

Build Vocabulary

Infer Meanings of Homonyms

Homonyms are words that sound the same and are often spelled the same, but have different meanings. Look at these homonyms:

can: meaning "be able to"

can: meaning "a metal container for food"

Use context clues in each sentence to choose the correct definition of each word. Write the word and definition in your Personal Dictionary.

1. We know it <u>well</u> that we cannot achieve success alone.
   a. a water hole made in the ground
   b. in a complete way, fully

2. We thank all the people in this country and the <u>rest</u> of the world.
   a. sleep, not work
   b. what is left over

Personal Dictionary

The Heinle Newbury House Dictionary

Activity Book p. 137

Student CD-ROM

Text Structure

Biography and Speech

"Nelson Mandela" is a **biography.** Remember, a biography is the true story of someone's life written by another person.

"The Inaugural Address, May 10, 1994" is a **speech.** A speech is spoken aloud to a group of people. People may write down the speech to remember it and so that others can read it. A good speech often has the features shown in the chart.

As you read or listen, notice how both the biography and the speech give you information about what Nelson Mandela is like.

Speech	
First-Person Pronouns	pronouns *we* and *us* to show that the speaker feels the same as the people listening
Repetition	repeated words in some sentences in order to make an idea clear
Simple Sentences	short sentences that are easy to understand
Strong Ending	a sentence that makes people feel a certain way, such as happy or excited

Student
CD-ROM

Reading Strategy

Draw Inferences

When you **draw inferences,** you use information in a text and what you already know to understand what you read.

Draw inferences as you read the selections.

1. Read the first sentence of the biography. What inference can you draw about Rolihlahla's family?
2. Use a chart like the one here to continue making inferences as you read both selections.

Text Information	What I Know	Inference I Can Draw
The family lives in a hut.	Rich families don't live in huts.	The family is probably poor.

Reading Log

Student
CD-ROM

NELSON MANDELA

an excerpt from a biography
by Jack L. Roberts

THE INAUGURAL ADDRESS
May 10, 1994

an excerpt from a speech
by Nelson Mandela

Nelson Mandela
an excerpt from a biography by Jack L. Roberts

1   *Twelve-year-old Rolihlahla* stood silently by his father's side in their tiny **thatched hut** near the Bashee River. The young tribal prince knew that this was an important day.

2   Rolihlahla's father was a poor but respected chief of the Tembu, one of many black African groups in the southeastern part of South Africa. But now this proud chief was sick, and certain he would die soon. So he had asked the **paramount** chief of the Tembu tribe to come to his family *kraal,* or farm.

Draw Inferences

What inference can you draw about what might happen to Rolihlahla?

South African kraal

---

thatched   with a roof of straw or leaves
hut   a very small, plain home

paramount   the highest ranking or most important

3   The dying man wanted to make sure that Rolihlahla, his only son, would have a good education. He wanted to make sure that Rolihlahla would be **raised** to become a future chief of the Tembu.

4   Rolihlahla's father spoke softly to the paramount chief, asking him to take Rolihlahla to raise. "I am giving you this servant, Rolihlahla," he said.

"I want you to make him what you would like him to be." Then he proudly added, "I can say from the way he speaks to his sisters and friends that his **inclination** is to help the nation."

> **Draw Inferences**
>
> What inference can you draw about the work that Rolihlahla will do?

---

raised   taught during his childhood

inclination   a natural liking for something

5   Sadly, Rolihlahla's father did not live to see his **prediction** come true. But **fortunately** for millions of people in South Africa and throughout the world, Rolihlahla's inclination was, **indeed,** to help the nation.

6   The young boy grew up to become better known throughout the world as Nelson Mandela, **civil rights leader** and hero to millions. He grew up to lead the struggle for **justice** and **racial** **equality** in South Africa. He became a **beloved** South African **patriot** whose struggle for freedom never weakened **despite** some twenty-seven years behind prison walls.

Draw Inferences

What inference can you draw about why Mandela was in prison?

---

prediction a statement about what will happen in the future

fortunately luckily

indeed truly

civil rights leader a leader who works to gain equal rights for all citizens

justice laws carried out fairly

racial equality when people of all races are treated the same

beloved very loved

patriot a person who is proud of his or her country

despite even though

7   At various times during his life, Nelson Mandela has been a prince, a **politician,** and a prisoner. And on May 10, 1994, he became president of South Africa.

8   Through it all, he has been **committed** to one goal for himself and the millions of black South Africans:

Nelson Mandela has always been a man **determined** to be free.

Draw Inferences

What inference can you draw about what Mandela is like? Write three words that you think describe him.

---

politician   a person who tries to get elected in government

committed   determined to do something

determined   set on doing something

About the Author   **Jack L. Roberts**

Jack L. Roberts has written many biographies about well-known and important people. In addition to his book about Nelson Mandela, Roberts has also written about Bill Clinton and Booker T. Washington.

➤ Do you think Jack L. Roberts wrote a biography of Nelson Mandela to describe Mandela as a person or to describe apartheid in South Africa? Explain.

The Inaugural Address, May 10, 1994

an excerpt from a speech by Nelson Mandela

1   . . . We **dedicate** this day to all the heroes and heroines in this country and the rest of the world who **sacrificed** in many ways and **surrendered** their lives so that we could be free.

> ### Draw Inferences
>
> What inferences can you draw about what happened to many of these "heroes and heroines"?

2   Their dreams have become **reality.** Freedom is their reward . . .

3   We understand it still that there is no easy road to freedom.

4   We know it well that none of us acting alone can achieve success.

We must therefore act together as   5
a **united** people, for national **reconciliation,** for nation building, for the birth of a new world.

Let there be justice for all.   6

Let there be peace for all.   7

Let there be work, bread, water   8
and salt for all.

Let each know that for each the   9
body, the mind and the soul have been freed to **fulfill** themselves . . .

Let freedom **reign** . . .   10

God bless Africa! . . .   11

---

inaugural address   a speech given by a new president on the day that he or she takes office

dedicate   name in honor of someone or something

sacrificed   gave up something important for a special purpose

surrendered   gave up

reality   what is real

united   joined together

reconciliation   an agreement made after an argument or fight

fulfill   satisfy, make happy

reign   rule, be everywhere

Nelson Mandela accepting the Nobel Peace Prize.

About the Author

Nelson Mandela (born 1918)

Nelson Rolihlahla Mandela was born in a village in South Africa on July 18, 1918. After the death of his father, Mandela was raised by a leading tribal chief. In 1942, Mandela earned a law degree from the University of South Africa. In 1944, he joined the African National Congress (ANC), a group that worked against South Africa's apartheid laws.

In 1962, the South African government put Mandela in prison because of his work to end apartheid. He spent about 27 years in prison and was finally released on February 11, 1990. In 1993, Mandela won the Nobel Peace Prize, an award given each year for a great achievement in bringing about peace in the world. In 1994 Mandela was elected president of South Africa. He was president until 1999 and worked to bring white and black South Africans together.

➤ What do you think was more important to Nelson Mandela when he wrote his inaugural address: thanking the people who worked to end apartheid or asking the South African people to work together?

Beyond the Reading

Reading Comprehension

Question-Answer Relationships (QAR)

"Right There" Questions

1. **Recall Facts** In "Nelson Mandela," what did Rolihlahla's father want for his son?

2. **Recall Facts** In "Nelson Mandela," what does Rolihlahla's father say the boy will do?

"Think and Search" Questions

3. **Draw Conclusions** In "Nelson Mandela," how does Rolihlahla "help the nation" when he grows up?

4. **Identify** In "The Inaugural Address, May 10, 1994," what things does Mandela wish for all South African people?

"Author and You" Questions

5. **Understand Author's Perspective** How do you think the author of "Nelson Mandela" feels about Mandela? Explain.

6. **Draw Inferences** Reread paragraph 1 of "The Inaugural Address, May 10, 1994." Who do you think these "heroes and heroines" are?

7. **Understand Author's Perspective** Suppose you are Nelson Mandela giving his inaugural speech. Describe your feelings and hopes for the future of South Africa.

"On Your Own" Questions

8. **Explain** Do you think that Nelson Mandela is a hero? Explain.

9. **Describe Character Traits** What three words best describe Nelson Mandela? Why do you think so?

Activity Book
p. 138

Student
CD-ROM

Build Reading Fluency

Echo Read Aloud

Effective readers learn to read with feeling. Echo reading helps you read with feeling and expression. Your teacher reads a line. Then the class reads (echoes) the same line aloud. Turn to page 260.

1. Listen to your teacher read.
2. Read the same line aloud with expression.
3. Continue listening and reading.

Listen, Speak, Interact

Create and Present Dialogue

Sometimes a biography has **dialogue**—what people in a text say to each other.

Even though a biography describes events that really happened, the dialogue does not always show *exactly* what the people said. Many events in a biography happened a long time ago, and people often cannot remember everything they said. The writer may write dialogue to show what the people possibly said.

1. With a partner, reread or listen to paragraph 4 of "Nelson Mandela." Rolihlahla's father tells the chief what he wants him to do. Discuss the father's perspective.

2. What do you think the chief said? Create four to six lines of dialogue for him and for the father.

3. Practice your dialogue with your partner. One of you is the chief, the other is the father.

4. Read your dialogue for the class. Act out your speech with expression. When you read, read only the words in quotation marks (" ").

Activity Book
p. 139

Elements of Literature

Analyze Style in a Speech

Style is the way writers use language. In Nelson Mandela's speech, some elements of his style are word choice, sentence length, and repetition. This speech has an inspiring style—it makes the listener want to take action.

1. Reread or listen to paragraphs 1 and 2. Find strong words in the paragraphs that make the audience pay attention. What effect do these words have on you?

2. Reread paragraphs 3 and 4. Read closely to find the repetition. What effect do you think the repetition has on the listener?

3. What other elements of style do you notice? How long are the sentences? What effect does this have?

Student
CD-ROM

Word Study

Identify the Suffix *-ion*

A **suffix** is a group of letters that is added to the end of a word. A suffix changes the meaning of a root word.

The suffix *-ion* usually changes verbs into nouns. Here the verb is the root word.

protect + -ion → protection

verb + suffix → noun

1. Complete a chart like the one here in your Personal Dictionary. Write the correct verb and suffix for each *-ion* word.

Verb	Suffix	*-ion* Word	Meaning
protect +	-ion ⇒	protection	action taken against harm
		education	
		prediction	

2. Use the verb to write what you think is the meaning of each *-ion* word. Be sure to spell the root word and suffix correctly. If the verb ends in *-e*, drop the *-e* before you add *-ion*.

3. Check your definitions of the *-ion* words in a dictionary.

Personal Dictionary

The Heinle Newbury House Dictionary

Activity Book *p. 140*

Student CD-ROM

Grammar Focus

Recognize Commands with *Let*

The verb *let* can be used to express a command or a strong desire. Nelson Mandela wants there to be peace, so he says, "Let there be peace."

Here are some more examples.

<u>Let</u> all children have a good education.

<u>Let</u> them all go to college.

<u>Let</u> there be jobs for them when they graduate.

Here are some ideas that you might use in a speech. On a piece of paper, restate them using *let*.

1. Every town should be safe.
2. The air in the cities should be clean.
3. Every worker should have a good-paying job.

Activity Book *pp. 141–142*

Student Handbook

Student CD-ROM

From Reading to Writing

Write a Persuasive Speech

Imagine that your classmates just elected you as class president. Write a short speech in which you describe how you want to improve your school. Write your speech so that it is appropriate for classmates.

1. Thank your classmates for electing you.
2. Write two sentences using *we* or *us* to persuade your classmates to work together.
3. Include three sentences that use *let* as a command to explain how your school should be.

4. End your speech by saying something great about your school, such as "Our school is the best!"
5. Read your speech aloud to your classmates. Use gestures and tone of voice to show meaning and to make your speech appropriate for your classmates.
6. If possible, use presentation software for your speech. Include visuals to support your statements to improve your school.

Activity Book
p. 143

Student Handbook

Across Content Areas

Read a Timeline

Read the timeline of events in the life of Nelson Mandela.

1. What is the total number of years that the timeline shows?

2. How many years after Mandela helped form the ANCYL did he become president of the ANCYL?
3. What happened in 1990?
4. How long was Mandela in prison?

Activity Book
p. 144

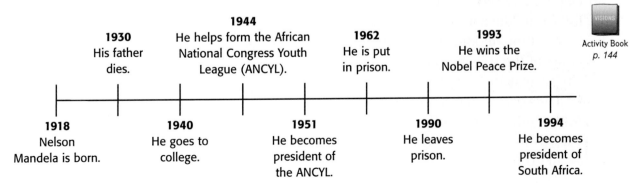

1930
His father dies.

1944
He helps form the African National Congress Youth League (ANCYL).

1962
He is put in prison.

1993
He wins the Nobel Peace Prize.

1918
Nelson Mandela is born.

1940
He goes to college.

1951
He becomes president of the ANCYL.

1990
He leaves prison.

1994
He becomes president of South Africa.

CHAPTER 4

My Father Is a Simple Man

a poem
by Luis Omar Salinas

Growing Up

a poem
by Liz Ann Báez Aguilar

Objectives

Reading Compare and contrast as you read two poems.

Listening and Speaking Discuss jobs.

Grammar Recognize reported speech.

Writing Write a poem.

Content Social Studies: Read advertisements for jobs.

Use Prior Knowledge

Discuss Role Models

Role models are people whom we want to be like. For example, a good teacher may be a role model for someone who wants to be a teacher.

1. Brainstorm role models in your life. List them on a piece of paper.
2. Choose one role model from your list. Complete a web like the one here. In the middle circle, write the name of the role model. In the outer circles, write at least three reasons why this person is your role model. Add as many circles as you need.
3. Discuss your role model with a small group.

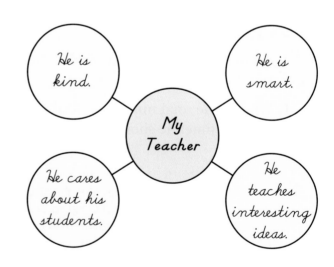

He is kind.

He is smart.

My Teacher

He cares about his students.

He teaches interesting ideas.

Build Background

Mexican-American Authors

In this chapter, you will read two poems by Mexican-American poets. Some Mexican-Americans write poetry, fiction, essays, and plays about their cultural experiences.

They write about growing up, their family, and Mexican-American traditions. Many of these writings mix the English and Spanish languages.

Content Connection

Before the mid-1800s, Mexico owned large parts of land in what is now the United States. When these places became part of the United States, many Mexican people became United States citizens.

Build Vocabulary

Use Word Squares to Remember Meaning

Using word squares can help you remember the meanings of new words.

1. Listen as your teacher discusses these words.

   scholar   perpetual   architect

2. In your Personal Dictionary, complete a word square for each word.
3. Write the word in the **word** box.
4. Use a dictionary or glossary to write the **meaning**.
5. Draw a **symbol** to remember the word.
6. Write a sentence with the word in the **sentence** box.

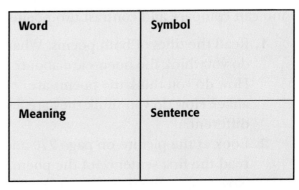

Word	Symbol
Meaning	Sentence

Personal Dictionary

The Heinle Newbury House Dictionary

Activity Book p. 145

Student CD-ROM

Text Structure

Poem

"My Father Is a Simple Man" and "Growing Up" are **poems.** Look at the features of these poems in the chart.

Poems can look very different from one another. As you read, notice how the punctuation and lengths of sentences are different in each poem.

Poem	
Content	The poet describes his or her thoughts, feelings, or experiences.
First-Person Pronouns	The poet often uses *I, we, me,* and *us* to show his or her ideas.
Images	Details help readers form pictures in their minds.
Stanzas	The poem is separated into groups of lines called stanzas.

Student
CD-ROM

Reading Strategy

Compare and Contrast

When you **compare,** you notice how two things are alike. When you **contrast,** you notice how two things are different. You can compare and contrast two poems.

1. Read the titles of both poems. What do you think the poems are about? How do you think the poems are alike? How do you think they are different?

2. Look at the picture on page 270 and read the first sentence of the poem. Now look at the picture on page 274 and read the first four lines. How are the two poems alike? How are they different?

3. Use a Venn Diagram like the one here to help you compare and contrast as you read each selection.

4. Use comparative adjectives when possible.

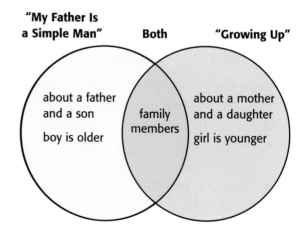

"My Father Is a Simple Man" **Both** "Growing Up"

about a father and a son

boy is older

family members

about a mother and a daughter

girl is younger

Student
CD-ROM

My Father Is a Simple Man

a poem
by Luis Omar Salinas

Growing Up

a poem
by Liz Ann Báez Aguilar

Audio
CD 2, Tr. 5

Compare and Contrast

Compare how the father walks with how the speaker of the poem walks.

My Father Is a Simple Man
a poem by Luis Omar Salinas

1 I walk to town with my father
to buy a newspaper. He walks slower
than I do so I must **slow up.**
The street is filled with children.

2 We argue about the price
of **pomegranates,** I **convince**
him it is the fruit of **scholars.**
He has taken me on this journey
and it's been **lifelong.**

---

slow up   move less quickly

pomegranates   round fruits with reddish skin and many juicy red seeds

convince   cause someone to believe that something is true

scholars   people who have learned much through study

lifelong   lasting your entire life

Compare and Contrast

Contrast what the poet says about pomegranates in stanza 2 with what he says about oranges in stanza 3.

3   He's sure I'll be healthy
so long as I eat more oranges,
and tells me the orange
has seeds and so is **perpetual**;
and we too will come back
like the orange trees.

4   I ask him what he thinks
about death and he says
he will gladly face it when
it comes but he won't jump
out in front of a car.

---

perpetual   continuing forever

5   I'd gladly give my life
for this man with a sixth
grade education, whose kindness
and **patience** are **true** . . .

Compare and Contrast

Compare and contrast the father and the son.

6   The truth of it is, he's the scholar,
and when the **bitter-hard** reality
comes at me like a **punishing**
evil stranger, I can always
remember that here was a man
who was a worker and **provider,**
who learned the simple facts
in life and lived by them,
who held no **pretense.**

---

patience the ability to bear pain or trouble while
    waiting for something
true real, honest
bitter-hard very difficult

punishing having the quality of causing pain
provider a person who supports his or her family
pretense a reason or an act that hides the real reason
    for doing something

7 And when he leaves without
   benefit of **fanfare** or **applause**
   I shall have learned what little
   there is about greatness.

---

fanfare   a loud, showy introduction to an event

applause   hand clapping to show that you like something

About the Author

Luis Omar Salinas (born 1937)

Luis Omar Salinas was born in Robstown, Texas. He lived in Monterrey, Mexico, until he was four. After his mother died, Salinas moved to California with his uncle. He grew up and went to school in California. He studied and taught writing at California State University. Today, Salinas continues to write powerful poetry that describes Mexican-American life.

➤ Listen to the audio recording of the poem to appreciate the author's message. What does he tell you about the father? How is the father a hero?

Audio
CD 2, Tr. 6

Growing Up
a poem by Liz Ann Báez Aguilar

Compare and Contrast

Compare and contrast the form of this poem with "My Father Is a Simple Man."

1 When I grow up,
   I want to be a doctor.

2 *M'ija, you will* **patch** *scraped knees*
   and wipe away children's tears.

3 But what if I become an **architect?**

4 *M'ija, you will build beautiful houses*
   where children will sing and play.

5 And what if I become a teacher?

6 *M'ija, you will teach*
   your students to read every day.

M'ija the Spanish term for "my daughter"   **architect** a person who designs buildings
patch fix or mend

7   But what if I become a famous **chef?**

8   *M'ija, your **arroz con pollo**
    will be eaten with **gozo.***

9   And Mami, what if I want to be like you someday?

10 *M'ija, why do you want to be like me?*

Compare and Contrast

In stanza 11, the poet compares Mami to a doctor, an architect, a teacher, and a chef. Explain how she does this.

11 Oh Mami, because you care for people, our house is built on love,
    you are wise, and your **spicy stew** tastes delicious.

---

chef   the leading cook in a restaurant

arroz con pollo   the Spanish term for "rice with chicken"

gozo   the Spanish term for "joy"

spicy   tasty, hot

stew   a thick soup of meat and vegetables

About the Author — Liz Ann Báez Aguilar

Liz Ann Báez Aguilar has written many poems and short stories. She enjoys doing community service. She sometimes visits sick people in the hospital. She also works with her church to take clothing and other things to orphanages in Mexico. (Orphanages are homes for children whose parents have died.) Aguilar currently teaches English at San Antonio College in Texas. She lives in San Antonio, Texas, where she was born.

➤ Based on "Growing Up," do you think Liz Ann Báez Aguilar believes that being a good mother is an important job? Explain.

Beyond the Reading

Reading Comprehension

Question-Answer Relationships (QAR)

"Right There" Questions

1. **Recall Facts** In "My Father Is a Simple Man," why does the speaker go to town with his father?
2. **Recall Facts** According to the father in "My Father Is a Simple Man," how will the speaker stay healthy?
3. **Recall Details** In "My Father Is a Simple Man," at which grade level did the father leave school?
4. **Summarize** Why does the daughter in "Growing Up" want to be like her mother?

"Think and Search" Questions

5. **Identify** What four jobs are mentioned in "Growing Up"?
6. **Draw Conclusions** Who are the two speakers in "Growing Up"?

"Author and You" Questions

7. **Understand Author's Perspective** Why do you think Liz Ann Báez Aguilar uses Spanish words in "Growing Up"?
8. **Recognize Character Traits** What three words do you think the speaker in "My Father Is a Simple Man" might use to describe his father? What does this say about their relationship?
9. **Recognize Character Traits** What three words do you think the daughter in "Growing Up" might use to describe her mother?

"On Your Own" Question

10. **Explain** Do you know someone you would call "great"? Why is that person "great"?

Activity Book
p. 146

Student
CD-ROM

Build Reading Fluency

Audio CD Reading Practice

Listening to the Audio CD for "My Father Is a Simple Man" is good reading practice. It will help you to become a fluent reader.

1. Listen to the Audio CD.
2. Follow along in your book on page 270.
3. Listen to the phrases, pauses, and expression of the reader.
4. Reread with expression paragraphs 1 and 2.

Listen, Speak, Interact

Discuss Jobs

"Growing Up" describes four different jobs: doctor, architect, teacher, chef. What do you know about these jobs?

1. The class will work in at least four groups. Each group is assigned one of the jobs described in "Growing Up."
2. With your group, answer the following questions about the job you were assigned. Many of these questions have more than one answer. List your answers on a piece of paper.

a. Describe the job. What do people who work this job do?
b. How do you think people learn to do this job?
c. Do you think that you would like this job? Why or why not?

3. Present your answers to the class. For the last question, each person in the group should present his or her own answer.

Elements of Literature

Recognize Imagery

Poets use **imagery** to help you form pictures in your mind as you read. We call these pictures **images.** Imagery can help you understand what a poet is describing, and it can also help you enjoy a poem.

In stanza 6 of "My Father Is a Simple Man," the poet uses the image of a "punishing, evil stranger." This image helps us understand that the poet is describing a bad and scary feeling.

1. With a partner, reread or listen to stanza 3 of "My Father Is a Simple Man." What images does the poet use? Compare answers with your partner.
2. Choose one image to draw in your Reading Log.
3. Discuss your drawing with a partner. How did this image help you understand what the poet describes?

Activity Book
p. 147

Student
CD-ROM

Word Study

Identify the Suffix -er

The suffix -er can change verbs into nouns. The suffix -er means "a person who does something." For example, *writer* means "a person who writes."

If a verb ends in -e, you drop the -e before you add the suffix -er.

Verb	Suffix	Noun	Definition
writẹ +	-er ⇒	writer	a person who writes
+	-er ⇒		
+	-er ⇒		
+	-er ⇒		

1. Find three examples of nouns that contain the suffix -er in the two poems. Look at stanza 6, line 6, of "My Father Is a Simple Man" and stanza 5 of "Growing Up."
2. Complete a chart like the one here in your Personal Dictionary. Use a dictionary to check your definitions.

3. Write a sentence of your own using each of the four words in the chart. Be sure to spell the root correctly.

Personal Dictionary

The Heinle Newbury House Dictionary

Activity Book p. 148

Student CD-ROM

Grammar Focus

Recognize Reported Speech

Read these two sentences.

My father says, **"I won't jump out in front of a car."**

My father says <u>that he</u> won't jump out in front of a car.

The first sentence is **direct speech.** It gives the actual words that the person said. Direct speech uses quotation marks.

The second sentence is **reported speech.** Notice that *I won't jump* changes to *<u>he</u> won't jump.* Also, reported speech does not use quotation marks. You can use *that* before the reported speech, or you can leave it out.

My father says he won't jump out in front of a car.

1. Rewrite the examples of direct speech as reported speech. Be sure to use correct subject-verb agreement.
   a. My father always says, "I want to be healthy."
   b. Every morning, my mother says, "I am going to make some stew."

Activity Book pp. 149–150

Student Handbook

Student CD-ROM

From Reading to Writing

Write a Poem

Write a poem about the role model that you described in Use Prior Knowledge on page 266.

1. Use your web from Use Prior Knowledge. Choose information from three circles to write three sentences. Separate your sentences into three stanzas.
2. In each sentence, use imagery to help your readers form pictures in their minds.

3. Write a title for your poem that describes your role model.
4. Use your best handwriting and copy your poem on a nice piece of paper. Illustrate or decorate your poem.
5. Create a classroom collection of everyone's poems. Make a cover and a table of contents.

Activity Book
p. 151

Student
Handbook

Across Content Areas

Read Advertisements for Jobs

Ads (advertisements) for jobs use a lot of **abbreviations,** or shortened forms of words.

1. Match these job ad abbreviations with their full forms.

p/t	experience
f/t	full time
wknds	hour
hr	part time
exp	weekends

2. Read the job ads below and answer these questions.
   a. Which ad gives the hourly pay, "baggers" or "store assistant"?
   b. Which job is only part time?
   c. Which job is only on weekends?
   d. Which job requires experience?

BAGGERS needed. P/t, f/t. $8.50/hr. Shop Here Supermarket. Apply 9 to 5, Mon. to Fri. 2435 Broadway.

STORE ASSISTANT, Cosmo Garden Center. Retail exp required. P/t, wknds. Call 981-350-5555.

Activity Book
p. 152

Apply and Expand

Listening and Speaking Workshop

Give a Descriptive Presentation

> **Topic**
>
> Choose a person that you know very well and admire. Describe that person in a presentation to the class.

Step 1: Identify what you know about the person and ask questions.

On a note card, answer the following questions. If you do not know an answer, ask someone who might know. Revise your questions as needed. Write your answers in complete sentences. Use one card for each question and answer.

1. What is the person's name?
2. How do you know the person?
3. What does the person look like?
4. What is the person like? For example, *funny, smart,* and *kind.*
5. Where does the person live?
6. What are the person's hobbies?
7. What is some other information, such as the person's job or where the person goes to school?

Step 2: Organize your presentation.

1. On another note card, write an opening that will get your audience's attention. For example:
   a. Use a quote that the person said.
   b. Give your opinion about something the person does well.

2. On your note cards, write numbers in the order in which you will present the information.

> **3.** He is my father.
>
> **2.** His name is Carlos Sanchez.
>
> **1. Opening**
>
> The person who I am going to describe is the best cook in the world.

Step 3: Show pictures that describe what you will say. You may:

1. Draw a picture or bring in a photograph of the person.
2. Draw a picture that shows one of the person's favorite hobbies.

Step 4: Practice your presentation.

1. Practice your presentation in front of a partner. Use the tips in the Presentation Checklist.
2. Ask your partner to complete the Active Listening Checklist.
3. Revise the presentation as needed.
4. Give your presentation to the class.

Step 5: Give your presentation.

1. Give your presentation. If possible, record it on video. Then watch your presentation and note how you could improve.

I. **Paragraph 1**
   A. Begin with a strong opening.
   B. Who is the person?
   C. When and where was the person born?

II. **Paragraph 2**
   A. Describe the first important event.
      1. What?
      2. When?
      3. Where?
      4. Why?

III. **Paragraph 3**
   A. Describe the first important event.
      1. What?
      2. When?
      3. Where?
      4. Why?

IV. **Paragraph 4**
   A. Describe the first important event.
      1. What?
      2. When?
      3. Where?
      4. Why?

V. **Paragraph 5**
   1. Tell the results of the event.
      1. What impact did the person have?
      2. Why is this person admired?

Step 4: Revise your draft.

1. Ask a partner to read your draft and then complete the Editor's Checklist on a piece of paper.
2. Discuss how you could improve your draft with your partner.
3. Make changes to improve your draft.

Step 5: Edit and proofread.

Use reference materials, such as a dictionary or grammar guide, to help you edit your biography. If you wrote your biography on a computer, run checks for spelling, punctuation, and grammar. Make changes if necessary. Remember to check paragraph indents.

Editor's Checklist

1. The biography has a strong opening.
   ____ Yes ____ No

2. The events are in correct time order. The writer uses transition words.
   ____ Yes ____ No

3. The writer includes details and adjectives.
   ____ Yes ____ No

4. The writer gives reasons for his or her opinions.
   ____ Yes ____ No

5. The writer uses a variety of sentence types: simple, compound, and complex.
   ____ Yes ____ No

Step 6: Publish your biography.

1. If you wrote your biography by hand, rewrite it in your best handwriting. If you wrote it on a computer, use a font and spacing that is easy to read.
2. Make a title page. Include the title and your name.
3. Draw a picture on the title page. The picture should describe something in the biography.
4. Make a copy of your biography for the person you wrote about. Ask if it describes him or her correctly.

The Heinle
Newbury House
Dictionary

Student
Handbook

Projects

These projects will help you learn more about different types of heroes.

Project 1: Interviews About Heroes

Interview five people about their heroes.

1. Copy the Interview Organizer on a piece of paper or use a computer. Prepare questions to fill in the chart.
2. Choose five people of different ages to interview. List their answers.
3. Write a summary of your chart.
   a. Did anyone have the same heroes?
   b. Were most of the heroes famous people or everyday people?
   c. Did the interviewees list similar qualities for their heroes?
   d. Did they have similar or different reasons for picking their heroes?
   e. Draw some conclusions. For example: "Most people chose ordinary people as their heroes."
4. Report your findings to your class. Make a record of the heroes. Analyze the record of these interviews. How many different heroes were identified? What do all the heroes have in common? Organize the records into famous people and everyday people.

Project 2: Be a Hero

There are ways you can be a hero in your school and community.

1. Research areas in your school and community where help is needed. Some ideas might be: clean up a nearby park; read to first-graders in an elementary school; play cards with senior citizens at the nursing center. Your teacher and school librarian will have some ideas.
2. Pick a project you can do by yourself or with a partner.
3. Organize and carry out your service project. How many people are needed to do what you have decided? What tools will you need? Who do you need to talk with to arrange things?
4. After you finish your service project, report back to your class. What did you do? What did you learn? How did the people you helped feel about you? Were you their hero?
5. Write a news report of your service project. Send it to your school newspaper. Remember to answer the *Wh-* questions: *who, what, when, where, why,* and *how.* Try to persuade the newspaper audience to find a community service project to do.

Interview Organizer				
Person's Name	Who is your hero?	Why is this person your hero?	Is your hero a famous or an everyday person?	Three words that describe qualities of a hero

Further Reading

Here is a list of books about heroes. Read one or more of them. Write your thoughts and feelings about what you read in your Reading Log. Answer these questions:

1. What makes the people heroes?
2. Which hero inspired you the most?

Pride of Puerto Rico:
The Life of Roberto Clemente
by Paul Robert Walker, Odyssey Classics, 1991. This book tells the life story of the legendary Pittsburgh Pirates right fielder, from his childhood to his tragic death.

Through My Eyes
by Ruby Bridges, Scholastic Trade, 1999. In this book, Ruby Bridges retells her experiences as the first African-American child to attend William Frantz Elementary School, a school for white children.

Heroes of the Day, Vol. 3
by Nancy Louis, ABDO Publishing Co., 2002. On September 11, 2001, real-life heroes saved many lives. This book describes the heroic actions of police officers, paramedics, emergency telephone operators, and ordinary citizens.

Women Warriors: Myths and Legends of Heroic Women
by Marianna Mayer, William Morrow & Co., 1999. This book contains 12 tales, folktales, and myths about female military leaders, warriors, goddesses, and other heroes.

Boys Who Rocked the World:
From King Tut to Tiger Woods
by Mattie Stepanek, Beyond Words Publishing Co., 2001. This book features the biographies of 30 boys who changed the world by the age of 20. The biographies include a wide range of people, from King Tut to Bill Gates.

Girls Who Rocked the World: Heroines from Sacajawea to Sheryl Swoopes
by Amelie Welden, Gareth Stevens, 1999. This book includes 35 biographies about girls who changed the world by the time they were 20 years old. The biographies include Anne Frank, Jane Goodall, and Joan of Arc.

B. Franklin, Printer
by David A. Adler, Holiday House, 2001. Printer, writer, scientist, inventor, patriot: everything Franklin did was marked by cheer, energy, and hard work. He organized the postal system and America's first subscription library. Now he is our favorite Founding Father.

Tallchief: America's Prima Ballerina
by Maria Tallchief with Rosemary Wells, Viking, 1999. Born with music in her body, Tallchief became the greatest American-born ballerina of her time, even though she didn't formally study ballet until age 18. This book details her growing-up years that inspired her dancing.

Companion
Web site

Reading Log

Heinle
Reading Library
The Red Badge
of Courage

UNIT 5

Explorations

Winged Shuttle Craft, Concept drawing by North American Rockwell Corporation.

View the Picture

1. What is this shuttle craft exploring?
2. Have you ever explored something? Have you explored a new part
    of your town? Have you read a new kind of book?

In this unit, you will read three nonfiction selections and one
science fiction short story. Each reading focuses on an exploration.
You will also learn the elements of these forms and how to write
them yourself.

Eye to Eye

an excerpt from a
personal narrative
by Sylvia Earle

Objectives

Reading Draw conclusions as you read a personal narrative.

Listening and Speaking Describe a place that you have explored.

Grammar Recognize and use the simple past tense.

Writing Write a personal narrative.

Content Science: Identify types of scientists.

Use Prior Knowledge

Explore What You Know About Whales

In "Eye to Eye," the author describes whales. What do you know about whales?

Read each statement. On a piece of paper, write *T* if you think the statement is true and *F* if you think the statement is false. Discuss your answers with a partner. Check them with your teacher.

1. Whales are fish.
2. There are many kinds of whales.
3. Whales can swim very fast.
4. Whales do not make sounds.
5. Most whales live in the same place their whole life.

Build Background

Humpback Whales

Humpback whales live in all of the world's oceans. They usually grow to about 40 to 50 feet (12 to 15 meters) long. Humpback whales can sing. Their songs have many different sounds. Humpback whales in the same area may sing the same songs and, over time, make the same changes to their songs.

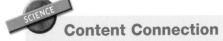

Content Connection

Many scientists believe that humpback whales sing to communicate with one another.

Build Vocabulary

Use Context to Identify Correct Homophones

Homophones are words that are pronounced the same but have different meanings. Homophones may also have different spellings.

main most important

mane a long strip of hair on the neck of some animals

Choose the correct homophone for the following sentences. Use the **context**—nearby words or the sentence meaning. Use a dictionary to pronounce each homophone.

1. I called to _____ if the store was still open.
   a. see find out about something
   b. sea a body of salt water
2. The _____ lives in the ocean.
   a. wail a cry of sadness
   b. whale a very large mammal shaped like a fish

The Heinle
Newbury House
Dictionary

Activity Book
p. 153

Student
CD-ROM

Text Structure

Personal Narrative

"Eye to Eye" is a **personal narrative.** A personal narrative describes real events that happened to the author. It tells those events as a story. As you read the selection, look for the features of a personal narrative shown in the chart.

As you read "Eye to Eye," notice that you learn about humpback whales and the author's feelings about these whales.

Personal Narrative	
Events	what happens to the author
First-Person Pronouns	*I, me, we,* and *us*
Descriptive Language	sense words that help readers see and feel what happens
Details	information about what the author knows or learns

Student
CD-ROM

Reading Strategy

Draw Conclusions

Authors do not always explain everything. Sometimes, you must **draw conclusions** to figure out what an author thinks or feels. To draw conclusions, use what the author writes and your experiences to determine what the author thinks or feels.

In Unit 4, you made inferences from what you read and your experiences. This is similar to drawing conclusions.

As you read "Eye to Eye," draw conclusions about the author, Sylvia Earle. Use a chart like this one. Write your conclusions in your Reading Log.

What the Author Writes	Your Experiences	Your Conclusion
As soon as I got home, I went to bed.	You know from your experiences that people go to bed when they are tired.	The author probably was tired.

Eye to Eye

an excerpt from a personal narrative
by Sylvia Earle

Audio
CD 2, Tr. 7

Prologue

Sylvia Earle is a scientist who studies ocean plants and animals. In "Eye to Eye," Earle is working with other scientists to study humpback whales. These scientists want to know more about the actions of these whales, such as why they sing and how they move underwater.

Draw Conclusions

How do you think Sylvia Earle feels as the whale swims toward her? Explain why you think so.

1   I was floating in clear, warm water along the coast of Maui, one of the Hawaiian Islands. Far below was the largest creature I had ever seen—a female humpback whale. She looked as big as a bus and was heading straight toward me. It was too late to worry about whether or not I was in her way or if whales have **brakes.**

2   A moment later her **grapefruit-size** eyes met mine. She **tilted** right, then left, as her 15-foot **flippers** and powerful tail **propelled** her past me far faster than humans can swim or run. I glanced at my own slip-on flippers, a wonderful **aid** for human feet underwater but no match for a whale's **built-in propulsion system . . .**

3   "Home" for whales is a place several thousand miles long, with the dining room at one end in cool, northern waters and the **nursery** at the other in the **tropics.**

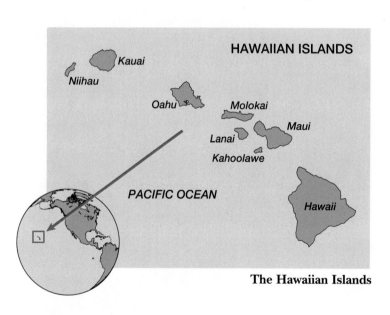

The Hawaiian Islands

---

brakes   tools that stop something

grapefruit-size   something the size of a grapefruit, a large, round fruit

tilted   leaned

flippers   wide, flat limbs on certain sea animals, used for swimming; objects that people wear on their feet to swim faster and more easily

propelled   moved something with force; thrust

aid   help, assistance

built-in   having as part of something; something that cannot be removed

propulsion system   a system used to get an object to start moving and keep it moving

nursery (in this reading)   the place where young whales grow up

tropics   the hot region of Earth

4   In Hawaii Al [Giddings, a photographer,] and I were in the nursery, trying to see if we could **record** the short **grunts** and **squeals** **associated** with certain whale behaviors . . .

5   It might seem easy, but when swimming underwater, it is almost impossible to determine the direction sounds are coming from. Often, many whales are **vocalizing** at once, and the sounds may travel many miles.

6   In the weeks that followed we heard whales singing day and night, and once while underwater, whalesong was so loud that the air spaces in my body **vibrated**—a feeling something like being next to a very loud drum or in the **midst** of an **orchestra** . . .

Draw Conclusions

Sylvia Earle listens to whale songs for weeks. What conclusions can you draw about her?

---

record   make a sound or video recording of something on a disk or tape
grunts   short, deep sounds, from the throat
squeals   high-pitched screams
associated   connected

vocalizing   speaking, singing
vibrated   shook
midst   the middle of a place or an activity
orchestra   a usually large group of musicians who play music on instruments, such as the violin and horns

About the Author

Sylvia Earle (born 1935)

As a child, Sylvia Earle loved nature and the ocean. When she grew up, Earle became a scientist. She studies plants and animals that live in the ocean. She has said, "I was swept off my feet by a wave when I was three and have been in love with the sea ever since . . . everywhere [there are] strange and wonderful forms of life that occur only underwater."

►Why do you think that Sylvia Earle wrote "Eye to Eye"? To teach people about humpback whales? Or to describe what it was like to study humpback whales? Explain.

Beyond the Reading

Reading Comprehension

Question-Answer Relationships (QAR)

"Right There" Questions

1. **Recall Facts** Who is the author of "Eye to Eye"?
2. **Recall Details** Where is Earle when she first sees the female humpback whale?

"Think and Search" Questions

3. **Recognize Cause and Effect** Why is it often difficult for Earle to tell where whale sounds are coming from?
4. **Explain** Reread paragraph 2. What helps humpback whales swim faster than humans?
5. **Identify** What does Earle use to help her swim underwater?

"Author and You" Question

6. **Paraphrase** Reread paragraph 6. Using your own words, describe what the whale songs sound like to Earle.

"On Your Own" Questions

7. **Evaluate** What do you think would be interesting about being an ocean scientist? What would be scary?
8. **Understand Author's Perspective** What question would you like to ask the author?

Activity Book
p. 154

Student
CD-ROM

Build Reading Fluency

Read Silently

Reading silently is good practice. It helps you learn to read faster. An effective reader reads silently for increasing lengths of time.

1. Listen to the audio recording of paragraphs 1 and 2 on page 292.
2. Listen to the chunks of words as you follow along.
3. Reread paragraphs 1 and 2 silently two times.
4. Your teacher will time your second reading.
5. Raise your hand when you are done.
6. Record your timing.

Listen, Speak, Interact

Describe a Place That You Have Explored

When you explore, you go somewhere new or do something to learn new things. What places have you explored?

1. On a piece of paper, brainstorm a list of places that you have explored; for example, a community park.
2. Choose one place on your list. Write a description of three things that you learned about this place.
3. In a small group, take turns describing the place that you explored. Ask and answer questions about each description.

Places That I Have Explored

- the park in my community
- Blue Beach
- a new store by my house

In the park in my community:

People play soccer in the park.

There's a statue of a horse.

There's a garden with roses.

Elements of Literature

Analyze Figurative Language

Sylvia Earle uses **figurative language** to help readers form images (pictures) in their minds.

One way to use figurative language is to use the words *like* or *as* to compare two things. This is called a *simile*.

The whale looked **as big as** a bus.

(the whale)—(big)—(a bus)

The author compares the size of the whale to a bus. It shows readers how big the whale is.

1. Write these sentences in your Reading Log.
   a. The whale's eyes were as large as grapefruits.
   b. The whale sounded like a loud, deep drum.
2. Complete a word web like the one shown. In the outer circles, write the two things that are being compared in each sentence. In the middle circle, write what quality describes the two things.

Activity Book
p. 155

Student
CD-ROM

Word Study

Recognize Compound Adjectives

Compound adjectives are adjectives that are made up of two or more words. Many compound adjectives contain a **hyphen** (-). You can often find the meaning of a compound adjective by looking at the words it contains.

The hour-long movie was very funny.

Hour-long contains *hour* and *long.* It means "lasting for an hour."

First Word	Second Word	Compound Adjective	Meaning
hour +	long ⇒	hour-long	lasting an hour
+	⇒		
+	⇒		
+	⇒		

1. Read these sentences.
   a. Her grapefruit-size eyes met mine.
   b. Her fifteen-foot flippers propelled her past me.
   c. I glanced at my own slip-on flippers.
2. In your Personal Dictionary, complete a chart like the one shown. Write the words that make up each of the compound adjectives.

Personal Dictionary

The Heinle Newbury House Dictionary

Activity Book p. 156

Student CD-ROM

Grammar Focus

Recognize and Use the Simple Past Tense

The **simple past tense** describes an action that began and ended in the past. Regular past tense verbs end in *-d* or *-ed.*

She tilt**ed** right, then left.

Some verbs are irregular. Their past tense forms are spelled differently. The verb *be* has two past tense forms.

Reread paragraph 6 of the selection and find the four past tense verbs in it.

Simple Form	Past Tense Form
go	went
meet	met
see	saw
hear	heard

Be: Past Tense Forms	
I/He/She	**was** at school yesterday.
You/We/They	**were** at school yesterday.

Activity Book pp. 157–158

Student Handbook

Student CD-ROM

From Reading to Writing

Write a Personal Narrative

On a piece of paper, draw a picture of an unusual animal. Then write a two-paragraph personal narrative about it.

1. Use the first-person pronouns *I, me, we,* and *us.* These pronouns show that you are describing what happened to you and what you saw.

2. Use figurative language. Compare the animal to something else.

3. Use comparative and superlative adjectives to describe great things about your animal. For example, your animal might be stronger than another animal, or it might be the strongest of a group.

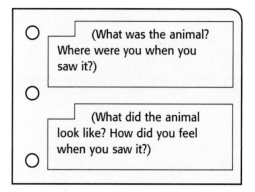

4. Enter your draft on a computer. Use spell check to check your spelling.

Activity Book   Student
p. 159   Handbook

Across Content Areas

Identify Types of Scientists

Sylvia Earle is a **scientist**—a person who works in science. There are many different types of scientists. Here is a list of some types:

biologist	a person who studies living things
botanist	a person who studies plants and trees
zoologist	a person who studies animals
marine biologist	a person who studies things that live in the ocean

Work with a partner to write a job application form. Suppose this form would be used to hire one of these scientists for your town. Organize the form to include sections for name, address, and experience. Also include a section for a description of the job. Revise your form as you think of more needs for the community.

Activity Book
p. 160

CHAPTER 2

The Fun They Had

a science fiction
short story
by Isaac Asimov

Objectives

Reading Make inferences from text evidence as you read science fiction.

Listening and Speaking Present advantages and disadvantages.

Grammar Use dependent clauses with *because*.

Writing Write an ending to a science fiction short story.

Content Science: Define Internet terms.

Use Prior Knowledge

Compare and Contrast Schools

Compare and contrast schools that you know about.

1. Work with a small group. Compare and contrast these topics:
   a. what the school buildings look like
   b. the number of students that go to the schools
   c. the subjects taught
   d. the ages of the students
2. On a separate piece of paper, complete a Venn Diagram like this one. Use the information from your discussion to complete the diagram with your group.

3. Discuss your Venn Diagram with the class.

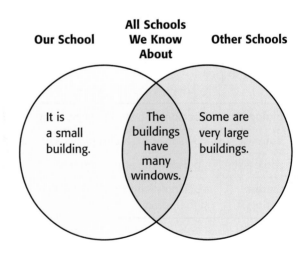

All Schools
Our School　**We Know**　**Other Schools**
About

It is a small building.

The buildings have many windows.

Some are very large buildings.

Build Background

Schooling in the United States

Schools in the United States have changed over the years. In the mid-1600s, people from England set up the first public schools paid for by the public. Many of the school buildings had only one room. Students of all ages learned together.

Content Connection

In the United States, **public schools** are free for students and are paid for by people in the community and the government.

In the mid-1800s, many schools put children into grades. Each grade had its own room and teacher. Many states wrote laws saying that all children must go to school. Today, all children in the United States must go to school. They learn many different subjects.

Build Vocabulary

Explore Multiple Meaning Words

Multiple meaning words are words that are spelled and pronounced the same but have different meanings. For example, *run* can mean "to move quickly on foot" or "to make a machine work."

I love to exercise. I <u>run</u> five miles a day.

You know from the first sentence that the person is talking about exercise. So, *run* in this sentence means "to move quickly on foot."

Decide which meaning the words have in these sentences.

1. The movie was very <u>funny</u>. I laughed until my sides hurt.
   a. causing laughter
   b. odd, strange
2. I liked the concert a lot. The last song was <u>awfully</u> good.
   a. badly, dreadfully
   b. very

The Heinle Newbury House Dictionary

Activity Book *p. 161*

Student CD-ROM

Text Structure

Science Fiction

"The Fun They Had" is **science fiction.** Science fiction is a made-up story that is based on scientific facts (information from science that is true). Look for the features of science fiction in the chart.

In "The Fun They Had," the author describes how machines can change school. Think about which changes you think are good changes as you read. Also think about changes that might cause problems.

Science Fiction	
Setting	often takes place in the future, a time that has not happened yet
Characters	see the world differently from how people do today
Scientific Facts	machines and ways of life that the author imagines

Student
CD-ROM

Reading Strategy

Make Inferences from Text Evidence

When you **make inferences from text evidence,** you use clues in a text. You also use your experience to understand a story better.

Suppose you are reading a story about a man who puts on a heavy coat, a hat, and boots. You can use these clues to make an inference that the story takes place in winter.

Use a chart like the one below as you read. This will help you make inferences.

Text Evidence	What I Know from My Experience	Inferences
The man puts on a heavy coat, a hat, and boots.	People wear this clothing when it is cold.	The story takes place in winter.

Student
CD-ROM

The Fun They Had

a science fiction story
by Isaac Asimov

1   Margie even wrote about it that night in her diary. On the page headed May 17, 2157, she wrote, "Today Tommy found a real book!"

2   It was a very old book. Margie's grandfather once said that when he was a little boy *his* grandfather told him that there was a time when all stories were printed on paper.

3   They turned the pages, which were yellow and **crinkly**, and it was awfully funny to read words that stood still instead of moving the way they were supposed to—on a screen, you know. And then, when they turned back to the page before, it had the same words on it that it had had when they read it the first time.

4   "Gee," said Tommy, "what a **waste**. When you're through with the book, you just throw it away, I guess. Our television screen must have had a million books on it, and it's good for plenty more. I wouldn't throw it away."

5   "Same as mine," said Margie. She was eleven and hadn't seen as many textbooks as Tommy had. He was thirteen.

6   She said, "Where did you find it?"

7   "In my house." He pointed without looking, because he was busy reading. "In the **attic**."

8   "What's it about?"

9   "School."

Audio
CD 2, Tr. 8

Make Inferences from Text Evidence

How often do you think Margie and Tommy read books? Why do you think so?

---

crinkly formed into folds or thin lines
waste a loss of something because it is not used well

attic a space, often used for storage, under the roof of a house

Make Inferences from Text Evidence

What inference can you make about how well Margie does in school? Which evidence did you use to make your inference?

10   Margie was **scornful.** "School? What's there to write about school? I hate school."

11   Margie always hated school, but now she hated it more than ever. The mechanical teacher had been giving her test after test in geography, and she had been doing worse and worse until her mother had shaken her head **sorrowfully** and sent for the County Inspector.

12   He was a round little man with a red face and a whole box of tools with dials and wires. He smiled at Margie and gave her an apple, then took the teacher apart. Margie had hoped he wouldn't know how to put it together again, but he knew how all right, and, after an hour or so, there it was again, large and black and ugly, with a big screen on which all the lessons were shown and the questions were asked. That wasn't so bad. The part Margie hated most was the **slot** where she had to put homework and test papers. She always had to write them out in a **punch code** they made her learn when she was six years old, and the mechanical teacher **calculated** the **mark in no time.**

---

scornful   showing dislike
sorrowfully   in a way that shows sadness
slot   a small opening, usually shaped like a rectangle
punch code   a way of showing information by making holes in a piece of paper; the paper is then read by machines

calculated   did math to figure something, such as a grade
mark   a grade, such as on a test
in no time   quickly, fast

13 The Inspector had smiled after he was finished and patted Margie's head. He said to her mother, "It's not the little girl's fault, Mrs. Jones. I think the geography **sector** was **geared** a little too quick. Those things happen sometimes. I've slowed it up to an average ten-year level. Actually, the overall **pattern** of her **progress** is quite **satisfactory.**" And he patted Margie's head again.

14 Margie was disappointed. She had been hoping they would take the teacher away altogether. They had once taken Tommy's teacher away for nearly a month because the history sector had **blanked out** completely.

15 So she said to Tommy, "Why would anyone write about school?"

16 Tommy looked at her with very **superior** eyes. "Because it's not our kind of school, stupid. This is the old kind of school that they had hundreds and hundreds of years ago." He added **loftily,** pronouncing the word carefully, "*Centuries* ago."

17 Margie was hurt. "Well, I don't know what kind of school they had all that time ago." She read the book over his shoulder for a while, then said, "Anyway, they had a teacher."

18 "Sure they had a teacher, but it wasn't a *regular* teacher. It was a man."

19 "A man? How could a man be a teacher?"

---

sector a section, or part

geared set up, prepared

pattern a repeated set of events, characteristics, or features

progress advancement, movement toward a goal

satisfactory good enough, acceptable

blanked out could not be seen

superior giving the feeling that you are better than others

loftily as if higher above, or better, than others

centuries time periods of 100 years

Make Inferences from Text Evidence

Which text evidence could you use to make the inference that Margie thinks Tommy is smart?

20   "Well, he just told the boys and girls things and gave them homework and asked them questions."

21   "A man isn't smart enough."

22   "Sure he is. My father knows as much as my teacher."

23   "He can't. A man can't know as much as a teacher."

24   "He knows almost as much, I **betcha**."

25   Margie wasn't prepared to **dispute** that. She said, "I wouldn't want a strange man in my house to teach me."

26   Tommy screamed with laughter. "You don't know much, Margie. The teachers didn't live in the house. They had a special building and all the kids went there."

27   "And all the kids learned the same thing?"

28   "Sure, if they were the same age."

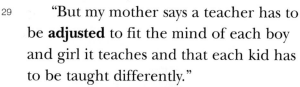

29   "But my mother says a teacher has to be **adjusted** to fit the mind of each boy and girl it teaches and that each kid has to be taught differently."

30   "Just the same, they didn't do it that way then. If you don't like it, you don't have to read the book."

31   "I didn't say I didn't like it," Margie said quickly. She wanted to read about those **funny** schools.

32   They weren't even half-finished when Margie's mother called, "Margie! School!"

33   Margie looked up. "Not yet, Mamma."

34   "Now!" said Mrs. Jones. "And it's probably time for Tommy, too."

---

betcha   informal pronunciation for "bet you," meaning that you think you are right and another person is wrong

dispute   argue against

adjusted   changed

funny   odd, strange

Make Inferences from Text Evidence

What text evidence supports the inference that Margie could be a good student if she wanted to?

35   Margie said to Tommy, "Can I read the book some more with you after school?"

36   "Maybe," he said **nonchalantly.** He walked away **whistling,** the dusty old book **tucked** beneath his arm.

37   Margie went into the schoolroom. It was right next to her bedroom, and the mechanical teacher was on and waiting for her. It was always on at the same time every day except Saturday and Sunday, because her mother said little girls learned better if they learned at regular hours.

38   The screen was lit up, and it said, "Today's **arithmetic** lesson is on the addition of **proper fractions.** Please **insert** yesterday's homework in the **proper** slot."

39   Margie did so with a sigh. She was thinking about the old schools they had when her grandfather's grandfather was a little boy. All the kids from the whole neighborhood came, laughing and shouting in the schoolyard, sitting together in the same schoolroom, going home together at the end of the day. They learned the same things, so they could help one another on the homework and talk about it.

---

nonchalantly   in a relaxed, carefree way

whistling   making a musical sound by blowing air through the lips

tucked   put beneath something else

arithmetic   math dealing with addition, subtraction, multiplication, and division

proper fractions   fractions (numbers smaller than whole numbers) in which the top number is smaller than the bottom number, for example ½

insert   put something into something else

proper   correct

40　　And the teachers were people . . .

41　　The mechanical teacher was flashing on the screen: "When we add the fractions ½ and ¼—"

42　　Margie was thinking about how the kids must have loved it in the old days. She was thinking about the fun they had.

Make Inferences from Text Evidence

What inference can you make about how Margie feels about going to school alone? Explain.

About the Author

Isaac Asimov (1920–1992)

Isaac Asimov was born in Russia. He moved to the United States as a young child. When he was 18, he sold his first science fiction story to a magazine. Later, Asimov studied science in college and became a college teacher. But his real love was writing. He wrote almost 500 books! Asimov once said, "All I do is write. I do practically nothing else . . . The longer I write, the easier it gets."

➤ Why do you think that Isaac Asimov wrote "The Fun They Had"? To explain his opinion? Or do you think he just wanted to write something that would be fun to read? If you could ask Isaac Asimov one question about this story, what would it be?

Beyond the Reading

Reading Comprehension

Question-Answer Relationships (QAR)

"Right There" Questions

1. **Recall Facts** What does Tommy find?
2. **Recall Details** What did Margie's grandfather tell her about books?
3. **Recall Details** What does the County Inspector fix at Margie's house?

"Think and Search" Questions

4. **Identify** Name three things that Margie learns about old schools.
5. **Compare and Contrast** How is Margie's mechanical teacher different from the teachers described in Tommy's book? How are the teachers similar?
6. **Recognize Character Traits** How did Tommy behave toward Margie? Was he kind to her? Did he make fun of her?

"Author and You" Questions

7. **Understand Plot** Why did someone write a book about old schools?

8. **Understand Author's Tone** From the tone of the story, do you think that Isaac Asimov liked the idea of mechanical teachers? Explain what effect this has on the text.
9. **Paraphrase** In your own words, tell what Margie's feelings were about school.

"On Your Own" Questions

10. **Evaluate** How does the illustrator show the mechanical teacher? Do all the pictures help you to better understand the story? Why or why not?
11. **Evaluate** Would you like to learn from a mechanical teacher? Why or why not?

Activity Book
p. 162

Student
CD-ROM

Build Reading Fluency

Rapid Word Recognition

Rapidly recognizing words helps increase your reading rate. It is an important characteristic of effective readers.

1. With a partner, review the words in the box.
2. Read the words aloud for one minute. Your teacher will time you.

wrote	through	once	page	once	wrote
diary	page	through	once	page	once
page	know	diary	wrote	know	diary
once	once	page	diary	wrote	know
know	diary	wrote	know	through	page

3. Count how many words you read in one minute.

Listen, Speak, Interact

Present Advantages and Disadvantages

What do you think about learning on a computer?

1. With a partner, make a list of advantages (things that are good) and disadvantages (things that are bad) about learning on a computer.

Learning on a Computer	
Advantages	Disadvantages
Computers are fun to learn on.	You can't talk to a computer as you can to a teacher.

2. Your teacher will lead a class discussion. As you present your ideas, your teacher will write them on the board.
3. As a class, choose three of the most important advantages and three of the most important disadvantages.
4. Now decide whether your advantages and disadvantages are facts (things that can be proven) or opinions (things that people think or believe).

Elements of Literature

Analyze Setting

Every story has a **setting.** Setting is the time and place of a story. In "The Fun They Had," the setting is an important part of the story. It puts the reader in a certain place and time. It shows how the characters' lives are different from people's lives today.

1. Work with a partner. Reread paragraphs 1, 32, and 37 and take notes on details that describe the setting. Answer these questions about the setting of "The Fun They Had." Write your answers in your Reading Log.

a. In what year does the story happen?
b. On what date does Tommy find the book?
c. Where are Tommy and Margie reading the book?
d. Where is Margie's schoolroom?

2. With a partner, discuss why the setting is important. How would this story be different if it were set in another time and place?

Reading Log

Activity Book
p. 163

Student
CD-ROM

Word Study

Use the Latin Root Words to Find Meaning

Root words are the words from which other words are made. Many English words are based on root words from other languages, such as Latin.

For example, the word *inspect* is based on the Latin root word *specere*. This word means "to look."

You can use this root word to help understand the word *inspect*. Do you see a word part from *specere* in *inspect*? *Inspect* means "to look at carefully."

Specere	
Word	Meaning
inspect	to look at carefully
inspector	a person who _____
inspection	the act of _____

1. Copy the chart in your Personal Dictionary. Each of the words comes from the word *specere*.

2. Use the meaning of *specere* to help you complete the definitions.

3. Check your answers in a dictionary.

Personal Dictionary The Heinle Newbury House Dictionary Activity Book p. 164 Student CD-ROM

Grammar Focus

Use Dependent Clauses with *Because*

A **clause** is part of a sentence. It has a subject and a verb. An **independent clause** can stand alone. A **dependent clause** cannot stand alone.

Writers often join two sentences with the word *because*. By adding *because,* a sentence becomes a dependent clause.

Independent Clause	Dependent Clause
Margie read the book,	because she wanted to learn about the past.

You use a comma before a dependent clause with *because.*

1. On a piece of paper, combine these sentences using *because.*
   a. They took his teacher away. The history sector had blanked out.
   b. Margie's mother told her to go to sleep. It was very late.

2. In each sentence, underline the independent clause one time and the dependent clause two times.

3. Write two sentences that have a dependent clause with *because.*

Activity Book pp. 165–166 Student Handbook Student CD-ROM

From Reading to Writing

Write an Ending to a Science Fiction Short Story

"The Fun They Had" ends with Margie thinking about what it would be like to go to school with other children. Write a paragraph about what happens next.

1. Brainstorm ideas for your paragraph. Your ideas can include a scientific idea or a tool that changes how characters live. Here is an example: Margie might build a time machine and travel to the year 2008.

2. Decide which characters will be in your paragraph. Will you also make up a new character?

3. Decide the setting. Does it take place in Margie's house? On a different planet?

4. Include a dependent clause with *because*. Use correct punctuation.

5. Use nouns correctly to show how many people, places, and things.

6. Use progressive verbs to tell about actions that are happening.

Student Handbook

Across Content Areas

Define Internet Terms

We use the Internet and the World Wide Web to learn about different topics. Here are some things to help you when looking for facts.

browser a tool that lets you visit sites on the Internet or World Wide Web

URL (uniform resource locator) the address of a Web page, such as http://www.heinle.visions.com

cursor an arrow or black line on a computer screen that shows where you are writing or clicking your mouse

links words or pictures on a Web page (usually underlined or a different color) that bring you to other pages when you click on them with your cursor

The picture below shows a Web page. Match the Internet terms with the information in the picture.

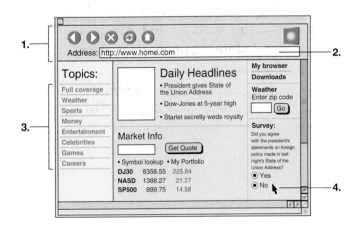

Activity Book
p. 168

CHAPTER 3

Using the Scientific Method

an excerpt from
a textbook
by Stephen Kramer

Objectives

Reading Recognize cause and effect relationships as you read an informational text.

Listening and Speaking Use information to raise unanswered questions.

Grammar Use *might* to show possibility.

Writing Write an informational text.

Content Science: Learn about sleep.

Use Prior Knowledge

Share Knowledge About Science Experiments

Science is the study of the natural world or the world around us. It explains why things are the way they are. "Using the Scientific Method" describes the steps for doing a science experiment.

A science experiment is a very careful plan or test. It helps scientists find out why something happens. It also can explain how something works.

What do you know about science experiments? Answer the questions below to gather your ideas:

1. Have you ever done a science experiment? What was it about?
2. What do you do in a science experiment? Ask questions? Make a plan? Observe or look carefully? Take notes?
3. With your class, discuss your experiences with science.

Build Background

The Scientific Method

Scientists are people who ask questions and find out why things happen. To do this, scientists use the **scientific method.** The scientific method starts with an idea. This idea is called a **hypothesis.** The hypothesis can be about why and how something happens or it also can be about how people act.

Scientists then do an experiment to test the idea. The facts from the experiment are called the results. The results help the scientists learn if their hypothesis is true.

Many famous people have used the scientific method to discover new things. Do you know any famous scientists?

Content Connection

Scientists began to use the scientific method during the 1600s.

Build Vocabulary

Use a Dictionary to Locate Meanings and Pronounce Words

The selection includes words related to **behavior**—ways of acting.

1. Look up these words in a dictionary. With your teacher, pronounce the words and read the meanings.

| Pronunciation | Meaning |

a. curious /ˈkyʊriəs/ *adj.* interested in knowing about things: *I am curious; where did you buy that beautiful dress?*

b. focus

c. frustrated

2. Match the underlined words in the sentences with one of the words you looked up in the dictionary.
   a. He will work for a long time putting the pieces of a puzzle together.
   b. He gets mad at the puzzle and throws the pieces across the room.
   c. Your older brother or sister might like to know.

Write a sentence using each behavior word. Be sure you spell each syllable in the word correctly.

The Heinle Newbury House Dictionary

Activity Book
p. 169

Student CD-ROM

Text Structure

Informational Text

"Using the Scientific Method" is an **informational text.** It gives true information about a real-life topic. There are different kinds of informational texts. The author of this selection gives the process (directions) for doing an experiment. In an informational text, authors often use graphic features such as bold and italic type, bullets, and lists with numbers to organize the information. Look for the features of an informational text that are listed in the chart as you read.

Informational Text	
Facts	tell information that is true
Graphic Features	show the organization of a reading

Student
CD-ROM

Reading Strategy

Recognize Cause and Effect Relationships

A **cause** is the reason why something happens. An **effect** is something that happens as a result of the cause. Authors sometimes present ideas using cause and effect. This helps them explain relationships.

Here are ways to find a cause and effect relationship. Ask "Did this happen *because* of that?" You might also ask "Did this *make* that happen?" If you can answer "yes" to these questions, you have found a cause and effect relationship.

Look at this sentence.

Ramona forgot to add sugar <u>so</u> the lemonade is not sweet.

Ramona forgot to add the sugar. This is the cause. The lemonade is not sweet. This is the effect. The lemonade is not sweet *because* Ramona forgot to add the sugar.

Look for cause and effect relationships as you read the selection. Remember to ask these questions to help you: "Did this happen *because* of that?" "Did this *make* that happen?"

Student
CD-ROM

Using the Scientific Method

an excerpt from a textbook
by Stephen Kramer

You can probably think of some questions that the scientific method could help you answer. Perhaps you have a younger brother. You know that he is much harder to get along with when he misses his afternoon **nap.** But what is it about his behavior that makes him harder to get along with? How does he act differently? Let's use the steps of the scientific method to see how you could find the answer.

1. *Ask a question.*

"How does my little brother act differently when he misses his afternoon nap?"

2. ***Gather*** *information about the question.*

Watch your brother on days when he takes a nap and on days when he misses his nap. Ask your parents or brothers or sisters how he acts differently.

3. ***Form*** *a hypothesis.*

"My little brother has less patience in the evenings on days he misses his nap than on days he takes a nap."

Audio
CD 2, Tr. 9

Recognize Cause and Effect Relationships

What is one cause that can have an effect on how the younger brother acts?

---

nap a short sleep
gather bring together

form make up

5 **4. Test** *the hypothesis.*

Perhaps you've noticed that some evenings your little brother will work for a long time putting the pieces of a **puzzle** together. Other times he gets mad at the puzzle and throws the pieces across the room. You might decide to **measure** your brother's patience by checking how long he will work on putting together a puzzle.

Recognize Cause and Effect Relationships

What causes the little brother to throw the pieces across the room?

a. Pick five days when your brother   6 takes a nap. After dinner on those days give him a puzzle to put together. Count how many pieces he uses before **giving up.** This is the **control group.**

b. Pick five days when your   7 brother misses his nap. After dinner on those days give him a puzzle to put together. Count how many pieces he uses before giving up. This is the **experimental group.**

Control Group of 5 Days: Naps   **Experimental Group of 5 Days: No Naps**

---

test   try out

puzzle   a game in which stiff paper that has been cut into pieces is put back together

measure   find the total or size of

giving up   stopping doing something

control group   a group of people or objects used in an experiment to compare all other groups to

experimental group   a group of people or things that is being compared to the control group

Of course, you would have to use puzzles that were all about the same **difficulty.** You would also have to be careful not to use one puzzle too many times, or your brother might begin to put it together more easily than the others.

However, if you did have enough puzzles, you could probably get a good idea of how much patience your brother had each evening. If your brother always put together more of the puzzle after taking a nap, he might also be more patient and easier to get along with. What if the **results** of your experiment don't **support** your hypothesis? Perhaps the number of puzzle pieces your brother puts together is not really a good measure of his patience. You might try to think of another way to measure how much patience he has.

Recognize Cause and Effect Relationships

If you used the same puzzle over and over, what would the effect on the experiment be?

---

difficulty   how hard something is to do

results   something that happens because of an action

support   agree with

10   If there is no evidence from any of your experiments to support your hypothesis, try a different one. A hypothesis you could test quite easily would be, "My brother cries more often in the evenings on days when he misses his nap."

Recognize Cause and Effect Relationships

What does the author say the effect is when the little brother misses his nap?

11   **a.** Pick five days when your brother takes a nap. Count the number of times he cries between 6:00 P.M. and 8:00 P.M. This is the control group.

b. Pick five days when your brother   12
misses his nap. Count the number of times he cries between 6:00 P.M. and 8:00 P.M. This is the experimental group.

Examine your results. Does your   13
brother really seem to cry more in the evenings on days when he misses his nap?

5. *Tell someone what you found.*   14

Your parents might be interested. Your older brother or sister might like to know. What you learned might make **babysitting** easier.

---

examine look at carefully

babysitting taking care of a child while the parents are away

15   Everywhere you look there are questions you could use the scientific method to answer.

16
- Which kind of food does your dog like best?
- Does your mother go to bed earlier on **weekday** nights or on **weekend** nights?
- Do you eat more food on days when you go to school or on days when you stay home?
- Does your father drive the car more on weekdays or on weekends?
- Do dishes really get cleaner if you wash them in hot water instead of cold water?
- Is your older sister more **likely** to help you if you say please?

Recognize Cause and Effect Relationships

What might be the effect of saying "please" to an older sister?

---

weekday   Monday, Tuesday, Wednesday, Thursday, or Friday

weekend   Saturday or Sunday

likely   to be expected

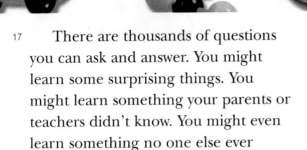

17   There are thousands of questions you can ask and answer. You might learn some surprising things. You might learn something your parents or teachers didn't know. You might even learn something no one else ever knew. That's what makes science exciting. There are all kinds of new **discoveries** to be made. All you have to do is ask the right question—and know how to answer it.

> **Recognize Cause and Effect Relationships**
>
> What makes science exciting?

---

discoveries   the finding of something new

About the Author

Stephen Kramer (born 1953)

Stephen Kramer has always loved science. He enjoys writing about it, too. Kramer also likes teaching science to fifth grade and high school students. He started a Web site for young people who like science. Kramer also likes to learn new things. He is learning to play the bagpipes (a musical instrument) for fun!

➤ Which of the following sentences do you think Stephen Kramer would most agree with? Why do you think so?

1. Science experiments are difficult and a lot of trouble to do.
2. Science experiments can be creative and fun.

Beyond the Reading

Reading Comprehension

Question-Answer Relationships (QAR)

"Right There" Questions

1. **Recall Facts** What is a hypothesis?
2. **Recall Facts** What tools are used to find out about the younger brother's patience?

"Think and Search" Questions

3. **Compare and Contrast** Compare the brother's behavior when he naps with his behavior when he does not nap.
4. **Identify Steps in a Process** Look at paragraph 6. What step comes after the younger brother is given the puzzle to put together?

"Author and You" Question

5. **Draw Conclusions** The experiment you read about shows the brother crying more often without a nap. What conclusion can you make?

"On Your Own" Questions

6. **Generalize** How could an experiment like this help a family?
7. **Ask Questions** What questions would you like to ask and explore? Do you think you can use the scientific method to find the answers? Why or why not?
8. **Revise Questions** Discuss one of your questions above with a partner. Do you need to revise your question? If so, do it.

Activity Book p. 170   Student CD-ROM

Build Reading Fluency

Read Aloud to Engage Listeners

Reading aloud helps increase your fluency and expression. Learning to read with expression makes others want to listen to you.

1. Listen to the audio recording of "Using the Scientific Method."
2. Turn to page 316 and follow along.
3. Pay attention to phrasing and expression.
4. With a partner, read aloud paragraph 1 three times.
5. Read in front of the class with expression.

Listen, Speak, Interact

Use Information to Raise Unanswered Questions

Stephen Kramer shows you how to use the scientific method to find the answers to two questions. He also gives some other questions you could answer using the scientific method.

1. Work with a small group. Reread the questions in paragraph 16 of the selection.
2. Choose one question from the list. Then talk about an experiment you could do to find out the answer.

3. Think of additional questions you could answer using the scientific method. Make a list of these questions with your group. Be sure to use a question mark at the end of each question. Which questions does your group find the most interesting? Which would you revise?
4. Present your best questions to the class. Make sure to use words from the reading selection in your questions and answers.

Elements of Literature

Recognize the Style of Direct Address

Style is how authors use language to express themselves. Style can include many elements, such as word choice and the use of long or short sentences.

In this selection, part of the style is **direct address.** This means that the author speaks directly to the reader using the pronoun *you.*

Perhaps you have a younger brother.
(paragraph 1)

The author also uses direct address by writing words the reader might say. These words are in quotation marks.

"My little brother has less patience in the evenings on days he misses his nap than on days he takes a nap."
(paragraph 4)

1. Look in paragraphs 2, 5, and 10. Find places in the selection where the author uses the pronoun *you.* Then find words the reader might say.
2. Why do you think the author writes the selection using this style? Does the style of direct address make the selection easier to understand? Why or why not?

Activity Book
p. 171

Student
CD-ROM

Word Study

Use Greek Word Origins

Learning about a word's history and origin can help you understand its meaning. English has many words that come from Greek. Read this sentence from the selection:

> What if the results of your experiment don't support your hypothesis?

The word *hypothesis* comes from the Greek word *thesis*, which means "to set down." When you form a hypothesis you "set down," or present, an idea.

1. Look at the chart. First look at the meanings of the Greek words. Use these meanings to determine the meanings of the English words.

Greek Words	Meaning of Greek Words	English Word
meta hodos	with (meta) a way (hodos)	method
bios graph	life writing	biography

Choose from these meanings:
a. the story of a person's life
b. a process for doing something

2. Write the words and their meanings in your Personal Dictionary.
3. Check your answers in a dictionary.

Personal Dictionary   The Heinle Newbury House Dictionary   Activity Book *p. 172*   Student CD-ROM

Grammar Focus

Use *Might* to Show Possibility

Look at this sentence from the text:

> If your brother always put together more of the puzzle after taking a nap, he might also be more patient.

The modal verb *might* means *it is possible*. Use *might* with the simple form of a verb.

Subject	Modal Verb	Simple Verb
he	might	be

Think about next weekend. On a piece of paper, write two sentences about things that you might do.

> *I might go to the mall with my family.*

Activity Book *pp. 173–174*   Student Handbook   Student CD-ROM

From Reading to Writing

Write an Informational Text

Work with a partner. Write three paragraphs that explain the process.

1. Brainstorm a list of things that you and your partner know how to do.
2. Choose one thing from your list. Write instructions on how to do it.
3. Use nouns correctly to show how many things are needed in each step.
4. Use the future tense with *will* to tell the reader how the process will help.

Activity Book
p. 175

Student
Handbook

How to _____

○ **Introduction**
Tell about the process that you will explain.

○ **Step-by-Step Instructions**
Explain how readers can do the process.
1. First step.
2. Second step.
(Use as many steps as you need to.)

○ **Conclusion**
Summarize your writing.
Tell how the process will help your readers.

Across Content Areas

Learn About Sleep

When we sleep, we are having a time of rest. We do not know what is going on around us. It may seem like we are not doing anything as we sleep. Yet, this time of rest is a very important part of our lives.

Read each sentence below. Match each underlined word with the correct definition.

1. When we sleep, we sometimes have <u>dreams</u> that we remember after we wake up.
2. Our bodies <u>repair</u> themselves as we sleep. This is why it is important to sleep enough when we are sick.
3. We need to sleep enough to have the <u>energy</u> to do activities.

Definitions
a. heal, or become healthy
b. the power, or ability, to work and play
c. pictures and stories that form in the mind during sleep

In a small group, create a form that lists everyone's sleep habits over one week. Organize the form to include the days of the week, hours of sleep, and dreams. Revise your form as you correct spelling and grammar mistakes.

Activity Book
p. 176

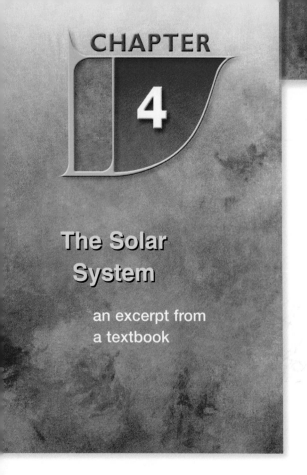

The Solar System

an excerpt from a textbook

Into the Reading

Objectives

Reading Summarize information as you read an excerpt from a textbook.

Listening and Speaking Paraphrase to recall information.

Grammar Identify superlative adjectives.

Writing Outline an informational text.

Content Science: Compare planet orbits.

Use Prior Knowledge

Summarize What You Know on a Chart

The reading selection in this chapter gives information about three planets: Mercury, Venus, and Mars.

1. On a piece of paper, complete a KWL (**K**now, **W**ant to Know, **L**earned) Chart like the one here.

2. In the first column, list what you know about each of these three planets. In the second column, list what you want to know.

3. After you read the selection, list what you learned about each of these planets in your KWL Chart.

	What I Know	*What I Want to Know*	*What I Learned*
Mercury	*It is close to the sun.*		
Venus		*Could humans live there?*	
Mars			

Build Background

Our Solar System

Our solar system is made up of the sun and all the objects that move around the sun. The sun is the star in the center of the solar system. Nine planets move around the sun. They are Mercury, Venus, Earth, Mars, Jupiter, Saturn, Uranus, Neptune, and Pluto.

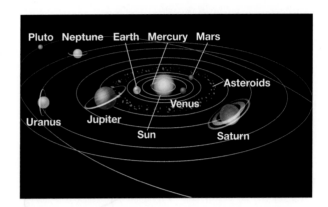

Content Connection

Smaller objects called comets and asteroids also move around the sun.

Build Vocabulary

Use Different Resources to Find Meaning

A **resource** is a tool that can help you research and find information.

1. A **table of contents** is a list of the sections or chapters of a book. It tells the page numbers where the section begins. Use the table of contents of this book to locate two favorite selections you read.
2. A **glossary** is a part of a book that gives the meanings of words. In this book, a glossary can be found at the bottom of each page of the reading selections. Find the word *gravity* in the glossary on page 330 of this book.

3. A **thesaurus** or **synonym finder** are books that you can use to find **synonyms** (words with similar meanings, such as *glad* and *happy*). Use a thesaurus or synonym finder to find a synonym for *vast*.
4. You can use the **Internet** to find a dictionary or a thesaurus. Type the keyword *dictionary* or *thesaurus* in a search engine to get started. Use a dictionary or the Internet to find the pronunciation of *mysterious*.

The Heinle
Newbury House
Dictionary

Activity Book
p. 177

Student
CD-ROM

Text Structure

Informational Text

"The Solar System" is an **informational text.** Informational texts give information about a certain topic. When you read a textbook, you are reading an informational text. Look for the features of informational texts listed in the chart.

As you read "The Solar System," notice how these features help you understand new information.

Informational Text	
Informational Writing	uses details and facts to explain what something is or how something works
Headings	titles that tell you what the part of the text is about
Pictures and Charts	drawings, charts, and photos that help you understand what you read

Student
CD-ROM

Reading Strategy

Summarize Information

When you **summarize information,** you say or write down the most important ideas in a reading or part of a reading.

Dogs make great pets for many reasons. Most are very smart and loving and like to play. They also protect your house. Finally, walking a dog is good exercise.

Summary: Dogs have several great qualities as pets.

Follow these steps as you read this selection:

1. Look for the most important information in the first and last sentences of each paragraph.
2. If you cannot summarize by reading these sentences, ask yourself, "What is the paragraph mostly about?"
3. Write a summary of each paragraph. Then write a summary of the entire selection.

Student
CD-ROM

The Solar System

an excerpt from a textbook

Starry Night, Vincent van Gogh, 1889.

The Inner Planets

What is it like on other planets?

1   It's a good thing that Earth is part of the solar system. Without the pull of **gravity** between the sun and Earth, Earth would find itself traveling off into space. Without the sun's light and energy, Earth would be a very cold and dark world. However, Earth does **orbit** the sun and so it has a place in the solar system. But Earth is not the only planet that is affected by the sun's **energy** and gravity.

Summarize Information

In writing, summarize how Earth is affected by the sun's energy and gravity.

Audio
CD 2, Tr. 10

2   People have always wondered what it's like on other **bodies** in the solar system. The moon is the only place people have been able to visit in person to answer that question. On July 20, 1969, **astronaut** Neil Armstrong was the first human to set foot on the moon.

Earth orbiting the sun

---

gravity   a natural force pulling objects to the ground
orbit   a path in space followed by a planet, moon, or space vehicle

energy   the power to do work
bodies   objects
astronaut   a person who flies into outer space

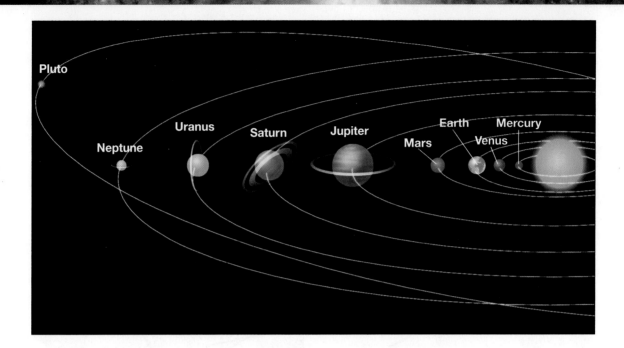

Pluto

Neptune

Uranus

Saturn

Jupiter

Mars

Earth

Venus

Mercury

3   Six other **missions** visited the moon after that to explore, collect **samples,** and **conduct experiments.** Space **probes** sent from Earth without **crews** have been able to travel **vast** distances through the solar system. The probes have found that the planets in the solar system are very different from one another.

Find Mercury, Venus, Earth, and Mars on the map. They are the inner planets because they orbit closest to the sun. The outer planets—Jupiter, Saturn, Uranus, Neptune, and Pluto— orbit much farther away. In this lesson, you will learn how being in the solar system affects the inner planets.   4

Summarize Information

Summarize orally the ways that people have learned about the planets in the solar system.

---

missions   groups of people sent somewhere for a purpose

samples   single things that show what larger groups are like

conduct   do something

experiments   tests done to see if something works or happens

probes   space vehicles

crews   workers on a space vehicle

vast   wide in area, immense

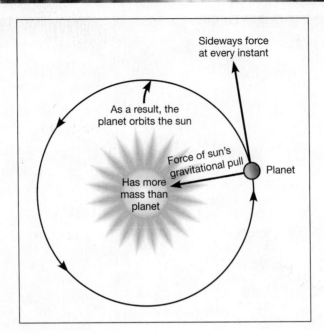

Sideways force
at every instant

As a result, the
planet orbits the sun

Force of sun's
gravitational pull

Planet

Has more
mass than
planet

The Sun—The Shining Sphere

5   The sun is the largest, brightest, and hottest object in the solar system. It is also the center of the solar system. The sun has more **mass** than all the other objects in our solar system put together. As a result, **gravitational force** causes all the planets to orbit around the sun—even planets as **distant** as Neptune and Pluto.

> **Summarize Information**
>
> What is the most important information in this paragraph? Write your answer.

The powerful sun is mostly made of a gas called hydrogen. In turn, the hydrogen is made of tiny **particles** called atoms. At the sun's center, hydrogen atoms may reach temperatures as high as 15 million degrees Celsius (°C). The higher the temperature, the faster the atoms move. Some of the atoms move so fast that they **smash** into each other and form a gas called helium. And when the hydrogen atoms change into helium, they also **release** energy. The energy heats up the sun and makes it **shine.** The sun has enough hydrogen to stay hot and shining for about 4 billion years.

6

---

mass   generally speaking the amount of matter (material) in an object

gravitational force   what causes one object to move toward another object because of gravity

distant   far away

particles   very small pieces of something

smash   hit against something

release   let something go

shine   send out light

Mercury—The Hot and Cold Planet

7   The closest planet to the sun is Mercury. Because it is so close to the sun, it is difficult to study Mercury from Earth. The brightness of the sun makes it hard to see. **Spacecraft** flying past Mercury have sent back to Earth pictures and information about this planet.

In some ways, Mercury is similar to our moon. This small planet is only a little larger than our moon and, like the moon, it is covered by dust, rocks, and bowl-shaped holes called craters. Thousands of meteorites (mē'tē ɹ ītz) —chunks of rock from outer space— formed the craters by **crashing** into Mercury. You can see Mercury's rocky surface and some of its many craters in the picture shown below.   8

> **Summarize Information**
>
> Write one sentence to summarize this paragraph.

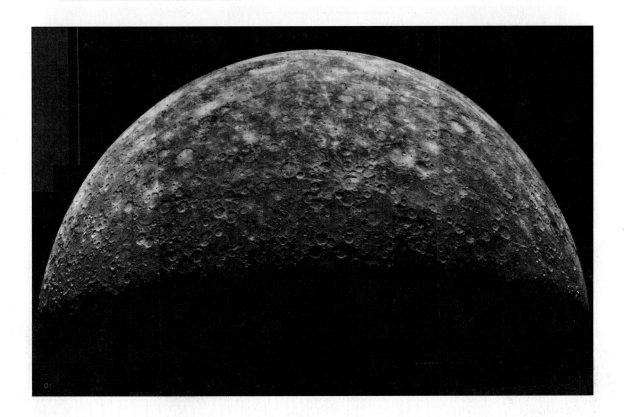

---

spacecraft   vehicles that fly in space

crashing   hitting onto something in a very hard way

9   When Mercury has **rotated** once around its **axis,** 59 Earth days have gone by. Long days combined with closeness to the sun and a very thin **atmosphere** explain how Mercury can be so hot and so cold. During the day, Mercury's thin atmosphere can't protect the planet from the sun's heating rays. The diagram below shows that daytime temperatures on Mercury can reach 407°C. At night, the atmosphere can't keep the heat in, so the temperature drops to about −183°C.

Summarize Information

Using your own words, orally summarize why Mercury is so hot during the day and so cold at night.

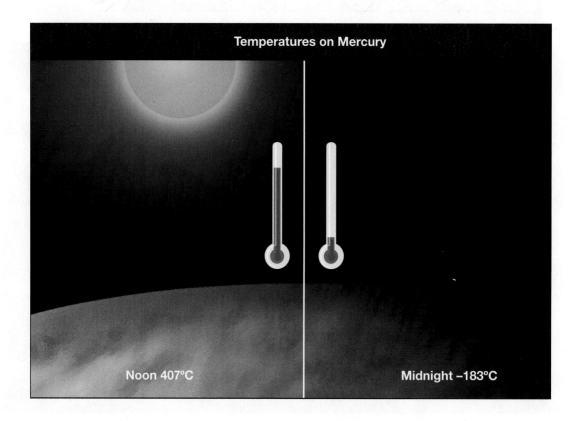

Temperatures on Mercury

Noon 407°C

Midnight −183°C

---

rotated moved around something, especially in a circle

axis a straight line around which an object turns

atmosphere the air space above Earth or another planet

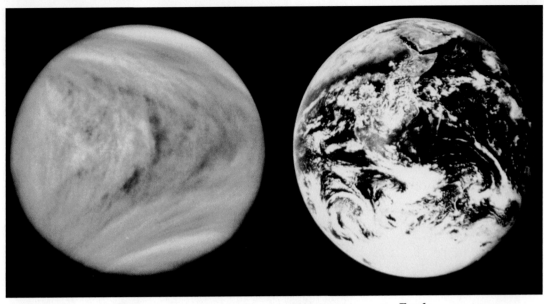

Venus   **Earth**

Venus—Cloudy Neighbor

10   Venus has a very thick atmosphere. The picture shows the thick, **swirling** clouds of **carbon dioxide** and acid that surround Venus. Powerful winds that move at speeds of over 300 kilometers per hour keep the clouds moving at all times. The atmosphere presses down on Venus like a very heavy blanket. In 1975, two large space probes from Earth landed on Venus. The probes lasted less than two hours before they were **flattened** by Venus's **crushing** atmosphere.

> **Summarize Information**
>
> In writing, summarize the most important information about Venus in this paragraph.

11   It takes Venus a little longer to rotate once around its axis than to **revolve** once around the sun. So, on Venus, a day is slightly longer than a year.

12   Compare the pictures of Venus and Earth. Venus is about the same size as Earth.

---

swirling   twisting and turning
carbon dioxide   a gas with no color, taste, or smell; people form carbon dioxide when they breathe out, but they cannot breathe in large amounts of carbon dioxide

flattened   made flat, crushed
crushing   able to crush or make flat
revolve   turn around something; move in a circle

Volcano on Venus

13   Like Earth, Venus has **mountains, valleys,** and **plains.** It even has a **volcano** bigger than any mountain on Earth. But Venus has no water. The heat on Venus is **unbearable**—about 450°C, enough to melt some kinds of metal! The thick atmosphere on Venus traps the sun's energy and holds it close to the surface, day and night. Venus is hotter than Mercury, even though Mercury is closer to the sun.

Life as we know it could not **survive** on Venus. Only rocks can **exist** in Venus's high temperatures and the crushing pressure of its atmosphere.

> **Summarize Information**
>
> Write a sentence summarizing how Venus is different from Earth.

---

mountains very high hills

valleys low areas of land between hills and mountains

plains wide areas of flat land

volcano a hill or mountain formed by hot, melted rock escaping from beneath the earth

unbearable something that cannot be dealt with, accepted, or tolerated

survive continue to live

exist be

Mars—The Red Planet

14   Mars is a little bit like Mercury, a little bit like Venus, and a lot like Earth. As you can see in the picture, Mars looks **reddish.** Mars is about half the size of Earth.

> **Summarize Information**
>
> Which sentence in this paragraph contains the most important information? Write your answer.

15   As on Mercury, craters **dot** the surface of Mars. The nights are much colder than the days. As on Venus, the atmosphere of Mars is mostly carbon dioxide. But Mars's atmosphere is not thick enough to **trap** the sun's heat.

16   Like Earth, Mars has changing seasons, and days that are about 24 hours long. The average winter temperature on Mars is a **chilly** −125°C. Summer temperatures can sometimes get as high as 0°C. Mars also has north and south **poles.** The poles are covered with caps of frozen carbon dioxide, called dry ice. When the poles heat up, the ice caps melt and get smaller. When the poles cool down, the ice caps get larger.

Mars seen from space

---

reddish   somewhat red
dot   mark with small points
trap   catch something

chilly   a little cold
poles   tops and bottoms of planets

17   Some of the ice at the poles may also be frozen water. Mars might have had a lot of water millions of years ago. The many valleys and canyons on the surface of Mars could have been formed by **rushing** rivers. The flat areas could be the bottoms of lakes that dried up long ago. However, the surface is now dry and the air contains only **traces** of **water vapor.** Notice in the picture below that the surface of Mars is dry, reddish, and dusty. The redness comes from **rusted iron** in the rocks.

Summarize Information

Orally summarize the most important information in this paragraph.

Mars Polar Lander

---

rushing moving quickly

traces very small amounts

water vapor water that has changed from liquid to gas, and usually cannot be seen

rusted iron iron (a metal) that is covered with a reddish-brown material

View of Mars from space probe

18　　Mars appears to be **lifeless** now. But does that mean there never was any life on Mars? In the summer of 1976, two space probes from Earth landed on the surface of Mars. The probes studied the air and the soil. They took pictures and sent the information back to Earth. Scientists found no signs of life after studying the information. Even so, some scientists think Mars could **support** life. Perhaps someday astronauts will go to Mars to try to answer this **mysterious** question.

> **Summarize Information**
>
> Write one sentence that summarizes this paragraph.

---

lifeless　without life
support　maintain, keep something going

mysterious　having no known cause

Beyond the Reading

Reading Comprehension

Question-Answer Relationships (QAR)

"Right There" Questions

1. **Recall Facts** List the inner planets.
2. **Recall Facts** Which gases create the light and heat from the sun?
3. **Recall Facts** What is the average winter temperature on Mars?

"Think and Search" Questions

4. **Explain** Why are Jupiter, Saturn, Uranus, Neptune, and Pluto called the outer planets?
5. **Identify Main Ideas** Why is it so difficult to study Mercury?
6. **Compare and Contrast** How is Mars the same or different from Mercury?
7. **Find Supporting Arguments** Why do scientists think that Venus cannot support life?

"Author and You" Question

8. **Describe** How does the author of "The Solar System" describe the atmosphere of Venus?

"On Your Own" Questions

9. **Evaluate** How does the illustrator's choice of pictures help you to understand the solar system?
10. **Evaluate Evidence** Based on "The Solar System," do you think that there was once water on Mars? Explain.

Activity Book
p. 178

Student
CD-ROM

Build Reading Fluency

Adjust Your Reading Rate to Scan

When you scan you adjust your reading rate to read fast. **Scanning** means glancing at the text for key words to help you answer questions. Work with a partner. Read aloud key words as you look for information. Write your answers on a piece of paper.

1. What astronaut first set foot on the moon?
2. Which planets are the "outer" planets?
3. What is the hottest object in the solar system?
4. What planet is closest to the sun?
5. Which planet has thick clouds of carbon dioxide?
6. Which planet looks reddish?

Listen, Speak, Interact

Paraphrase to Recall Information

Paraphrasing is another way to think about a reading selection and the information in it.

1. With a partner, reread the information in Build Background on page 327.
2. Close your books. On a note card, write the information that you learned in your own words.
3. Check your paraphrase against the original text. Is your paraphrase accurate?

Summarizing	Writing or saying the main ideas of a selection, or part of a selection. A summary is *shorter than* the original selection.
Paraphrasing	Retelling a selection or part of a selection in your own words, in writing or orally. A paraphrase can be *about the same length as* the original selection.

4. Share your paraphrase with the class. How are the paraphrases alike? How are they different?

Elements of Literature

Explore Graphic Aids

A **graphic aid** is a picture that tells you more about the information in a text. Many textbooks have graphic aids such as photographs, charts, and diagrams. Graphic aids help readers understand new and sometimes difficult information.

For example, paragraph 13 describes how Earth and Venus are similar and different. The photograph on the same page *shows* what Venus really looks like. This helps you understand the similarities and differences.

1. Reread paragraphs 3, 4, 7, and 8 without looking at the graphic aids. In your Reading Log, list any questions that you have about what you read.
2. When you have finished reading, look at the graphic aids for each of these paragraphs.
3. Examine how each of the graphic aids work to influence you.
4. Think about how the graphic aids helped you answer your questions. Which graphic aids helped you the most? Why?

Reading Log   Activity Book *p. 179*   Student CD-ROM

Word Study

Recognize Words and Sounds with the Spelling *oo*

Some English words have two written vowels, but they are pronounced as one sound. The letters *oo* in the word *moon* are a diphthong. *Moon* contains two *o* vowels, yet you pronounce only one sound. It is only one syllable.

In English, *oo* is pronounced one of two ways. These two different sounds can be heard in the words *moon* and *good*. You must learn which way to pronounce *oo* for each word you read.

1. With a partner, pronounce each word in the chart. Use a dictionary to help you.
2. If you do not know the meanings of any of the words, use a dictionary and write the words' meanings in your Personal Dictionary.

Words Pronounced Like *Moon*		Words Pronounced Like *Good*	
cool	school	took	look
too	tool	book	cook
boot	root	foot	

3. Choose two *oo* words and write a sentence using each word.

Personal Dictionary   The Heinle Newbury House Dictionary   Activity Book *p. 180*   Student CD-ROM

Grammar Focus

Identify Superlative Adjectives

Superlative adjectives are adjectives that describe a noun compared with two or more other nouns. Superlative adjectives often end in *-est*. Look at this example:

Kai is the smart**est** person in the class.

The superlative adjective *smartest* describes Kai. It compares Kai with all the other people in the class.

1. Find two sentences that contain superlative adjectives in "The Solar System." Look in paragraphs 4 and 5.

2. Copy the sentences on a piece of paper. Underline the superlative adjectives.

3. Write the root word for each adjective. Note that adjectives ending in *-e* drop the *-e* before adding *-est*.

Activity Book *pp. 181–182*   Student Handbook   Student CD-ROM

From Reading to Writing

Outline an Informational Text

An **outline** shows the main ideas and supporting details in a text. Use Roman numerals (I, II, III, etc.) for main ideas. Use capital letters for subtopics, and use numbers for details.

1. With a partner, reread aloud paragraphs 7 and 8. Adjust your reading rate so that you can outline as you read. Read more slowly.
2. On a piece of paper, copy and complete this outline.
3. Use a computer to prepare and print your final outline.
4. Compare and contrast your outlines.

> **Mercury**
> I. Location
>   A. Closest planet to the sun
>   B. ____
>   1. Brightness of the sun—hard to see
>   2. Pictures from spacecraft
> II. Mercury compared to Earth's moon
>   A. ____
>   B. Surface
>   1. Dust
>   2. ____
>   3. ____

Activity Book
p. 183

Student
Handbook

Across Content Areas

Compare Planet Orbits

Read the list below. It shows about how long it takes for each planet to orbit around the sun in Earth years.

Mercury	88 days	Venus	224 days
Earth	1 year	Mars	2 years
Jupiter	12 years	Saturn	30 years
Uranus	84 years	Neptune	165 years
Pluto	247 years		

Note: There are about 365 days in 1 Earth year.

1. Which planet orbits around the sun in the shortest amount of time?
2. Which planet orbits around the sun in the longest amount of time?
3. Is Neptune closer to or farther from the sun than Venus? How do you know?

Work with a partner to write a news story about travel to other planets. Write a title and two paragraphs to organize your news story. Revise it as you correct spelling and grammar mistakes.

Activity Book
p. 184

Apply and Expand

Listening and Speaking Workshop

Give an Oral Report About Your Community

> **Topic**
>
> Imagine that you are speaking to people who want to explore your community. Give an oral presentation in which you describe interesting places or things in your community.

Step 1: Choose a topic to present.

1. On a piece of paper, list three topics that you could present.
2. Choose the topic that you can research and that you know the most about.

Step 2: Brainstorm three details that support your topic.

Use a chart like this one to organize your ideas.

Topic: The Best Things to Do in My Community
Detail: go swimming at the pool
Detail: go boating on City Park Lake
Detail: watch a baseball game at the park

Step 3: Think of an opening statement that will get the audience interested.

1. Ask a question, such as "Would you like to hear about the best things to do in my community?"

2. Give an opinion, such as "My community is a great place to have fun."
3. Compare your community to another place or thing. For example, "There are as many ways to have fun in my community as there are stars in the sky."

Step 4: Write your ideas on note cards.

Give examples and details.

Step 5: Find or draw a picture that shows something that you will describe.

Step 6: Practice your presentation.

1. Practice your presentation in front of a partner. Use your note cards to help you remember what to say.
2. Ask your partner to complete the Active Listening Checklist. You will answer the Speaking Checklist.
3. Use the checklists to make your presentation better.

Step 7: Give your presentation.

1. Speak clearly and slowly. Make sure everyone can hear you.
2. Use your voice to show that you are excited about your topic.
3. If possible, record your presentation on audio or video. Review your presentation. How can you improve?

Active Listening Checklist

1. The opening statement was interesting: Yes / No

2. The details and supporting evidence helped me to understand the topic: Yes / No

3. The most interesting thing that I learned was _____ .

4. I understood the purpose of the presentation: Yes / No

Speaking Checklist

1. Did I prepare note cards on main points and details?

2. Did I speak clearly and loudly enough for people to hear me?

3. Did I hold up a picture to show what I was describing?

4. Did I use gestures?

Student Handbook

Viewing Workshop

View and Think

Discuss What People Are Exploring

People all over the world are exploring places such as the solar system to learn more about them. People are also exploring new ideas in computers, medicine, and science in order to make our lives better.

1. Go to a library. Find an article about a new idea or place that people are exploring today. You may use the Internet to search for an article. Use these keywords: *scientific discoveries, explorations, science news.*

2. Take notes and summarize as you read the article.

   a. What new idea or place is the article about?

   b. What did you learn about this idea or place from the article?

   c. Is it important to study this new idea or place? Why or why not?

3. Look for stories that tell about the new idea or place. Compare and contrast your article with the stories you find.

4. Make a chart with your class to show what you and your classmates found.

Further Viewing

Watch the *Visions* CNN Video for Unit 5. Do the Video Worksheet.

CNN Video

Writer's Workshop

Write a Research Report

> **Prompt**
>
> In this unit, you learned about whales. Think of an animal that you would like to know more about. Write a research report about it.

> Question: What does the animal eat?
> Summary: Many snakes eat birds and mice.
> Source: www.snakesaregreat.com

Step 1: Brainstorm what you would like to know about the animal.

1. What does the animal look like?
2. Where does the animal live?
3. What does the animal eat?
4. What interesting or amazing things does the animal do?

Step 2: Research the animal and find answers to your questions.

1. Find multiple sources about the animal. Use books from a library, or find information on the Internet. Use the animal's name as a keyword for your Internet search.
2. Use headings, tables of contents, and graphic features (maps, pictures, charts) to locate and organize information. Ask your teacher or librarian to help you interpret the information in the graphic features.
3. Revise your questions as you find information. Continue to research the answers.
4. Review your notes and your own knowledge to ask any questions you still need answers to.

Step 3: Record and organize information.

1. Evaluate your research. Decide if the information you find is useful.
2. Find information that answers your questions. Paraphrase it on a note card. *Be sure to use your own words.* Write your questions to help you organize your notes.
3. List the sources where you found the information. Use the citation format in your Student Handbook.
4. Use your own words to note additional information that is important or interesting.
5. Choose the information you will include in your report. The report outline in the next step will help you organize the information you paraphrased.

Step 4: Write a draft.

1. Write the introduction.
   a. Tell what your report is about.
   b. Explain why people should learn about the animal.
2. Write a **body** of three paragraphs. Each of these paragraphs explains a different idea.

a. In each paragraph, state one idea about the animal.

b. Give details or examples that support each idea.

3. Write the conclusion. Explain why you think the animal is interesting.

4. Include a drawing of the animal.

5. List the sources you used, such as books or Web sites.

6. Give your report a title.

Title _____

| Tell what animal your report is about. _____ |

Explain why people should learn about the animal. _____

Idea 1: _____

Details and examples: _____

Idea 2: _____

Details and examples: _____

Idea 3: _____

Details and examples: _____

Explain why you think the animal is interesting. _____
_____

Sources: www.snakesaregreat.com
The Big Book of Snakes

Step 5: Revise and edit your draft.

1. Read your draft. Be sure you used details and examples in your body paragraphs. Did I correctly use the information that I found in my sources?

2. If you use a computer, use software, such as an online dictionary or thesaurus, to check your work. Also use the spell check and grammar check to revise and edit your draft.

3. Exchange drafts with a partner. Proofread each other's drafts. Then complete the Editor's Checklist for your partner's draft on a piece of paper.

4. With your partner, discuss how you could make your draft better.

5. Revise your draft to make it better. Also refer to the sources you used to help you clarify ideas and revise text.

✓ **Editor's Checklist**

1. The writer explained what the report is about. Yes / No

2. The writer explained why people should know about the animal. Yes / No

3. The writer used details and examples in each body paragraph. Yes / No

4. The writer listed sources. Yes / No

5. The writer used visuals. Yes / No

Step 6: Publish.

1. Rewrite your report in your best handwriting, or use a computer to type your report. Check for spelling and grammar errors.

2. Read your report to the class. Ask your science teacher to post it on the wall of your science class.

Projects

These projects will help you learn more about explorations. Ask an adult for help if you need it.

Project 1: Explore Sources to Answer Science Questions

A source is a place where you can get information and answers to questions.

1. Work with a partner. Think of a science question. Write the question on a note card.
2. Go to a library. Ask the librarian where to find these sources:
   a. encyclopedias
   b. Internet access
   c. newspapers
   d. science books
   e. science magazines
3. List two sources that you could use to answer the question.

Question: Why do plants need sunlight to grow?

Sources: 1. An encyclopedia
                2. A person who grows plants

---

4. Report your question and answer to the class. Tell where you found the answer.
5. Think of a new question you formed as you researched. Use the information you found and your own knowledge. Where do you think you will find the answer?

Project 2: Give a Presentation About an Explorer

An explorer is a person who goes to a new place in order to learn about it.

1. Choose a famous explorer to research. Choose one from the list below or choose one on your own.
   a. Neil Armstrong
   b. Sacagawea
   c. Ferdinand Magellan
2. Research the explorer. Look for articles and stories about the explorer to compare and contrast how different sources tell information about him or her. You can use resources from a library. You can also use the Internet. (Use the explorer's name as a key word.)
3. Evaluate your research. Make sure the information you found is useful. Ask yourself the questions below. Write your answers on note cards to help you summarize and organize information. Write the answers in complete sentences.
   a. Where did the explorer go?
   b. When did the explorer go?
   c. What is this explorer famous for?
   d. Why is this explorer interesting?
4. Give a presentation on the explorer to the class. Use your note cards.
5. Use visuals such as photos, drawings, timelines, charts, and maps. Use these features to summarize and organize the information you found. Include captions that explain the visuals. Write the captions in complete sentences.
6. E-mail or write a letter to a friend or family member to further share your research.

Further Reading

The books below discuss exploration and discoveries. Read one or more of them. Write your thoughts and feelings about what you read in your Reading Log. After you read, answer these questions:

1. Which discovery did you find the most interesting?
2. Would you like to explore one of these places or ideas?
3. Can you connect the ideas and issues in these books to those found in the reading selections in this unit?

Dive!: My Adventures in the Deep Frontier
by Sylvia A. Earle, National Geographic Society, 1999. Sylvia Earle describes exploring oceans, learning about whales, and living in an underwater laboratory.

How to Think Like a Scientist: Answering Questions by the Scientific Method
by Stephen Kramer, HarperCollins Children's Books, 1987. This book teaches how the scientific method works by exploring everyday problems and questions.

Hallucination Orbit: Psychology in Science Fiction
edited by Isaac Asimov, Martin H. Greenberg, and Charles G. Waugh, Farrar, Straus and Giroux, 1983. Twelve science fiction stories explore how the human brain responds to strange situations. Authors include Roald Dahl, Isaac Asimov, and Jerome Bixby.

Exploring the Titanic
by Robert D. Ballard, Econo-Clad Books, 1999. The *Titanic* is a ship that sank in 1912. In 1986, it was discovered 12,690 feet (3,870 meters) below the ocean. This book describes the *Titanic,* the night it sank, and how the ship was explored more than 70 years later.

Can You Hear a Shout in Space?: Questions and Answers About Space Exploration
by Melvin Berger and Gilda Berger, Scholastic, Inc., 2001. This book describes what it is like to be in space. The book also talks about how the human body reacts to zero-gravity conditions.

1,000 Inventions & Discoveries
by Roger Francis Bridgman, DK Publishing, Inc., 2002. From millions of years ago to the present, there have been discoveries that have changed the world we live in. Each chapter of this book details an important period in the history of discoveries.

We Have Conquered Pain: The Discovery of Anesthesia
by Dennis Brindell Fradin, Simon & Schuster Children's, 1996. Four different doctors—Horace Wells, William Morton, Crawford Long, and Charles Jackson—claim to have discovered anesthesia in the 1840s. This book explores what each one did and how they fought for credit of the discovery.

Companion
Web site

Reading Log

Heinle
Reading Library
The Invisible Man

UNIT 6

Connections

Excavation of the Sphinx, Ernst Koener, 1883.

View the Picture

1. Describe what you see in the picture.

2. How does this picture show the theme of "connections"?

In this unit, you will read fiction, a biography, and informational texts. You will also practice writing these forms.

Into the Reading

Esperanza Rising

an excerpt from a novel
by Pam Muñoz Ryan

Objectives

Reading Make inferences as you read an excerpt from a novel.

Listening and Speaking Distinguish between facts and opinions.

Grammar Identify possessive adjectives.

Writing Write a fiction story.

Content Social Studies: Learn about land forms.

Use Prior Knowledge

Describe a Place That You Like to Visit

What place do you like to visit? Is it indoors or outdoors? How would you describe it?

1. Copy this Sunshine Organizer. Use it to describe the place that you like to visit.
2. With a partner, ask and answer questions about the place. For example:

What do you do there?

Who do you see?

When do you like to go there?

How do you get there?

Who? What? When? Where? Why? How?

My Place
_____

Build Background

Growing Grapes

The selection you will read takes place in a vineyard. A vineyard is an area of land where people grow grapes. Grapes grow on vines. Vines are plants that have long, thin stems. Grapes are grown around the world. They have been grown for thousands of years.

Content Connection

The word *vineyard* comes from *vine* and *yard* (an area of land).

Build Vocabulary

Understand Words in Context

Read each sentence and use the **context** to help you understand the underlined word. The context is the information around the word. Check your answers with a partner. If you are not sure about an answer, look the word up in a dictionary.

1. The girl loved to walk with her father, <u>gazing</u> up at him as he spoke to her.
   a. looking at him for a long time
   b. looking away from him
2. He gently touched a green <u>tendril</u> that grew from the vine.
   a. piece of clothing
   b. a thin part of a plant
3. Little by little, she <u>inched</u> next to him.
   a. sat down
   b. moved very slowly
4. Her father told her to <u>be patient</u>, so she waited and lay silent.
   a. wait calmly for something
   b. sing a song

Write the words and their meanings in your Personal Dictionary.

Personal Dictionary

The Heinle Newbury House Dictionary

Activity Book *p. 185*

Student CD-ROM

Text Structure

Fiction

"Esperanza Rising" is from a novel, a story that fills a book. A novel is **fiction.** The author makes up the story. In this selection, you will find the features of fiction listed in the chart.

As you read the selection, look for the main character's traits and motivation. Also look for how the character changes.

Fiction	
Characters	the people in a story
Plot	the things that happen in a story
Character Traits	a character's qualities, such as friendly or honest
Character Motivation	the reason a character does something
Character Changes	changes in a character as the events take place

Student CD-ROM

Reading Strategy

Make Inferences

To understand characters in a story, you should **make inferences** about them. When you make an inference, you use the information in the text and your knowledge and experience to make a guess. Look at this example:

Tim yawned and closed his eyes.

Inference: Tim is tired.

1. Read the sentences in the chart. Do you agree with all these inferences?
2. As you read the selection, make inferences about the characters. Write your inferences in your Reading Log.

Text	Possible Inferences
Rita went to the window and looked outside. She gazed at her friends who were skateboarding. Sadly, she returned to her desk and opened her book.	**a.** Rita had to study. **b.** Rita doesn't like to study. **c.** Rita would like to be with her friends. **d.** Rita likes skateboarding.

Reading Log

Student CD-ROM

Esperanza Rising

an excerpt from a novel
by Pam Muñoz Ryan

Aguascalientes, Mexico
1924

1   "Our land is alive, Esperanza," said Papa, taking her small hand as they walked through the gentle **slopes** of the vineyard. Leafy green vines draped the **arbors** and the grapes were ready to drop. Esperanza was six years old and loved to walk with her papa through the winding rows, gazing up at him and watching his eyes dance with love for the land.

2   "This whole **valley** breathes and lives," he said, sweeping his arm toward the distant mountains that guarded them. "It gives us the grapes and then they welcome us." He gently touched a wild tendril that reached into the row, as if it had been waiting to shake his hand. He picked up a handful of earth and studied it. "Did you know that when you lie down on the land, you can feel it breathe? That you can feel its heart beating?"

3   "Papi, I want to feel it," she said.

4   "Come." They walked to the end of the row, where the **incline** of the land formed a grassy **swell.**

5   Papa lay down on his stomach and looked up at her, patting the ground next to him.

6   Esperanza smoothed her dress and knelt down. Then, like a caterpillar, she slowly inched flat next to him, their faces looking at each other. The warm sun pressed on one of Esperanza's cheeks and the warm earth on the other.

7   She giggled.

8   "Shh," he said. "You can only feel the earth's heartbeat when you are still and quiet."

> **Make Inferences About Characters**
>
> How does the way Papa touches the tendril tell you about his feelings?

---

slopes   areas at an angle, like a hill
arbors   shelters of vines; frameworks covered with vines
valley   a low area of land between hills and mountains

incline   a hill
swell   a rounded hill

9   She swallowed her laughter and after a moment said, "I can't hear it, Papi."

10   "*Aguántate tantito y la fruta caerá en tu mano,*" he said. "Wait a little while and the fruit will fall into your hand. You must be patient, Esperanza."

11   She waited and lay silent, watching her Papa's eyes.

12   And then she felt it. Softly at first. A gentle **thumping.** Then stronger. A **resounding thud,** thud, thud against her body.

13   She could hear it, too. The beat rushing in her ears. *Shoomp, shoomp, shoomp.*

14   She stared at Papa, not wanting to say a word. Not wanting to lose the sound. Not wanting to forget the feel of the heart of the valley.

15   She pressed closer to the ground, until her body was breathing with the earth's. And with Papa's. The three hearts beating together.

16   She smiled at Papa, not needing to talk, her eyes saying everything.

17   And his smile answered hers. Telling her that he knew she had felt it.

Make Inferences About Characters

Was Esperanza patient? What tells you this?

---

thumping   a heavy sound
resounding   loud or booming

thud   the sound that a falling heavy object makes when it hits the ground

About the Author   Pam Muñoz Ryan (born 1951)

Pam Muñoz Ryan's grandparents moved from Mexico to the United States in the 1930s. Her grandmother told stories about her life. Pam Muñoz Ryan uses parts of her grandmother's stories in "Esperanza Rising."

➤Why do you think Pam Muñoz Ryan uses her grandmother's stories in "Esperanza Rising"? What strategies do you think she uses to write?

Beyond the Reading

Reading Comprehension

Question-Answer Relationships (QAR)

"Right There" Questions

1. **Recall Facts** What does Esperanza's father grow on his land?
2. **Recall Facts** What does Esperanza hear when she lies down?

"Think and Search" Questions

3. **Explain** Why does Papa tell Esperanza to be patient?
4. **Resolve Problems** In paragraph 9, what problem does Esperanza have? How does she resolve it?

"Author and You" Questions

5. **Make Inferences About Characters** How does Esperanza feel at the beginning of the selection? How do you know this?

6. **Analyze Character Changes** How does Esperanza change at the end of the selection? How do you know this?

"On Your Own" Questions

7. **Analyze Character Traits** *Esperanza* means "hope" in Spanish. Do you think Esperanza has hope? Why?
8. **Compare Your Experiences** What family stories do you have? Make connections between one of your stories and "Esperanza Rising" by comparing the two.
9. **Draw Conclusions** What is the purpose of this story—to entertain you or to persuade you to do something? How do you know?

Activity Book
p. 186

Student
CD-ROM

Build Reading Fluency

Read Silently and Aloud

Reading silently for practice then reading aloud helps you read with expression and understanding.

1. Listen to the audio recording for "Esperanza Rising" on page 356.
2. Follow along with the reading.
3. Read silently paragraphs 1 and 2 two times.
4. With a partner read aloud both paragraphs.
5. Your partner will time your last reading.
6. Record your timing.

Listen, Speak, Interact

Distinguish Between Facts and Opinions

A **fact** is a statement that can be proved. An **opinion** is what someone thinks or believes.

1. Reread or listen to "Esperanza Rising."
2. Write down two facts found in the story. Also write down two of your opinions about the story.

For example:

Esperanza is six years old. (fact)

Esperanza is a good daughter. (opinion)

3. Read one of your facts or opinions to a partner. Your partner will tell you if it is a fact or an opinion.

Elements of Literature

Analyze Characters

Authors help you understand characters by describing how they behave.

"Our land is alive, Esperanza," said Papa, taking her small hand . . .

From Papa's actions, you can make an inference that he is a loving father. This is one of his traits.

Reread or listen to the story and **analyze the characters.** Copy and fill in the chart.

Activity Book
p. 187

Student
CD-ROM

	Esperanza	Papa
Traits What do they look like? How do they behave?		
Motivation Why do they do certain things?		*wants to teach Esperanza*
Conflict What problems do they have?		
Point of view What are their opinions? What do they like or not like?		
Relationships How do they feel about each other?	*admires her father*	
Changes How do they change?		

Word Study

Distinguish Denotative and Connotative Meanings

All words have **denotative** meanings—the meaning that you find in the dictionary. Some words also have **connotative** meanings—attitudes or feelings connected to the word. For example:

"Esperanza . . . loved to walk with her papa, . . . <u>gazing</u> up at him . . ."

Gazing means *looking for a long time.* *Gazing* has the connotative meaning that you like or admire what you are looking at.

1. Copy the chart. Read the words and the meanings. Write *D* if the meaning is *denotative.* Write *C* if it is *connotative.*

Word	Meanings
a. drape	_____ hang from with beauty
	_____ hang from
b. tendril	_____ a young, tender green stem
	_____ a green stem

2. With a partner, choose one of the words and write a sentence using the connotative meaning.

The Heinle Newbury House Dictionary

Activity Book
p. 188

Student CD-ROM

Grammar Focus

Identify Possessive Adjectives

A **possessive adjective** shows who or what owns something.

Jimmy brought <u>his</u> dog.

The possessive adjective *his* shows who owns the dog.

1. Find three examples of possessive adjectives in paragraphs 1, 2, 5, 10, and 17 of the story.

2. Write two sentences with possessive adjectives. Be sure to spell *its* correctly. Do not use the apostrophe (') as in *it's (it is).*

Possessive Adjectives	
I	my
you	your
he	his
she	her
it	its
we	our
they	their

Activity Book
pp. 189–190

Student Handbook

Student CD-ROM

From Reading to Writing

Write a Fiction Story

Write a story about how a character changes as events happen.

1. Make up a character. Use note cards to write down what they are like.
2. Decide on a character and a setting (the time and place) for your story.
3. Organize your story into three paragraphs. Remember to indent.
4. Use past tense verbs to show events that already happened.

Activity Book
p. 191

Student Handbook

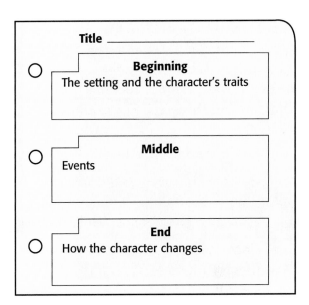

Title _____

○ **Beginning**
The setting and the character's traits

○ **Middle**
Events

○ **End**
How the character changes

Across Content Areas   SOCIAL STUDIES

Learn About Land Forms

Earth is made up of different **land forms.** The words below are some types of land forms.

mountain very high formation of land and rock

plateau a high area of flat land that has a drop on at least one side

valley a low area of land between high areas of land

plain a wide area of flat land

The diagram here shows the shapes of different types of land forms. Copy the diagram and write the types of land in the

correct places. Match the land form word with the correct type of land.

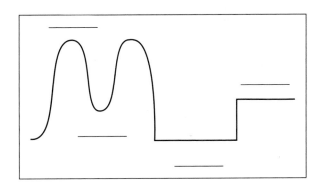

Activity Book
p. 192

CHAPTER

2

Honus and Me

an excerpt from a novel
by Dan Gutman

Objectives

Reading Identify the main idea and details as you read fiction.

Listening and Speaking Use persuasion.

Grammar Understand the past perfect tense.

Writing Write a paragraph.

Content Math: Use multiplication.

Use Prior Knowledge

Discuss Objects That You Would Like to Collect

Many people collect objects such as dolls or stamps as a hobby. They collect these objects because they like them. They usually keep these objects together as a group.

1. Work with three or four classmates.
2. Using one piece of paper and a pencil, write one kind of object that you collect or would like to collect.

3. Pass the paper and pencil to the next person. Each person will write what he or she collects or would like to collect.
4. After everyone has written an object, tell the group why you are interested in collecting your object.
5. Ask your group members questions about the objects that they are interested in.

Build Background

Baseball Cards

Baseball cards are small cards with pictures of famous baseball players on them. The cards list facts about these baseball players. People began making baseball cards in the 1800s.

Most baseball cards do not cost a lot of money. Cards that are very old can be very valuable (cost a lot of money).

Content Connection

Honus Wagner was a baseball player in the early 1900s. One of his cards is probably the most valuable baseball card in the world.

LIONS

First Base

Arturo Ricardo

Build Vocabulary

Learn Words About Emotions

Emotions are feelings that people have. These words describe different emotions:

joyful very happy

confused not knowing what to do

guilty feeling that you have done something wrong or bad

confident feeling that you are very good at doing something

1. Copy the following sentences in your Personal Dictionary.
2. Complete each sentence with an emotion from the list.

a. Monica is not sure if she should stay or go. She is ____ .
b. Yuri feels bad. He was mean to his brother. He feels ____ .
c. Li is very happy because she won the game. She is ____ .
d. Antonio thinks that he will do very well on the test. He is ____ .

Personal Dictionary

The Heinle Newbury House Dictionary

Activity Book p. 193

Student CD-ROM

Text Structure

Fiction

"Honus and Me" is **fiction.** It is an excerpt from a novel. Remember that a novel is a fictional story that fills a book. Look for the features of fiction listed in the chart as you read the selection.

Look for the conflict as you read or listen to "Honus and Me." Pay attention to the conflict and to point of view as you read. Who has the conflict? How would the story be different if told from the perspective of Joe's mother?

Student
CD-ROM

Fiction	
Narrator	The narrator tells the story.
First-Person Point of View	When the narrator is a character in the story, the story is written in the first-person point of view. The narrator uses the pronouns *I, me, we,* and *us.*
Plot	The plot is made up of events in the story.
Conflict	The characters must solve a problem. The conflict can be between two characters or within one character.

Reading Strategy

Identify the Main Idea and Details

The **main idea** is the most important idea in a paragraph. It is often the first sentence. **Details** are facts or examples. They help you understand the main idea.

Maria likes to help people. She teaches children how to read. She also helps me with my homework. When I was sick, she cooked dinner for me.

Main Idea	Maria likes to help people.
Details	She teaches children how to read. She helps me with my homework. When I was sick, she cooked dinner for me.

To Find the Main Idea	1. Read the whole paragraph. 2. Ask, "What is this paragraph about?"
To Find Details	1. Think about the main idea. 2. Find facts or examples that explain the main idea.

Student
CD-ROM

Honus and Me

WAGNER, PITTSBURG

an excerpt from a novel
by Dan Gutman

Audio
CD 2, Tr. 12

Prologue

Joe Stoshack is the main character of "Honus and Me." Joe is in the seventh grade. He loves to collect baseball cards.

Joe lives with his mother. They do not have a lot of money. Joe sometimes works to get money. He gives some of the money to his mother. He uses the rest to buy baseball cards.

Miss Young is Joe's **elderly** neighbor. She has a job for Joe. She wants Joe to throw out everything in her **attic.**

Joe goes to Miss Young's house. He is cleaning out her attic. Suddenly, Joe sees a small piece of paper on the floor. He bends down and picks it up . . .

1   I turned over the card and looked at the other side. I **couldn't believe my eyes.**

2   It was a picture of a man's face. I **gasped. Instinctively,** I looked around to see if anybody was watching. Of course nobody was there.

3   The man in the picture was a young man, with short brown hair parted in the middle. He had a **solemn** expression on his face, with his head **swiveled** slightly so he

> **Identify the Main Idea and Details**
>
> The main idea of this paragraph is what the man in the picture looks like. What details help you understand the main idea?

---

elderly   old, aged

attic   a space under the roof of a house; people often put things that they do not use in an attic

couldn't believe my eyes   couldn't believe what I saw

gasped   breathed in quickly, usually because of surprise

instinctively   done from feeling, not from what you learned

solemn   serious

swiveled   turned

was looking off to the left. His shirt collar was navy blue, and the shirt was muddy gray. It had four white buttons.

4 On the right side of his chest were the letters "PITTS" and on the left were the letters "BURG." There was no H.*

5 The **background** of the card was **burnt-orange.** There was a thin white border on all four sides. Across the bottom border, centered in the middle, were these magic words . . .

WAGNER, PITTSBURG

6 My breath came in short **bursts.** I suddenly felt warm. My heart was **racing.** My *brain* was racing. The **tingling sensation** was all over me, and stronger than I had ever experienced it.

7 No doubt about it. I had just **stumbled upon** a T-206 Honus Wagner card—*the most valuable baseball card in the world.*

* From 1890–1911, the city of Pittsburgh, Pennsylvania, was spelled "Pittsburg."

Identify the Main Idea and Details

The main idea of this paragraph is that Joe is very excited. What details show that Joe is very excited?

---

background   something behind something else
burnt-orange   an orange color that has a little red in it
bursts   things that happen suddenly and with force
racing   going very quickly

tingling sensation   a feeling that you get when you are excited, as if sharp things are touching your skin
stumbled upon   found by accident

8　　Every serious **collector** knows the **legend** behind the Wagner card. These early baseball cards were printed by tobacco companies and were included with their products. All the players agreed to be on the cards except for Honus Wagner, the **star shortstop** of the **Pittsburgh Pirates.**

Identify the Main Idea and Details

What is the main idea of this paragraph?

9　　Wagner was against cigarette smoking, and he didn't want his name or picture used to sell tobacco. He forced the American Tobacco Company to **withdraw** his card— but they had already started printing them. A small number of the cards reached the **public** before the card was **discontinued.**

---

collector　a person who collects something, such as baseball cards

legend　a story about a person; the story may include real events and made-up events

star　very famous

shortstop　a position in baseball

Pittsburgh Pirates　a baseball team

withdraw　take back

public　the people in a country or an area

discontinued　stopped being made

10   That's why the Honus Wagner card is so valuable. Only about forty of them are known to **exist** in the whole world, most of them in bad **condition.**

11   I just found No. 41, and it was *mint.* Nobody had *touched* it in over eighty years.

Identify the Main Idea and Details

What is the main idea of this paragraph?

12   I knew the piece of **cardboard** in my hand was **worth** thousands of dollars, but I didn't know exactly how *many* thousands. I remembered that a few years ago some famous athlete had bought one at an **auction,** but I couldn't **recall** who he was or how much he paid for it. It was a **huge** amount of money, that was for sure.

13   All my problems, I suddenly realized, were solved. Or so I thought.

exist be

condition how something is; for example, how something looks

mint in new or excellent condition

cardboard flat, stiff, thick paper

worth how much money someone will pay for something

auction a sale where items are sold to the person who offers to pay the most money

recall remember

huge very large

Identify the Main Idea and Details

What details show that Joe thinks the baseball card is very important?

14 I **slipped** the card in my backpack, being careful not to bend any of the corners or **damage** it in any way. A tiny **nick** in a card this rare might **decrease** its value by thousands of dollars.

15 Quickly, I gathered up the rest of the **junk** in the attic and **hauled** it out to the **curb.**

16 I had almost forgotten about Miss Young, but she called me over just as I was about to run home.

17 "Aren't you forgetting something, Joseph?"

18 She held out a five-dollar bill and shakily placed it in my **palm.** She grabbed my other hand and looked me in the eye.

19 "Thank you for helping out an old lady," she said seriously. "And because you did such a fine job, I want you to have *ten* dollars. I bet that's a lot of money to a boy your age."

---

slipped put in quickly and carefully
damage hurt, ruin
nick a small cut or mark
decrease lessen

junk things that are no longer useful to someone
hauled carried
curb the edge of a sidewalk
palm the inside part of the hand

20   Ten **bucks?** In my head I was thinking that I had a **fortune** in my backpack.

21   "Yeah, I could use ten dollars," I **sputtered.** "Thanks Miss Young."

22   "Buy something nice for yourself," she called out as I **dashed** away. "Money won't do *me* any good."

23   "I will," I called out as I left. "Believe me, I *will.*"

24   Mom wouldn't be home from work for an hour or so. I grabbed my bike, hopped on, and started **pedaling** east on Chestnut Street past Sheppard Park and Founders Square.

25   As I **cruised** down the streets I was filled with an **overwhelming** feeling of joy. Happiness washed over my body. Nobody could touch me. Nobody could hurt me. Nobody could tell me what to do. It was a feeling I had never experienced before.

> **Identify the Main Idea and Details**
>
> What is the main idea of this paragraph?

---

bucks   informal word for "dollars"
fortune   a very large amount of money
sputtered   spoke in an unclear way
dashed   left quickly

pedaling   moving the pedals of a bicycle with your feet
cruised   moving on a vehicle at a fast but comfortable speed
overwhelming   great; feeling an emotion very strongly

26   I didn't know if I should tell the whole world about my good **fortune,** or if maybe I shouldn't tell *anybody* in the world.

27   As I **whizzed** down the street, I felt like everyone was looking at me. I felt like everyone must somehow know what had happened to me. They knew what I had in my backpack. It was as if the news had instantly been picked up on **CNN** and **broadcast** around the **globe.**

Identify the Main Idea and Details

What is the main idea of this paragraph?

28   Those feelings lasted about a minute, when a different feeling came over me. A bad feeling. The baseball card wasn't mine to take, really. It was Miss Young's card. If anybody **deserved** to get rich from it, it was *her*. She had been nice enough to pay me *double* for cleaning out her attic, and I had **stolen** her fortune.

---

fortune luck
whizzed moved very quickly
CNN a news company
broadcast shown on television or played on the radio

globe world
deserved should; had a right to; was worthy of
double two times as much
stolen taken without permission or payment

29   Almost as quickly, my brain came up with reasons I shouldn't feel badly. Miss Young herself said that money wouldn't do her any good, so why *shouldn't* I keep the card? After all, *she* told me to throw the stuff away. If I hadn't found the card, *she* wouldn't have found it. It would have ended up buried in a **landfill** someplace, worth nothing to anyone.

30   **Finder's keepers,** right?

31   And besides, I thought, Miss Young isn't going to live much longer.

32   I felt bad, again, thinking that last thought.

33   I was feeling very **mixed up.** Deep inside I knew the right thing would be to give Miss Young back her baseball card.

---

landfill   a place where garbage is buried and covered with dirt

finder's keepers   a saying; it means that the person who finds something gets to keep it

mixed up   confused, unsure of what to do

About the Author

Dan Gutman (born 1955)

Dan Gutman grew up in New Jersey. He became a writer when he was about 25 years old. He wrote for newspapers and movies. He even started a magazine for video games. Later, Gutman began writing about one of his favorite things—sports. Today, Gutman loves to write fiction for young people. He also visits schools to talk to students. He explains how reading and writing are fun.

➤ What advice do you think Dan Gutman would give Joe? Why do you think so?

Beyond the Reading

Reading Comprehension

Question-Answer Relationships (QAR)

"Right There" Questions

1. **Recall Facts** Whose picture is on the baseball card that Joe finds?
2. **Recall Facts** What words are written at the bottom of that baseball card?
3. **Recall Facts** Where does Joe find the baseball card?
4. **Recall Facts** How much money does Miss Young give Joe?

"Think and Search" Questions

5. **Analyze Reasons** Why is the Honus Wagner card so valuable?
6. **Draw Conclusions** Why does Miss Young say, "Money won't do me any good"?
7. **Explain** Honus Wagner wanted the American Tobacco Company to stop making his baseball card. Why?

8. **Recognize Character Change** What is the first feeling that Joe has after he leaves Miss Young's house? How does his feeling change?

"Author and You" Questions

9. **Find Supporting Arguments** What are Joe's reasons for giving back the baseball card?
10. **Character Conflict** How do you think Joe will resolve his conflict? What will he do with the card?

"On Your Own" Question

11. **Support Your Opinion** What would you do with the baseball card? Why?

Activity Book
p. 194

Student
CD-ROM

Build Reading Fluency

Rapid Word Recognition

Rapidly recognizing words helps increase your reading rate. It is an important characteristic of effective readers.

1. With a partner, review the words in the box.
2. Read the words aloud for one minute. Your teacher will time you.
3. Count how many words you read in one minute.

believe	bursts	slightly	there	slightly
watching	there	bursts	slightly	there
there	breath	watching	believe	breath
slightly	slightly	there	watching	believe
breath	watching	believe	breath	bursts

Listen, Speak, Interact

Use Persuasion

People often use **persuasion** when they want other people to do or think something.

1. Copy and complete the paragraph.
2. Work with a partner. Suppose your partner is Joe. Persuade your partner to give back the baseball card. Use what you wrote in your paragraph.
3. As you speak, look at your partner. Use gestures to help make your point.

Joe, you should _____ _____. This is the right thing to do because _____.

You should also do this because _____.

If you do this, you will feel _____ because _____.

Elements of Literature

Recognize Style, Tone, and Mood

Authors use **style, tone,** and **mood** to express themselves and help readers understand and enjoy their writing.

Read the following paragraphs aloud with a partner. Then answer the questions together.

1. Read paragraph 25. In this paragraph, the author uses short sentences. How does this style help show Joe's feeling?
2. Read paragraphs 8 and 9. What is the author's tone? Does he seem to approve or disapprove of Honus Wagner?
3. Read paragraphs 1 and 2. What mood does the author create at this point in the story? Fear? Suspense? Happiness?

Style	How the author uses language, for example: Long or short sentences Use of figurative language Informal or formal language
Tone	The author's attitude, for example: Positive attitude Negative attitude
Mood	The feeling the author wants you to get, for example: Suspense (wanting to know what happens next) Excitement Fear

Activity Book
p. 195

Student
CD-ROM

Word Study

Use a Thesaurus or Synonym Finder

A **thesaurus** and a **synonym finder** are books that list synonyms. **Synonyms** are words that have similar meanings. You can also use the Internet to locate synonyms. Do a search using the keyword *thesaurus* or *synonym*.

1. Read the following sentences. Look at the underlined words. Write one synonym for each underlined word. Use a thesaurus or synonym finder.

   a. Happiness washed over my body.

   b. I had found the most valuable baseball card in the world.

   c. A tiny nick might decrease its value by thousands of dollars.

2. In your Personal Dictionary, copy and complete a chart like the one here.

Word	Synonym
fast	quick
happiness	
valuable	
decrease	

Personal Dictionary

The Heinle Newbury House Dictionary

Activity Book p. 196

Student CD-ROM

Grammar Focus

Understand the Past Perfect Tense

When authors want to show that a past action took place before another action, they use the **past perfect tense.**

> I remembered that a few years ago some famous athlete had bought one.

The verb *had bought* is in the past perfect tense. This tense shows that the *buying* took place before the *remembering*.

To form the past perfect tense, use the auxiliary *had* plus the past participle. To form most past participles, add *d* or *ed* to the simple form of the verb. Some verbs have irregular past participles, such as *be/been*.

On a piece of paper, copy these sentences. Underline the past perfect tense verbs.

1. He forced the . . . Company to withdraw his card—but they had already started printing them.

2. Nobody had touched it in over eighty years.

3. She had been nice enough to pay me *double* for cleaning her attic.

Activity Book pp. 197–198

Student Handbook

Student CD-ROM

From Reading to Writing

Write a Paragraph

In "Honus and Me," Joe finds something very special. Write a paragraph about an object that you would like to find.

1. Answer these questions:
   a. What is the object? Describe it for people who do not know what it is.
   b. Why would you like to find this object? How is it special?
   c. How would you feel if you found this object? Happy? Excited?
2. Use figurative language. Use a dictionary to find the denotative meaning of words. Then think about the connotative meaning.
3. Use the past perfect tense to show a past action that took place before another action.

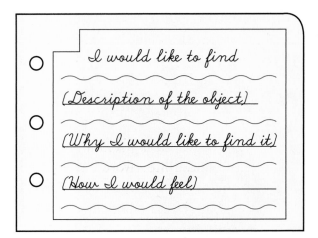

I would like to find

_____

(Description of the object)

_____

(Why I would like to find it)

_____

(How I would feel)

_____

Activity Book
p. 199

Student
Handbook

Across Content Areas

Use Multiplication

In "Honus and Me," Miss Young pays Joe ten dollars instead of five dollars. Ten dollars is two times five dollars.

When you see the word "times" in math, it usually means that you have to **multiply.** The symbol $\times$ is used to mean "multiply."

$$2 \times 5 = 10$$

"$2 \times 5 = 10$" is an example of an **equation.** To read this equation aloud, you would say, "Two times five equals ten."

Answer these questions:

1. On another day, Miss Young paid Joe $15 instead of $5. Complete the equation: _____ $\times$ 5 = 15.
2. How would you say the equation in **1**? Complete the sentence: Three _____ five _____ fifteen.

Activity Book
p. 200

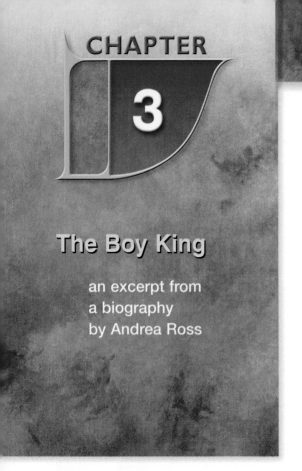

Objectives

Reading Identify cause and effect as you read a biography.

Listening and Speaking Ask and answer interview questions.

Grammar Understand modal auxiliaries.

Writing Write a biography.

Content Social Studies: Identify symbols.

Use Prior Knowledge

Leaders

A leader is a person who guides and connects with a group of people. There are different types of leaders. The president of a country guides the country's government and people. Your teacher guides your learning.

Leaders That I Know About	
Title	Name
Principal	Mrs. Rivera

1. Think of leaders that you know about from your country, state, community, or school.
2. Write the titles and names of these leaders in a chart like the one shown. A title tells the kind of ruler the person is, for example, president, king, principal.

3. Share the information from your chart with the class.
4. Compare leaders in your culture with leaders in other cultures. How are they the same? How are they different?

Build Background

Ancient Egypt

Egypt is a country on the continent of Africa. People who live in Egypt are called Egyptians. Thousands of years ago, kings and queens in Egypt were called pharaohs. The word *pharaoh* means "great house" in Egyptian. Very large buildings called temples and pyramids were built to remember pharaohs.

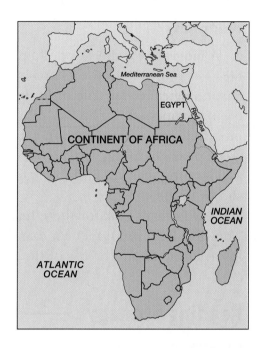

Content Connection

A **continent** is a very large area of land. It is surrounded by large bodies of water (oceans or seas).

Build Vocabulary

Look Up Syllables and Meanings of Words

Dividing a word into **syllables** is one way to learn to pronounce it. A syllable is a part of a word. For example, *teacher* has two syllables, *teach-er*. *Principal* has three syllables, *prin-ci-pal*. The dictionary breaks the words up into **syllables.** This helps you pronounce the words. For example:

Tut•ankh•a•men (an early king of Egypt)

1. Use a large dictionary to look up the words in the box.
2. Write the words, divided into syllables, in your Personal Dictionary.
3. Read the meaning in the dictionary. Then write it in your own words.
4. Work with your teacher to learn to pronounce the words. Listen for these words as you listen to the audio recording of the selection.
5. Listen to distinguish each sound in each word. Try to produce the sounds in the words that you hear.

archaeologist	antelope
hieroglyphics	papyrus

Personal Dictionary

The Heinle Newbury House Dictionary

Activity Book p. 201

Student CD-ROM

Text Structure

Biography

A **biography** is the story of a person's life. The author tells the events in chronological order (the order in which events happened). "The Boy King" is a biography about a young boy. This boy was a pharaoh in Egypt many years ago. In a biography, you will find the features shown in the chart.

As you read, look for these features. They will help you understand and recall information about the life of the boy king.

Biography	
Events in Chronological Order	things that happen in a person's life; they are presented in the order they happen
Dates	dates of birth, death, and important events
Details	information about the time and place in which the story happens

Student
CD-ROM

Reading Strategy

Identify Cause and Effect

A **cause** is the reason why something happens. The **effect** is what happens because of the cause.

I am going to the library because I want a book.

Cause: I want a book.

Effect: I am going to the library.

Some words that often show cause and effect are *because*, *since*, *so*, and *when*.

1. Read this sentence. What is the cause? What is the effect?

   When José doesn't sleep enough, he gets tired.

2. Look for causes and effects as you read or listen to "The Boy King." Write the causes and effects in your

Reading Log. Use a chart like the one shown.

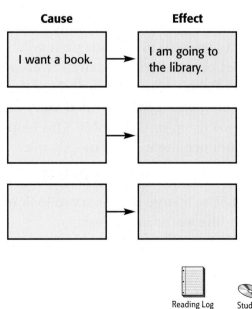

Reading Log   Student
CD-ROM

THE BOY KING

an excerpt from a biography
by Andrea Ross

1   How would you like to wake up one morning and be told that you are the ruler of your country? That is what happened over three thousand years ago to an Egyptian boy who was about nine years old.

2   Around 1370 **B.C.** a boy was born in a royal palace in Egypt. His name was Tutankhaten, which means "the living image of the sun god." He lived in a town in Egypt named El-Amarna during his early childhood, probably in the same palace as the pharaoh Akhenaten, and his wife, Queen Nefertiti. Most **historians** think Tutankhaten and Akhenaten were brothers, though no one knows for sure.

3   The walls of the palace were painted in rich, bright colors. The floors were decorated with colored clay tiles, and the furniture was covered with real gold. Beautiful gardens and pools around the palace helped keep the air cool.

4   In **ancient** Egypt the average **life span** was short by today's standards. Every boy in line for the throne had to be trained in case the time ever came for him to become a pharaoh.

Tutankhaten most likely started studying when he was about four years old. His education would have included learning hieroglyphics and mathematics. He would have written on papyrus, and if his answers were wrong, his **tutor** would have marked them in red ink.

> ### Identify Cause and Effect
>
> What would be the cause of getting marks in red ink?

Audio
CD 2, Tr. 13

B.C. Before Christ, the years before the birth of Christ in the Christian calendar

historians people who teach, study, and write about history

ancient very old

life span the number of years a person lives

tutor a teacher who helps students individually

5   Tutankhaten probably spent lots of time practicing sports. He would have learned to wrestle, swim, shoot a bow and arrow, and drive a two-horse chariot. When he stayed indoors, he might have played a game called *senet* that is not unlike today's checkers.

6   Eventually Tutankhaten's brother Akhenaten died. Tutankhaten was next in line for the throne, and he became the new king. He was about nine years old at the time. As part of becoming the new pharaoh, Tutankhaten had to marry his seven-year-old niece, the daughter of Akhenaten. Since she was the royal **heiress,** their marriage gave Tutankhaten the **right** to the throne.

> **Identify Cause and Effect**
>
> What was the effect of Tutankhaten marrying?

---

heiress   a female legally in line to receive property   **right**   ownership

7   Tutankhaten **ruled** successfully for the next few years with his wife. When he was about thirteen, the **temples** of Egypt displayed an **announcement** that praised all the things he had done to help the **kingdom.** These announcements were carved on flat pieces of stone. When he turned sixteen, Tutankhaten was considered a man and ruled the kingdom alone.

8   Tutankhaten was a great sportsman and seemed to like hunting particularly. Some of the objects from his **tomb** show him in a chariot aiming his bow at **ostriches.** He probably also hunted **gazelles** and **antelopes.**

Eventually, Tutankhaten decided to change his name to Tutankh*amen.* Amen was the god of Thebes, the city his family was from.   9

> **Identify Cause and Effect**
>
> How did the pharaoh's family background affect his decision to change his name?

---

ruled   governed, usually as a king or dictator

temples   buildings for religious worship

announcement   a formal letter or paper that makes public some information

kingdom   a country ruled by a king or queen

tomb   a burial room or grave with a monument over it

ostriches   large, flightless, African birds with long legs and necks

gazelles   animals like small deers

antelopes   any of various fast, hoofed, four-legged animals with horns

10   When Tutankhamen was about seventeen, scholars think he somehow **suffered** a head **injury.** Perhaps he was **wounded** in **battle,** or maybe he was hurt while hunting. He might even have had enemies who were trying to kill him. We don't know for sure if this **wound** caused his death, but it is likely that he never recovered from it.

11   More than three thousand years later, an English **archaeologist** named Howard Carter found Tutankhamen's tomb. It **yielded** some of the most beautiful Egyptian treasures ever found and made the pharaoh's name famous all over the world. Though his rule was **short-lived**, Tutankhamen, "the boy king," will never be forgotten because of the riches he left behind.

> **Identify Cause and Effect**
>
> How did Howard Carter help the world remember Tutankhamen?

---

suffered experienced pain, loss, or hardship
injury a wound or damage
wounded injured
battle a fight between enemy soldiers
wound a cut or other hurt cutting into the body

archaeologist a person who studies human life and civilizations through items of the past such as buried houses, statues, pots, and so on
yielded produced
short-lived not lasting long

About the Author   Andrea Ross

Andrea Ross was born in New York. She started writing at the age of seven. Since then, she has written plays, stories for children, and a book for young adults. Ross says that writing "is like sunshine to my soul."

➤ What questions do you think Andrea Ross researched to write this selection?

Beyond the Reading

Reading Comprehension

Question-Answer Relationships (QAR)

"Right There" Questions

1. **Recall Facts** How old was Tutankhamen when he became king?
2. **Recall Facts** What does Tutankhaten, the Boy King's original name, mean?

"Think and Search" Questions

3. **Make Inferences** Why do historians think Tutankhamen and Akhenaten were brothers?
4. **Analyze Cause and Effect** Why is Tutankhamen still famous today?

"Author and You" Questions

5. **Use Multiple Sources** How do you think Tutankhamen died? Draw a conclusion using information in this selection together with information from library books, encyclopedias, and the Internet.

6. **Compare Cultural Traditions** Compare and contrast the cultural tradition of leadership in Tutankhamen's time with today.
7. **Make Connections** Compare Tutankhamen's life with your own. What connections can you make with him?

"On Your Own" Questions

8. **Explain** If you were Tutankhamen, what do you think you would like best about being pharaoh? Explain your choice.
9. **Explain** What do you think you would like least about being pharaoh? Explain your choice.
10. **Speculate** Do you think that you would make a good leader? Why or why not?

Activity Book
p. 202

Student
CD-ROM

Build Reading Fluency

Repeated Reading

Repeated reading helps increase your reading rate and builds confidence. Each time you reread you improve your reading fluency.

1. Turn to page 382.
2. Your teacher or a partner will time you for six minutes.

3. With a partner, take turns reading paragraphs 1–2 aloud.
4. Stop after six minutes.

Listen, Speak, Interact

Ask and Answer Interview Questions

Suppose you are a news reporter. You have a chance to interview Tutankhamen to learn more about his life.

1. Write some questions you want to ask Tutankhamen. Some questions that are often asked in interviews are:
   a. When were you born?
   b. Where were you born?
   c. What do you do every day?
   d. What are some things that you like?
   e. How did you get your head injury?

2. Think about how Tutankhamen might answer. Use the reading to help you guess.
3. Ask your interview questions to a partner. Your partner will play the role of Tutankhamen and answer the questions.
4. Record your interview on video or audio. Review your recording. Is your interview believable? What would you do to improve it?

Elements of Literature

Discuss Themes Across Cultures

A reading presents a **theme.** A theme is an important topic that the author mentions several times in a reading selection.

1. With a partner, reread aloud paragraphs 4 to 9 of "The Boy King."
2. As you finish a paragraph, write down its main idea.
3. Use your main ideas to identify one theme in this part of the reading.

4. Discuss how the theme you identified is the same or different across other cultures.
5. Share with the class the theme that you found in "The Boy King."

Activity Book
p. 203

Student
CD-ROM

Word Study

Recognize the Suffix *-ian*

A **suffix** is a group of letters added to the end of a root word.

Most histor**ian**s think Tutankhaten and Akhenaten were brothers.

Historians has the suffix *-ian*. This suffix can mean "a person who works with or studies something." The root of *historians* is *history*. A historian is a person who studies history, or past events.

1. Read the words in the box. Read the root words below each word. Use a dictionary if you don't know a root word.

musician	mathematician	librarian
music	mathematics	library

2. What is the meaning of each word? Use the meaning of the suffix to help you. Check your ideas in a dictionary.

3. Ask your teacher to help you pronounce the words.

The Heinle
Newbury House
Dictionary

Activity Book
p. 204

Student
CD-ROM

Grammar Focus

Understand Modal Auxiliaries

Read these sentences from the selection and notice the words in **bold** type:

He **would** have learned to wrestle, swim, . . . and drive a two-horse chariot. When he stayed indoors, he **might** have played a game called *senet* . . .

In grammar, words like *would* and *might* are called **modal auxiliaries.** Modal auxiliaries are often used in the **perfect** form to express past time.

Complete each sentence with *might* or *would.*

Perfect Modal Auxiliaries			
Subject	**Modal Auxiliary**	**Have**	**Past Participle**
They	might *or* would	have	learned many sports.

1. In my school, you ____ have studied U.S. history in eighth grade.

2. He ____ have given the book to Yeny.

Activity Book
pp. 205–206

Student
Handbook

Student
CD-ROM

From Reading to Writing

Write a Biography

Write a short biography of a friend.

1. Interview a friend to find out about his or her life. Ask these questions:
   a. When were you born?
   b. Where were you born?
   c. Where do you live now?
   d. Where do you go to school?
   e. What is your family like?
   f. What are your favorite things to do?
   You may ask other questions.

2. Write your friend's answers on a piece of paper. Use your interview answers to write three paragraphs.
3. Form compound sentences with *and* or *but*.
4. Combine some of your sentences to form complex sentences with *because, if, when*.
5. Use transition words such as *then, next, finally*.

Activity Book
p. 207

Student
Handbook

Across Content Areas

Identify Symbols

Hieroglyphics are **symbols** that show meanings. A symbol is a picture, sign, or mark that stands for something else.

People in Egypt used hieroglyphics to write words long ago. In English writing, we use the letters of the alphabet to write words. However, we also use symbols to give information.

1. Copy the chart on a piece of paper.
2. Read the sentences in the first column. Use context clues to figure out what the symbols mean.
3. Choose the correct word from the box. Write the word in your chart.
4. What other symbols do you know?

	Symbol	Meaning
I paid $5 for lunch.	$	
The postcard had this message: I ♥ New York.	♥	
We moved the car when we saw this sign: ⃠	⃠	

dollars
love
not allowed

Activity Book
p. 208

CHAPTER 4

It Could Still Be a Robot

an excerpt from an
informational book
by Allan Fowler

High-Tech Helping Hands

an excerpt from an
informational article
by Jane McGoldrick

Objectives

Reading Paraphrase to recall ideas as you read an informational text.

Listening and Speaking Talk about advantages and disadvantages.

Grammar Use adverbs of frequency.

Writing Write a persuasive essay.

Content Science: Read an FAQ web page.

Use Prior Knowledge

Talk About Machines

Machines are tools that help people do things. For example, a car is a machine that helps people travel. Most people use many machines in their lives.

1. With a partner, think of different types of machines that people use. What machines help people do these things?
   a. research information
   b. travel long distances
   c. cook
   d. communicate
2. Write your ideas in a web. Add other machines as supporting evidence that people use many machines.

3. Present your web to the class. Tell about how these machines help people.

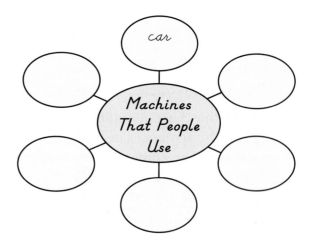

Build Background

Robots

You will read two selections about robots. Robots are special types of machines. They are controlled by computers. They are programmed to do certain jobs. This means that robots are made with instructions that tell them to do something. Most robots are made to help people do things. Some can be used to do dangerous jobs. Other robots can explore places that are far away. Robots can even help people who are disabled (not able to do certain tasks).

Content Connection

The first robots were made in the 1950s. They were used to help make things like cars.

Build Vocabulary

Distinguish Denotative and Connotative Meanings

In Chapter 1 of this unit, you learned about **denotative** and **connotative meanings.** Turn to page 360 and review that information.

Sometimes two words have similar denotative meanings, but their connotative meanings are different. Read these two sentences and then look at the chart:

They were **chatting** at the party.

They were **gossiping** at the party.

Word	Denotative Meaning	Connotative Meaning
chat	to talk	to talk informally
gossip	to talk	to tell private, untrue, or hurtful things

Read the meanings of these pairs of words. Which word has a connotative meaning? Which word has a denotative meaning?

1. **a.** device—an electrical or mechanical machine
   b. gadget—a small tool or machine that is often inexpensive and sometimes unnecessary
2. **a.** fume—a bad gas or smell
   b. smell—something that you sense with your nose or a feeling about something

Activity Book
p. 209

Student
CD-ROM

Text Structure

Informational Text

You will read two selections, "It Could Still Be a Robot" and "High-Tech Helping Hands." Both selections are **informational texts.** Informational texts explain a subject. These selections have the graphic features listed in the chart.

As you read, record sentences that give facts and examples. Notice how the graphic features help you understand what you read.

Informational Text	
Facts	things that are true
Examples	details that show how information is true
Graphic Features	photographs, drawings, and charts

Student
CD-ROM

Reading Strategy

Paraphrase to Recall Ideas

To **paraphrase** is to say or write something you read in your own words. Paraphrasing important parts of a text as you read can help you remember the information.

As you read "It Could Still Be a Robot" and "High-Tech Helping Hands," paraphrase some of the paragraphs. To paraphrase, do the following:

1. Read the paragraph until you are sure you understand it.
2. Close your book.

3. On a piece of paper, write the information that you read in your own words.
4. Open your book again and compare your paraphrase to the paragraph. Did you include all of the information?
5. Revise your paraphrase.

Student
CD-ROM

It Could Still Be a Robot

an excerpt from an informational book
by Allan Fowler

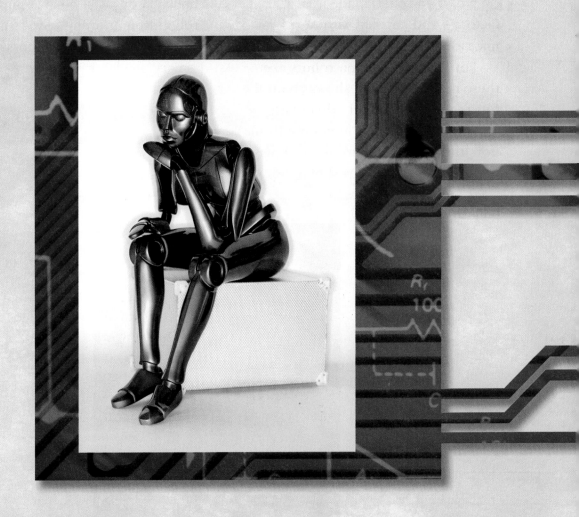

High-Tech Helping Hands

an excerpt from an informational article
by Jane McGoldrick

It Could Still Be a Robot

an excerpt from an informational book by Allan Fowler

1   It's shaped like a person. It walks like a person. It talks like a person and makes choices like a person. It seems to be alive. Is it a real person?

2   No, it's a robot, made in a factory—and covered with metal instead of skin.

3   You might have seen robots like these in movies or TV shows about the future or about life on other worlds.

4   Maybe someday, a long time from now, there will be androids—robots that look and act like real people.

5   Not yet, though. Most of the robots we have today don't look anything like people.

6   A robot could be an arm without a body . . . or just a box . . . and still be a robot. Robots aren't alive—since a robot is a machine. A robot is a "smart" machine.

> **Paraphrase to Recall Ideas**
>
> Paraphrase paragraphs 4, 5, and 6.

Audio
CD 2, Tr. 14

7   Robots can do many of the things that people do, and some things people can't do.

8   But each robot is built to do only one thing or certain types of things.

9   Robots often do jobs that are unsafe for people to do.

10   **Factories** use robots to pour hot metal.

11   Your family's car was probably spray painted by a robot, because paint fumes are bad for people's health.

> ### Paraphrase to Recall Ideas
>
> Paraphrase paragraphs 9, 10, and 11.

12   Robot hands pick up things that are dangerous for people to touch.

13   Robots are used for tasks that would be boring or tiring for people.

14   Robots never get bored or tired.

15   They also do certain jobs better or faster than human beings can do them.

16   No person can handle very tiny objects as easily as these robot fingers can.

17   Some robots help people do things they cannot do for themselves.

18   Some robots move around. A robot might roll on wheels . . . or travel under water . . . or even fly like this robot plane that has no human pilot . . . and still be a robot.

---

factories   buildings where things are made

19   But you won't often see a robot walking on two legs.

20   That's easy for you but hard for a robot.

21   Robots can go places where human beings can't go, such as the ocean bottom or the planet Mars.

22   At the end of a robot arm, there might be a hand with fingers . . . or a claw . . . or some kind of tool. It depends on what work the robot was built to do.

23   Robots today are run by computers. If its computer **program** is changed, a robot might be able to change from one type of job to another.

24   This rolling robot has an electronic "eye," like a camcorder or a TV remote control.

25   The "eye" can tell if something is blocking the robot's path.

> **Paraphrase to Recall Ideas**
>
> Paraphrase paragraph 22.

---

program   a code of instructions for a computer

26   Then the robot can move around whatever is in its way.

27   Other robots are guided by sound or touch. So a robot could be said to see, hear, or feel . . . and still be a robot.

28   A robot might be keeping your school building from getting too warm or too cold. A robot might open doors for people . . . solve hard math problems . . . draw pictures . . . play a musical instrument . . . or spin tops . . . and still be a robot.

29   But it can't feel great or feel bad . . . enjoy a joke, a story, or a song . . . taste food . . . or love someone. Only human beings can do those things.

Paraphrase to Recall Ideas

Paraphrase paragraph 29.

About the Author   Allan Fowler

Allan Fowler was born in New York. He used to work for advertising agencies (companies that give information about products and services). He currently works as a freelance writer and lives in Chicago, Illinois. In addition to writing, Allan Fowler enjoys traveling.

➤ Why do you think Allan Fowler wrote this selection? To inform, to entertain, or to persuade?

High-Tech Helping Hands
an excerpt from an informational article
by Jane McGoldrick

1   Krista is deaf and blind. To communicate, she often uses fingerspelling—forming shapes that stand for letters in the palm of the hand of her "listener." Krista helps **engineers** who work at the A.I. DuPont Institute in Wilmington, Delaware. They develop and test equipment to help people with **disabilities.** Krista is one of about a dozen young people with disabilities from the area who serve as **consumer** researchers before the **devices** are ready to be sold.

Paraphrase to Recall Ideas

Paraphrase the last sentence of paragraph 1.

---

2   "We ask the researchers to attend team meetings and give us ongoing **feedback,**" says director Richard Foulds. "They're a major part of our team."

3   Bern Gavlick, 16, has been testing a robot arm that attaches to his wheelchair. Because of his **cerebral palsy,** Bern cannot easily control the movements of his **limbs.** The arm can take a book off a shelf or open a door for him. Julia Nelson, 16, also has cerebral palsy. She tested a video game system designed for fun and fitness. "I love trying out the latest products," says Julia. "As a disabled teen, I'm looking to a future of trying to be independent," she adds. "It gives me hope that there are people working on products to help me achieve that goal."

Audio
CD 2, Tr. 15

---

engineers   people who design machines or other products

disabilities   illnesses or injuries that severely affect the brain or body

consumer   someone who uses or buys things

devices   equipment or machines designed for special purposes

feedback   response

cerebral palsy   a disease that affects the brain, muscles, and speech

limbs   arms and legs

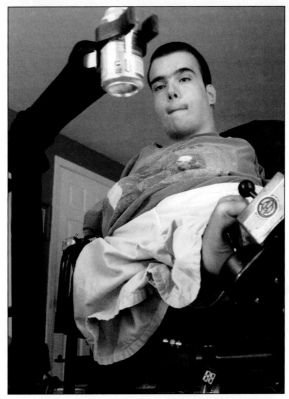

Robotic limbs help people with disabilities achieve independence.

About the Author — Jane McGoldrick

Jane McGoldrick loves reading. When she was a little girl, she used to hide in a quiet place of her home and read all her favorite books. McGoldrick has written magazine articles for children and adults as well as books for children. In addition to writing, McGoldrick completed advanced university work in English and psychology. (Psychology is the study of how people act.)

➤ Why do you think Jane McGoldrick wrote this selection? Did she want to inform, to entertain, or to persuade?

Beyond the Reading

Reading Comprehension

Question-Answer Relationships (QAR)

"Right There" Questions

1. **Recall Facts** Do most robots look like people?
2. **Recall Facts** Why are robots used to spray paint cars?
3. **Recall Facts** Where can robots go that people cannot?

"Think and Search" Questions

4. **Explain** How can an electronic "eye" help a robot?
5. **Explain** What can a robot's hands and fingers do that a person's cannot?
6. **Draw Conclusions** Is a robot the same thing as a computer?

"Author and You" Questions

7. **Compare** Do you think robots are as smart as people? Why or why not?

8. **Identify Main Ideas** How can robots help people with disabilities?
9. **Make Connections** Use the information in the selections to make connections between robots and your life. Do you know someone who could use a robot to help them?

"On Your Own" Questions

10. **Predict** What kinds of things do you think androids might do?
11. **Find Similarities and Differences Across Texts** How are the robots described in the two selections similar? How are they different?

Activity Book
p. 210

Student
CD-ROM

Build Reading Fluency

Reading Chunks of Words

Reading chunks or phrases of words is an important characteristic of fluent readers. It helps you stop reading word by word.

1. With a partner, take turns reading aloud the underlined chunks of words.
2. Read aloud two times each.

It's shaped   like a person.   It walks
like a person.   It talks   like a person
and makes choices   like a person.   It seems
to be alive.   Is it   a real person?   No,
it's a robot,   made in a factory
—and covered with metal   instead of skin.

Listen, Speak, Interact

Talk About Advantages and Disadvantages

An advantage is a good feature or benefit. A disadvantage is something that is negative and does not help.

1. Work with a group. Talk about the advantages and disadvantages of using robots. Use the following questions to help you brainstorm ideas.
   a. How can robots help us learn new things?
   b. What are some problems we can solve by using robots?
   c. What might happen if a robot broke down (stopped working)?
   d. Can using robots take jobs away from people?
2. Summarize your group's ideas and have one person present them to the class.

Elements of Literature

Analyze Text Evidence

Writers of informational texts often use examples to show how an important idea is true. Examples are **text evidence** because they support an important idea in the text.

> **Important Idea** Robots do jobs that are unsafe for people.

> **Evidence That Supports an Important Idea** Robots pour hot metal in factories.

Read the numbered sentences. Each one is an important idea. Choose the evidence—sentence **a** or sentence **b**—that best supports each important idea.

1. Robots are not real people.
   a. Some robots are covered with metal.
   b. Some robots are in movies.
2. Some robots move around.
   a. Some robots pick up tiny objects.
   b. Some robots roll on wheels.
3. Some robots go places where human beings cannot go.
   a. Some robots open doors for people.
   b. Some robots go to the planet Mars.

Activity Book
p. 211

Student
CD-ROM

Word Study

Learn Adverbs of Frequency

Frequency is how often something happens. Some words to describe frequency are on the diagram.

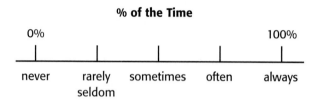

% of the Time

0%   100%

never   rarely   sometimes   often   always
           seldom

Copy the following sentences. Fill in each blank with an adverb of frequency that describes you.

1. I ＿＿ eat carrots because they are good for me.
2. I'm ＿＿ late for school because I ＿＿ get up early.
3. I ＿＿ help my little brother with his homework.

The Heinle
Newbury House
Dictionary

Activity Book
p. 212

Student
CD-ROM

Grammar Focus

Use Adverbs of Frequency

A **verb** is a word that tells the action of a sentence. **Adverbs of frequency** tell how often an action happens.

Robots <u>often do</u> jobs that are unsafe for people to do.

These charts show where to put adverbs of frequency in a sentence.

Rewrite these sentences and add an adverb of frequency.

1. He visits his grandmother on weekends.
2. Lon lies.
3. My room is messy.
4. I watch that TV show.

With the Verb *Be*			
Subject	**Verb**	**Adverb**	
She	is	never rarely sometimes often always	late.

With Other Verbs			
Subject	**Adverb**	**Verb**	
I	rarely	walk	to school.

Activity Book
pp. 213–214

Student
Handbook

Student
CD-ROM

402   **Unit 6**   Connections

From Reading to Writing

Write a Persuasive Essay

An essay is a piece of writing that is three to five paragraphs long. Essays can describe, tell a story, explain, or persuade.

Write a three-paragraph persuasive essay. Explain why people should use robots.

1. Paragraph 1: **Introduction**
   a. Tell what your essay is about.
   b. Write a sentence that tells why people should use robots. This is your **thesis statement.**

2. Paragraph 2: **Body**
   a. Write details that support your thesis statement. Use the advantages you talked about in Listen, Speak, Interact.
   b. Include examples.
3. Paragraph 3: **Conclusion**
   a. Restate your thesis.
4. Be convincing! You want readers to agree that people should use robots.

Activity Book
p. 215

Student
Handbook

Across Content Areas

Read an FAQ Web Page

Internet sites often have **FAQ** pages. FAQ stands for Frequently Asked Questions. Usually an FAQ page is a list of questions. You click on the question to find its answer.

Read each numbered item below. Then find the question in the FAQs that you would click on to find the answer.

1. You want to know more about the word *robot.*
2. You are interested in the history of robots.
3. You want to know if robots are used in farming.

4. You are interested in how much people depend on robots.

FAQ's
Where does the word *robot* come from?
What do robots look like?
How are robots used?
When were the first robots built?
How many robots are there in the world?
How can I build a robot?

Activity Book
p. 216

Apply and Expand

Listening and Speaking Workshop

Give a Persuasive Speech

Topic

Your school has decided to require students to wear uniforms. Some students think that this is a good idea. Others do not. What is your opinion? Present your opinion to the class. Use the Internet to find facts, examples, or quotations from experts to support your position.

Step 1: Plan your speech.

1. Make a list of reasons for and against the topic.
2. Decide whether you are for or against the issue.

Arguments For	Arguments Against
Wearing school uniforms saves money.	Not wearing school uniforms teaches students to be individuals.

Step 2: Write your speech.

Introduction

1. Present the issue and your position.
2. Give a reason on the other side of the issue. Then explain why that reason is not a good one.
3. Explain that there are many good reasons to support your position.

Reasons and Supporting Evidence

1. Give three good reasons to support your position.
2. Use phrases like, "I am in favor of . . ." "I do not agree that . . ."
3. Support each of your reasons with examples or evidence.
4. Be careful not to exaggerate. You want to convince the listeners to believe you.

Conclusion

1. Tell what the issue means to you.
2. Urge your listeners to support you.

Step 3: Practice your speech.

1. Write a note card for each topic.
2. Use the Speaking Checklist.
3. Ask a partner to listen to you and give you feedback using the Active Listening Checklist.
4. Revise your speech based on your partner's feedback.

Step 4: Present your speech.

1. Speak clearly and loudly enough for everyone to hear you.
2. Use expression to show that you are convinced of your opinion.
3. If possible, record your speech on audio or video. You might also use presentation software. Present your speech to the class to support your position.

Student
Handbook

Viewing Workshop

View and Think

Compare Presentations of Technology

Science fiction movies often show worlds with new technology. Robots and computers are examples of technology.

1. Go to your library and borrow a video that shows a future world with technology. Watch the video and take notes about the technology that you see.

2. Watch television news for reports about how technology is helping people. Take notes.

3. What is the purpose of the video? To inform, entertain, or persuade? What is the purpose of the television news reports? What tells you this?

4. What did you like about the video and television news reports? What did you not like?

5. Compare how the video you watched and television news present information about technology. What ideas and points of view are presented? How do they influence you? How is the television news similar to the technology you saw in the video? How do the video and television news reports affect how you feel about technology?

Further Viewing

Watch the *Visions* CNN Video for Unit 6. Do the Video Worksheet.

CNN Video

Writer's Workshop

Write a Persuasive Letter to the Editor

Prompt

Some schools provide a laptop computer (a small computer that you can carry) to every class. Do you think this is a good idea? Work with a partner to write a letter to the editor of your school or local newspaper. In your letter, state your position and try to persuade your readers that you are right.

Step 1: Brainstorm.

1. Make a list of all the reasons for or against this issue.
2. Decide what your position is on this issue.
3. Write your position in one or two lines.
4. Think of reasons to support your position. Write them in a chart like this.

Arguments For	Arguments Against
Every student would have access to the Internet.	It's very expensive to buy a computer for every student.

Step 2: Arrange your ideas in logical order.

1. What is your most important idea?
2. What is the least important idea?
3. Choose the ideas you want to include and number them in importance.

Step 3: Write a draft.

1. If possible write your draft on a computer.
2. Follow this model.

```
                        (Your Street)
                   (Your City, State)
                              (Date)
(Newspaper Name)
(Newspaper Address)
To the Editor:
   [State the issue and why you
think it is important.]
      [State your opinion.]

   [Give at least three reasons
to support your opinion.]


   [Summarize your position and
ask the readers to support your
position. Ask them to take
action.]
Sincerely,

[Your name]
```

Step 4: Revise and edit.

1. Combine some of your sentences with conjunctions like *and, but, because, if,* or *when.*
2. Blend your paragraphs using transition words.
3. Read your letter carefully to find and correct typing or spelling errors. Use the spell check and grammar check on the computer to help you. Also use software, such as an online dictionary or thesaurus, to check spellings and definitions.
4. Check carefully for correct capitalization, punctuation, and use of apostrophes.
5. Use resources such as your Student Handbook.
6. Make sure your ideas are clear.
   a. Elaborate (explain) any difficult words or phrases.
   b. Delete (remove) any text that does not make sense or that is repeated.
   c. Add text to clarify.
   d. Rearrange sentences so that your ideas follow a logical order.
7. Make a second draft. Read it with your partner. Give each other feedback.

Step 5: Publish.

1. Prepare a final draft of your letter.
2. Create a class collection of the persuasive letters. Review them for their strengths and weaknesses.
3. Choose several letters to e-mail to the editor of your school or local newspaper. Set your goals as a writer based on your writing and the writing of your classmates.

The Heinle Newbury House Dictionary

Student Handbook

Projects

These projects will help you learn more about making connections. You can make connections to the past by learning a story about your culture. You can make connections to the future by making a new robot.

Project 1: Tell a Story About Your Culture

Many families tell stories about something that happened in their culture. For this project, you will tell a story about your culture to a small group.

1. Think of an older family or community member you could interview.
2. Plan how you will interview this person. You may interview on the phone, in person, through the mail, or through e-mail.
3. Ask this person to share a story about something important that happened in the past. He or she may also share something funny that happened.
4. Ask the person some questions. You may want to ask:
   a. Who was with you?
   b. What happened?
   c. When did this event happen?
   d. Where did this event happen?
   e. Why was this event important?

You may think of more questions as you get information. Revise your questions as needed.

5. Take notes as the person tells the story. You may also want to record him or her speaking on audio or video. This will help you remember the story.
6. Work with a small group. Exchange stories. Tell the group the person's story. Then listen as your classmates share their stories.

Project 2: Make an Advertisement of a Robot

Work with a small group to design a new robot. Make an advertisement to tell about your robot. An advertisement is a notice or sign that tells about a product.

1. In a small group, brainstorm ideas.
2. Think about a task that many people need help with. Here are some examples: Students need help carrying books to school. People need help doing chores.
3. Think about how a robot could help people do this task. Review the ideas in Chapter 4 to help you.
4. Use poster board to make an advertisement for the robot.
   a. Give your robot a name. Draw the robot on a piece of poster board.
   b. Write a few exciting phrases to tell how the robot helps people.
   c. Use capitalization and punctuation to clarify and enhance your message.
   d. Be persuasive. You are making the advertisement so that people will want to buy the robot.
   e. Hang your poster in the class.

Further Reading

The books listed below discuss the theme of connections. Choose one or more of them. Write your thoughts and feelings about what you read in your Reading Log. Take notes about your answers to these questions:

1. How is the theme of connections found in the books you read?
2. Make notes of something interesting you learned from what you read.

Esperanza Rising
by Pam Muñoz Ryan, Scholastic, Inc., 2002. Esperanza and her mother are forced to move from Mexico to Southern California. This is the true story of the author's grandmother, Esperanza Ortega.

Honus and Me
by Dan Gutman, Camelot, 1998. Joe finds a very valuable baseball card of Honus Wagner. Joe discovers that the baseball card allows him to travel through time. He travels back to 1909. He meets Honus Wagner and plays in the World Series.

Do You Remember the Color Blue?: And Other Questions Kids Ask About Blindness
by Sally Hobart Alexander, Puffin, 2002. The author of this book lost her sight at the age of 26. She describes how she adjusted to her loss of vision. She also describes what it is like to be blind.

History of Automobiles
by David Corbett, Barron's Educational Series, Inc., 1999. Automobiles play a huge role in today's world. This book follows the history of the automobile.

How to Build a Robot
by Clive Gifford, Franklin Watts, 2001. This book explains the process of making a robot that can walk and talk. It also explains the history of robots.

Phineas Gage
by John Fleischman, Houghton Mifflin, 2002. In 1848, Phineas Gage had a 13-pound iron rod shot through his head. He survived, but his personality changed. This change led scientists to study how brain damage affects people.

Tutankhamen's Gift
by Robert Sabuda, Scott Foresman, 1997. This book is a biography of the Egyptian pharaoh Tutankhamen. Tutankhamen became ruler at the age of ten.

Companion Web site

Reading Log

Heinle Reading Library Moby Dick

Skills Index

Purpose

build reading fluency, 294, 400

determine purpose, 23, 223, 259, 345

distinguish intonation patterns, 159, 161

distinguish sounds, 15, 159, 161, 342, 379

eliminate barriers, 23, 282, 408

organize, 68, 222, 280, 344, 404

persuade, 173, 375, 404–405

produce intonation patterns, 159, 161, 322

produce sounds, 15, 159, 161, 322, 342, 379

recall details, 141, 187, 276

summarize, 64, 114, 144, 172, 189, 195, 198, 203, 238, 276, 328, 331, 334, 338, 341, 401

take notes, 39, 93, 222, 341, 348, 404, 408

understand major idea, 38, 69, 145, 158, 238, 345, 405

understand supporting evidence, 63, 187, 340, 344, 345, 374, 390, 401, 404

■ Reading

Comprehension

analyze, 22

  characters, 4, 6, 16, 56, 64, 65, 102, 115, 178, 186, 203, 238, 308, 358, 359

  reasons, 374

  settings, 309

  text evidence, 238, 300, 340, 401

  text types, 64

author

  feelings/perspective, 7, 21, 38, 63, 262, 275, 276, 290, 292–293, 294, 308, 321, 373

  purpose, 9, 23, 37, 101, 113, 139, 140, 171, 185, 217, 259, 293, 307, 357, 397, 399

  strategy, 173, 314, 357

build background, 3, 15, 27, 43, 55, 77, 93, 107, 119, 133, 153, 163, 177, 191, 207, 231, 243, 253, 267, 289, 299, 313, 327, 353, 363, 379, 391

captions, 134, 141, 147

cause and effect, 22, 56, 58–63, 114, 172, 178, 180–185, 294,

314, 316–321, 380, 382–385, 386

chronology, 42, 43, 53, 67, 244, 246–247, 248, 251, 282, 283, 380

compare and contrast, 4, 6, 8, 10, 15, 22, 38, 44, 46–49, 50, 64, 88, 92, 108, 120, 128, 140, 172, 218, 225, 268, 269–275, 308, 322, 340, 345, 348, 400

connect, 3, 15, 27, 38, 43, 50, 54, 55, 77, 88, 93, 107, 119, 128, 129, 133, 152, 153, 163, 177, 189, 191, 202, 207, 218, 231, 239, 243, 251, 253, 267, 289, 299, 313, 326, 327, 349, 353, 358, 363, 379, 386, 389, 390, 400, 409

details, 4, 120, 187, 208, 221, 294, 308, 344, 364, 380, 403

dialogue, 65, 178, 263

draw conclusions, 10, 50, 88, 114, 120, 122–127, 128, 140, 172, 248, 262, 276, 284, 290, 292–293, 322, 358, 374, 400

draw inferences, 22, 38, 88, 114, 128, 140, 154, 156–157, 158, 186, 202, 238, 253, 254, 256–260, 262, 290, 300, 302–307, 354, 356–357, 358, 386

evaluate, 64, 224, 238, 294, 308, 340

experience for comprehension, use of, 2, 38, 162, 172, 190, 218, 358

explain, 38, 88, 129, 140, 145, 158, 186, 202, 217, 259, 262, 276, 293, 294, 340, 358, 374, 386, 400

fact and opinion, 51, 94, 96–101, 309, 359, 392

generalize, 322

graphic organizers, 26, 328, 341, 346

  bar graph, 13

  charts, 12, 16, 26, 40, 42, 51, 56, 68, 70, 104, 107, 115, 119, 132, 143, 145, 148, 152, 159, 162, 176, 187, 189, 190, 226, 240, 242, 244, 250, 254, 264, 267, 278, 284, 290, 296, 300, 324, 326, 328, 341, 342, 344, 346, 354, 359, 360, 376, 378, 380, 388, 389, 392, 402, 406

diagrams, 4, 44, 141, 298, 327, 331, 332, 361, 402

drawings, 280, 328, 347, 392

maps, 3, 41, 43, 55, 77, 93, 107, 119, 133, 163, 175, 191, 241, 243, 292, 346

pie charts, 143

Sunshine Organizer, 352

symbols, 119, 267, 389

Venn Diagram, 4, 44, 223, 268, 281, 298

visuals, 327, 330–339, 341, 344, 346, 347, 348, 351, 392

headings, 134, 147, 148, 208, 219, 328, 346

identify, 10, 22, 24, 39, 43, 50, 55, 56, 58–63, 89, 90, 93, 102, 104, 108, 114, 116, 120, 128, 164, 202, 206, 218, 248, 262, 276, 280, 289, 294, 308, 322, 340, 342, 380, 389, 400

  steps in a process, 102, 218

images, 4, 28, 30–37, 76, 78, 80–87, 268, 277, 279, 295

interpret, 10, 187, 346

knowledge for comprehension, use of, 2, 14, 26, 42, 54, 76, 92, 102, 106, 118, 132, 152, 162, 176, 190, 206, 230, 242, 252, 266, 288, 298, 312, 326, 352, 362, 378, 390

main idea and details, 108, 109–113, 114, 128, 208, 210–217, 218, 340, 343, 364, 366–373, 387, 400

make judgments, 172

make modifications

  asking questions, 16, 38, 64, 102, 232, 295, 322, 323, 341, 348

  rereading aloud, 16, 18–21, 309, 343, 387

  searching for clues, 77, 88, 107, 191, 207, 253, 289, 353, 389

  translating, 16, 18–21, 203, 328

  using reference aids, 24, 40, 55, 93, 104, 116, 142, 231, 251, 278, 313, 324, 342, 353

mental images, 4, 28, 30–37, 76, 78, 80–87, 268, 277, 279, 295

monitor comprehension, 10, 22, 38, 50, 64, 88, 102, 114, 128, 140, 158, 172, 186, 202, 218, 238, 248, 262, 276, 294, 308, 322, 340, 358, 374, 386, 400

Word Identification

adjectives, 296, 342, 360
context, 77, 88, 107, 191, 207, 253, 289, 353, 389
derivations, 12
dictionary, 27, 40, 41, 55, 70, 93, 104, 116, 119, 130, 142, 147, 160, 163, 177, 191, 220, 221, 225, 231, 240, 264, 267, 278, 283, 289, 310, 313, 324, 327, 342, 347, 353, 377, 379, 388, 407
glossary, 267, 327
language structure, 12, 24
letter-sound correspondences, 342, 379
meanings, 12, 24, 40, 43, 52, 70, 77, 78, 93, 104, 116, 119, 130, 142, 177, 220, 221, 231, 250, 253, 267, 278, 289, 296, 299, 310, 311, 313, 324, 325, 327, 353, 360, 379, 388, 389, 391
prefixes, 104, 204, 250
pronunciation, 3, 39, 220, 231, 289, 313, 327, 342, 379, 388
root words, 52, 90, 104, 204, 240, 264, 278, 342, 388
  Greek, 90, 220, 324
  Latin, 221, 310
suffixes, 40, 52, 240, 264, 278, 388

■ Writing

Connections

authors
  challenges, 171
  feelings/perspective, 7, 21, 38, 63, 262, 275, 276, 290, 292–293, 294, 308, 321, 373
  purpose, 9, 10, 23, 37, 101, 113, 139, 140, 171, 185, 217, 259, 293, 307, 345, 357, 397, 399
  strategies used, 173, 314, 357, 359
collaboration with other writers, 117, 118, 152, 176, 252, 298, 325, 362, 390, 406
correspondence
  e-mail, 348, 407, 408
  mail, 161, 225, 348, 408

Forms

advertisement, 279, 408
biography, 251, 282–283, 389
editorial, 406–407
fable, 117
fiction, 67, 311, 361
forms, 205, 297, 325
historical fiction, 67
informational text, 143, 221, 325, 343
instructions, 51, 325
interview, 144, 284, 408
job application form, 297
legend, 241
letter, 53, 161, 224–225, 348, 406–407
letter to the editor, 406–407
literature review, 175, 222–223, 224–225
lyrics, 161
narrative, 13, 25, 41, 53, 67, 70, 105, 131, 297
narrative fiction, 67, 131
news report/story, 105, 148, 284, 343
opinion, 175, 280
order form, 205
paragraph, 41, 105, 175, 282, 311, 325, 377, 389
personal narrative, 13, 41, 53, 70, 105, 297
persuasive
  essay, 403
  letter to the editor, 406–407
  poster, 408
  speech, 265, 404
poem, 28, 39, 91, 279
poster, 72, 148, 408
presentation, 280–281, 347, 348, 404
questions, 144, 284, 344, 348, 408
radio program, 226
report, 72, 143, 148, 222–223, 284, 343, 346–347
research paper, 346–347
review, 175, 222–223, 224–225
rules, 146
science fiction, 311
song, 161, 223
speech, 265, 348, 404
story, 25, 105, 311, 343
storyboard, 226
summary, 148, 189, 325, 345, 348

Inquiry and Research

cluster map, 146
concept map/web, 3, 54, 76, 91, 92, 146, 230, 252, 266, 279, 295, 390
evaluation, 146, 308, 348
learning log, 11, 65, 103, 115, 129, 134, 149, 159, 187, 227, 239, 277, 285, 290, 295, 309, 341, 349, 354, 380, 409
on-line searches, 221, 282, 345, 346
organize ideas, 3, 54, 76, 91, 92, 105, 117, 146, 148, 161, 164, 230, 241, 251, 252, 266, 280, 282, 295, 325, 328, 344, 345, 346, 348, 352, 361, 390, 406
outline, 134, 136–139, 282, 283, 343, 346–347
periodicals, 148, 348
presentations, 280–281, 323, 346–347, 348, 390, 404
prior knowledge, 2, 14, 26, 42, 54, 76, 92, 102, 106, 118, 132, 152, 162, 176, 190, 206, 230, 242, 252, 266, 279, 288, 298, 312, 326, 352, 362, 378, 390
questions, 7, 9, 41, 94, 284, 293, 307, 321, 322, 323, 341, 345, 346, 348, 377, 385, 389, 408
scientific questions, 322, 323, 341, 348
sources, citation of, 221, 346, 347
summarize ideas, 146, 148, 189, 203, 224, 325, 326, 328, 330, 332–333, 335–337, 339, 341, 345, 348
take notes, 39, 93, 141, 222, 280, 282, 341, 344, 345, 348, 404, 408
technology presentations, 68, 147, 265, 280, 343, 344, 404
timelines, 164, 244, 265, 282

Literary Devices

descriptive language, 28, 290, 297
figurative language, 290, 295, 297, 377
first person point of view, 11, 13, 44, 53, 205, 221, 249, 254, 268, 290, 297, 364
point of view, 13, 290, 359, 364

Purpose

appropriate form, 12, 52, 130, 204, 324, 325, 342
appropriate literary devices, 11, 13, 28, 44, 53, 205, 221, 249, 254, 268, 290, 295, 297, 359, 364, 377
audience and purpose, 70, 147
  appropriate style, 323, 375, 404
  appropriate voice, 344, 345, 404
ideas, 3, 54, 76, 91, 92, 117, 118, 146, 230, 252, 266, 282, 295, 324, 328, 344, 345, 346–347, 390, 406
precise wording, 405
purposes
  compare, 297, 343, 344, 345, 378

Credits

Pp. 381–385, THE BOY KING. Reprinted by permission of SPIDER magazine, December 2000, Vol. 7, No. 12 © 2000 by Andrea Ross. Audio rights: From "The Boy King" from SPIDER magazine, December 2000, Vol.7, No. 12. Copyright © 2000 by Andrea Ross. Used by permission of the author.

Pp. 394–397, IT COULD STILL BE A ROBOT. From *It Could Still Be a Robot* by Allan Fowler. Copyright © 1997 by Children's Press®, a division of Grolier Publishing Co., Inc. Reprinted by permission.

Pp. 398–399, HIGH-TECH HELPING HANDS, by Jane McGoldrick. "High-Tech Helping Hands" from *National Geographic World,* March 1996. Copyright © 1996 by National Geographic Society. Reprinted by permission.

Illustrators

Mark Andresen: p. 356 (© Mark Andresen/Scott Hull Associates); **Don Baker:** pp. 316–320 (© Don Baker/Kolea Baker); **Kristin Barr:** p. 7 (© Kristin Barr/Irmeli Holmberg); **Clem Bedwell:** pp. 110–112 (© Clem Bedwell/Wilson-Zumbo Illustration Group); **Bob Dombrowski:** pp. 193–200 (© Bob Dombrowski/Artworks Illustration); **Andrea Eberbach:** pp. 80–86 (© Andrea Eberbach/Scott Hull Associates); **George Hamblin:** pp. 301–306 (© George Hamblin/Wilkinson Studios, LLC); **Ken Joudrey:** pp. 270–272 (© Ken Joudrey/Munro Campagna); **John Kastner:** pp. 30–37 (© John Kastner/The Beranbaum Group); **William Low:** pp. 121–126 (© William Low/Morgan Gaynin Inc.); **Ron Mahoney:** pp. 366–372 (© Ron Mahoney/Wilkinson Studios, LLC); **Mapping Specialists, Ltd.:** pp. 3, 41, 43, 55, 77, 93, 107, 119, 133, 163, 175, 191, 241, 243, 253, 292, 379; **Kay McCabe:** p. 247 (© Kay McCabe/The Beranbaum Group); **Precision Graphics:** pp. 131, 311, 327, 331, 332, 334; **Elizabeth Rosen:** p. 274 (© Elizabeth Rosen/Morgan Gaynin Inc.); **Elizabeth Sayles:** pp. 57–62 (© Elizabeth Sayles/Cornell & McCarthy, LLC); **Winson Trang:** pp. 180–184 (© Winson Trang/Square Moon); **Paula Wendland:** pp. 18–20 (© Paula Wendland/Wilkinson Studios, LLC); **Kris Wiltse:** pp. 234–237 (© Kris Wiltse/Morgan Gaynin Inc.); **Jean Wisenbaugh:** pp. 49, 53 (© Jean Wisenbaugh/Lindgren & Smith)

Author Photos

p. 7 (Ralph Fletcher); p. 9 (Carmen Lomas Garza); p. 21 (Andrew Matthews); p. 37 (Miriam Nerlove); p. 87 (Madeleine Dunphy); p. 113 (Lynette Dyer Vuong); p. 127 (Paul Fleischman); p. 139 (Mary Pope and Will Osborne, © Paul Coughlin); p. 171 (Zlata Filipovic, © Alexandra Boulat/SIPA Press); p. 185 (Suzanne Barchers); p. 201 (Edite Cunhã); p. 261 (Nelson Mandela, © Reuters NewMedia Inc./CORBIS); p. 273 (Luis Omar Salinas, © Arte Publico Press Photo Archives); p. 275 (Liz Ann Báez Aguilar); p. 293 (Sylvia Earle, © Macduff Everton/CORBIS); p. 307 (Isaac Asimov, © Douglas Kirkland/Corbis); p. 321 (Stephen Kramer, © Chris Kramer); p. 357 (Pam Muñoz Ryan); p. 373 (Dan Gutman); p. 385 (Andrea Ross); p. 399 (Jane McGoldrick)

Photos

Art Resource: (All © Art Resource) p. i-1 (*Children asking for 'posada' (La procesion),* Diego Rivera, oil on canvas, © Schalkwijk/Art Resource, NY); p. 329 (© The Museum of Modern Art/Licensed by SCALA/Art Resource, NY); p. 383 (© Scala/Art Resource, NY)

Bridgeman Art Library: p. 355 (*Vineyard, Provence,* by Eric Hains, oil on canvas © Bridgeman Art Library)

Cape Cod Times: p. 399 (© Vincent DeWitt/Cape Cod Times)

CORBIS: (All © Corbis) p. 5 (© Paul Barton/CORBIS); p. 29 (© Paul Barton/CORBIS); pp. 45 & 46 (© Richard T. Nowitz/CORBIS); p. 47 (© Vanni Archive/CORBIS); p. 48 (© Jonathan Blair/CORBIS); p. 63 (© David Samuel Robbins/CORBIS); pp. 74–75 (*Tiger in a Tropical Storm (Surprise!)* by Henri Rousseau © National Gallery Collection; By kind permission of the Trustees of the National Gallery, London/CORBIS); p. 79 (© Philadelphia Museum of Art/CORBIS); p. 95 (© Lucidio Studio Inc./CORBIS); p. 96 (© Alan Schein

Photography/CORBIS); p. 98 (© John Henley/CORBIS); p. 99 (© Dean Conger/CORBIS); p. 100 (© John-Marshall Mantel/CORBIS); p. 109 (© Tim Davis/CORBIS); p. 136 (© Michael & Patricia Fogden/CORBIS); p. 137 (© Kevin Schafer/CORBIS); p. 138 (© Australian Picture Library/CORBIS); pp. 150–151 (© Flip Schulke/CORBIS); p. 155 (© James Marshall/CORBIS); p. 179 (© Christie's Images/CORBIS); p. 206 (© Tom & Dee Ann McCarthy/CORBIS); p. 213 (© Michael Keller/CORBIS); pp. 228–229 (© Philadelphia Museum of Art/CORBIS); p. 233 (© Dallas and John Heaton/CORBIS); p. 245 (© Bettmann/CORBIS); p. 246 (© Bettmann/CORBIS); p. 251 (© David Butow/CORBIS SABA); p. 255 (© David Turnley/CORBIS); p. 256 (© Jonathan Blair/CORBIS); p. 257 (© Charles O'Rear/CORBIS); p. 258 (© Peter Turnley/CORBIS); p. 260 (© David Turnley/CORBIS); p. 261 (© Reuters NewMedia Inc./CORBIS); p. 269 (© Paul Barton/CORBIS); pp. 286–287 (*Drawing of a Winged Shuttle Craft* © Bettmann/CORBIS); p. 288 (© Amos Nachoum/CORBIS); p. 289 (© Brandon D. Cole/CORBIS); p. 291 (© Amos Nachoum/CORBIS); p. 330 (© 1996 CORBIS; Original image courtesy of NASA/CORBIS); p. 333 (© CORBIS); p. 335 (© NASA/Roger Ressmeyer/CORBIS); p. 337 (© Stocktrek/CORBIS); p. 338 (© AFP/CORBIS); pp. 350–351 (© Christie's Images/CORBIS); p. 353 (© Bernardo Bucci/CORBIS); p. 365 (© Kit Kittle/CORBIS); p. 382 (© Sandro Vannini/CORBIS); p. 384 (© Roger Wood/CORBIS); p. 395 (© Reuters New Media Inc./CORBIS)

Getty Images: (All © Getty Images) p. 135 (© Joel Sartore/Getty Images); p. 209 (© SW Productions/Getty Images); p. 210 (© Jodi Cobb/National Geographic/Getty Images); p. 336 (© Jim Ballard/Getty Images); p. 381 (© Getty Images); p. 393 (© Zac Macaulay/Getty Images); p. 394 (Craig van der Lende/Getty Images)

Index Stock Imagery: (All © Index Stock Imagery) p. 14 (© 2002 Indexstock.com); p. 17 (© 2002 Indexstock.com); p. 396 (© 2002 Indexstock.com)

Magnum Photos: p. 170 (© Paul Lowe/Magnum Photos)

Photo Edit: (All © Photo Edit) p. 211 (© Jeff Greenberg/Photo Edit); p. 212 (© Michael Newman/Photo Edit); p. 214 (© Michelle D. Bridwell/Photo Edit); p. 216 (© Michael Newman/Photo Edit); p. 315 (© David Young-Wolff/Photo Edit)

NASA: p. 339 (© NASA/Spacepix.net)

SIPA Press: p. 165 (© Alexandra Boulat/SIPA Press); p. 166 (© Alexandra Boulat/SIPA Press); p. 167 (© Alexandra Boulat/SIPA Press); p. 168 (© Alexandra Boulat/SIPA Press); p. 171 (© Alexandra Boulat/SIPA Press)